Jonathan Magonet
Gabriel Josipovici
John Barton

ıow he was a Hebrew?

For Jo
With fond memories of
times together with you and Willie

Jont
M Jont

Jonathan Magonet
Gabriel Josipovici
John Barton

How did Moses know he was a Hebrew?

Reading Bible stories from within

Hakodesh Press

Imprint

Any brand names and product names mentioned in this book are subject to trademark, brand or patent protection and are trademarks or registered trademarks of their respective holders. The use of brand names, product names, common names, trade names, product descriptions etc. even without a particular marking in this work is in no way to be construed to mean that such names may be regarded as unrestricted in respect of trademark and brand protection legislation and could thus be used by anyone.

Cover image: www.ingimage.com

Publisher:
Hakodesh Press
is a trademark of
Dodo Books Indian Ocean Ltd., member of the OmniScriptum S.R.L Publishing group
str. A.Russo 15, of. 61, Chisinau-2068, Republic of Moldova Europe
Printed at: see last page
ISBN: 978-620-2-45553-4

Zugl. / Approved by: Portrait by Leonard Glaser

Dedication

To my wife Dorothea

and our grandchildren Ephra and Arava.

I hope they will enjoy their Saba's writings

when they, in time, will read with adult eyes.

1

Contents

Acknowledgments

The articles in this collection have evolved over several years of teaching Biblical narratives in a variety of contexts. Some, like those on Avimelech and Jephthah (chapters 11 and 12) derive from a course taught to rabbinic students at Leo Baeck College. In recent years I have learned much from teaching Biblical narrative and poetry to rabbinic students at the Levisson Institute in Amsterdam at the invitation of my fellow Leo Baeck graduate Rabbi David Lillienthal, and at the Ecole Rabbinique de Paris, at the invitation of my former student Rabbi Pauline Bebe.

The chapter on how Moses learned that he was a Hebrew, was given as a memorial lecture for the late Professor Leon Yudkin z.l. The theme suggested itself as a tribute to Leon's studies on the changing nature of Jewish identity in the twentieth century.

Other chapters had their origin in interfaith contexts. The one on 'Rabbinic readings of Ruth' was given at the annual International Jewish-Christian Bible Week which I helped co-found over fifty years ago and which continues to be a special place for teaching and learning. I am always indebted to the late Anneliese Debray, whose courage and imagination initiated the Week at the Hedwig Dransfeld Haus (HDH) in Bendorf, near Koblenz, and to Dr Uta Zwingenberger, who offered a new home, when the HDH was forced to close, and has supervised the Week's continuing development at Haus Ohrbeck., Osnabrück.

Some chapters developed in a more academic context and were tried out during periods as a guest professor at the Kirchliche Hochschule in Wuppertal, at the University of Oldenburg, as the Schalom ben Chorin Visiting Professor at the universities of Augsburg and Würzburg. But the bulk of them found their final form during my annual visit for the past ten years as a guest professor at

Seinan Gakuin University, Fukuoka, Japan. Each year I have given public lectures on Biblical, Jewish and interfaith topics. A collection of these were translated into Japanese and edited by Yoichi Kobayashi-sensei and published as a book *Rabbino Seishokaishak: Yudaiyakuo to Kiristokuo no Taiwa* (Shinkhyo Shupansha, Fukuoka 2012). He subsequently translated other Biblical lectures and was succeeded in this task by Hiroshi Hihara-sensei, both of whom raised valuable questions and gave helpful critical comments in the process. I am grateful to both for their advice and companionship.

A final context which has helped me refine my readings of Biblical texts has been a variety of adult education courses I have taught over the years, both at weekend seminars in Germany and weekly study sessions organised through the Leo Baeck College 'Lehrhaus' programme, or by Liberal and Reform Jewish congregations in the UK. To one such regular lunchtime course at Wimbledon (Reform) Synagogue I am indebted for the photograph on the back cover that was taken discretely during a class by Leonard Glaser, who has kindly given permission for its reproduction here.

I am particularly grateful to Gabriel Josipovici and John Barton who read the manuscript and generously agreed to write, respectively a Foreword and Afterword to the book.

My special thanks must go to Anna Gaina and all associated with Hakodesh Press for making this publication possible.

Jonathan Magonet

Foreword

Gabriel Josipovici

In the 1970s I started teaching a course on 'The Bible and English Literature' at the University of Sussex. It was a course I had dreamed up with my friend and colleague Stephen Medcalf, both of us inspired by the first two chapters of Erich Auerbach's *Mimesis* and driven by the belief that it was impossible to understand much English literature before 1800 without some knowledge of the Bible. Two things at once became clear to me: you couldn't really get a grip on the Hebrew Bible without some knowledge of biblical Hebrew; and most of the secondary literature was of little use to anyone with our sorts of interests because it tended to be the product of a desire either to find the 'truth' behind the Bible stories or to sort out the various strands of tradition out of which the Bible was constructed, the so-called 'Documentary Hypothesis'. This literature sprang mainly out of a German Protestant tradition, harking back to the first Reformers' own concerns in their battles with an ossified Catholicism. However, in books like Martin Buber's *Moses* and in the notes and letters of Franz Rosenzweig I began to glimpse the possibilities of other approaches, while through my discovery of the great Italian Jewish biblical scholar Umberto Cassuto I discovered that the Documentary Hypothesis might possibly be no more than a mirage.

And then, in 1981, came Robert Alter's *The Art of Biblical Narrative*, the first to really open the window onto the landscapes Auerbach had allowed us to glimpse. Alter, though a professor of comparative literature at Berkeley, with books on the novel and on Stendhal to his credit, was, it seemed, also steeped in the Jewish tradition, as of course were Buber and Cassuto, ready to quote medieval rabbinic commentaries when it suited his argument but not wedded to their theological positions. And though not interested in engaging with the validity or otherwise of the Documentary Hypothesis, he made it clear that it had nothing to offer those who were interested in the nature and quality of the biblical narratives and might in fact be an actual hindrance to them. For example, instead of seeing the almost identical repetition of certain scenes and even speeches as evidence of a failure to properly integrate the various strands of narrative tradition he asked us to start with the belief that these authors and editors knew what they were doing and it might help our understanding to examine such episodes for minute differences, which would give us clues as to their meaning. Cassuto had already explored such things in his examination of the opening chapters of the Bible in his commentary on Genesis, but Alter took this much further. Again, instead of reading the episode of Judah and Tamar (Genesis 38) as a clumsy intrusion of an alien story into the narrative of Joseph and his brothers, he showed us how central it was to that very narrative. He made clear that these early writers knew exactly what they were doing even if their notions of narrative and its possibilities differed from our own, which had been moulded by two centuries of novel-reading.

The effect of all this, like Auerbach's close syntactic analysis of Genesis 22, was immensely liberating and spurred me on in my desire to write something about the overall shape of this strange book we call the Bible, made up of so many different genres and, in its Christian guise, constructed out of two vast entities. I had been encouraged in this by meeting a young graduate student of English, Francis Landy, who had come to Sussex to write a thesis on *The Song of Songs* under the supervision of one of the few people to be equally at home in the English literary tradition and the Jewish, David Daiches, Professor of English at Sussex and himself the son of a former rabbi of Edinburgh; and by a fortuitous meeting with Jeffrey Newman, who had trained at Leo Baeck College for Reform and Liberal rabbis in London. To my delight I found that my instinctive approach to the Bible chimed with their own perspectives, and both became good friends and mentors. Both also talked to me with admiration and respect about Jonathan Magonet, who was at the time lecturer in Bible at Leo Baeck. Quite independently of Alter, I discovered, Jonathan had, in 1977, published his doctoral thesis, *Form and Meaning: Studies in Literary Techniques in the Book of Jonah*, a book which exemplified all the virtues of Alter's approach – an inwardness with the Jewish commentary tradition along with a healthy scepticism about the wilder speculations of the rabbis, driven by their theological orientation; the detailed examination of words and phrases; the awareness of larger structural patterns; and, most important of all, the recognition that only by accepting these narratives as highly sophisticated artefacts could one actually grasp their human and theological dimensions. The book was a further confirmation to me that I was on the right path, though I would always lack the command of Hebrew and rabbinic tradition that both Alter and Magonet demonstrated on every page.

Jonathan has had a busy public life, first as lecturer and then as head of Leo Baeck College, as a key figure in many of the initiatives that have sprung up in the past fifty years throughout Europe for greater Jewish-Christian-Moslem co-operation and understanding, and as one of the editors of several new prayer-books. This has not stopped him from publishing a number of books on the Bible, such as *A Rabbi Reads the Torah* and *A Rabbi Reads the Psalms,* but, as the titles suggest, these, though packed with insights and based on formidable learning, have been kept deliberately short and simple. Yet he has not ceased, in public lectures and journal articles, to explore in greater depth various issues raised by the Hebrew Bible, and it is some of these he has now brought together in this book.

Reading them together one sees a number of unifying threads, the elaboration of themes that have concerned him since his work on the Book of Jonah. The first of these is that every word counts and that it has to be the Hebrew word, for translation cannot catch the nuances of the original or the subtle ways the biblical writers used them to reinforce their points. Thus in the story of the Tower of Babel (Genesis 11) we are told at the start: 'And they said to one another, come, let us make bricks, and burn them thoroughly.' (v.3) The Hebrew for 'to one another', '*ish el re'ehu*' means, literally, 'each man to his neighbour'. At the end (v.7), God, incensed at their arrogance, says to himself: 'Go to, let us go down, and there confound their language, that they may not understand one another's speech.' The Hebrew here is '*asher lo yishm'u ish s'fat re'ehu*', literally 'that they may not hear/understand the language of their neighbour.' The repetition of that word, '*re'ehu*' at start and finish alerts us to the fact that what the fiasco of the tower has done is to make men unable to talk/listen to one another, to treat one another as neighbours should be rightly treated. Obvious enough when it is pointed out but focusing on the word and its repetition in the Hebrew helps us understand the concision and artistry of these writers, and the way they use language to develop their themes.

But Jonathan has not finished. The men's 'Come, let us make bricks', '*hava nilv'nah*', he points out, finds its aural echo in God's '*hava… v'navla*', 'come … let us confound', but with a crucial inversion. Hebrew words normally have a root of three letters, in this case l-v-n/n-v-l, so that those alert to the sound of Hebrew will instinctively grasp that 'God will literally turn their words/deeds (the Hebrew *davar*, tellingly, can be either) back to front'.

These authors are not only masters of word-play, Jonathan shows us, but of larger structures too. Drawing on the work of his friend Jan Fokkelman and others, Jonathan explores the use of concentric circles, familiar to Homeric scholars, in these narratives (ABCDE/A'B'C'D'E'). In an illuminating exploration of the relation of Genesis 12 and 22 (the calling of Abraham and the binding of Isaac), he points out that the phrase *lekh lekha*, 'get up and go' with the second word meaning something like 'please' (yet not quite a plea and not quite a command, giving the phrase what he calls 'persuasive force'), occurs in precisely this form nowhere else in the Bible, thus alerting us to the link between the two episodes. And he proceeds to show how chapters 12 to 16 are mirrored by 17 to 22, with the story of Ishmael occupying the pivotal point at 16. But why Ishmael and not Isaac, the one who inherits and is the link between Abraham and Jacob? Because, suggests Jonathan, what we are shown is a kind of wrong turn in history, one which is then corrected, though not without peril, in the second part of the larger narrative.

Jonathan is in fact fascinated by this notion of history in these narratives being 'corrected' rather than moving in simple linear fashion. He shows how this may work across books as well as within them. Thus he sees both *Ruth* and *Esther* as 'attempts to "replay" and then "repair" earlier failures or mistakes.' How can Ruth be the ancestor of King David? She is a Moabite, and thus a descendant of the incestuous union of Lot and his daughters; Boaz is a descendant of the equally scandalous union of Judah and his daughter-in-law Tamar. Their union, in much more open and propitious circumstances, undoes, in a sense, what has occurred before. Similarly the Book of Esther echoes and undoes the failures of Saul. Mordecai is a descendant of the Benjamite 'Kish', the name of Saul's father and tribe and Haman is a descendant of Agag, the Amalekite grandson of Esau. Where Saul disobeyed God's command to exterminate Agag and his people Mordecai avenges himself and the Jewish people on Haman and on his children. 'What has been done cannot be undone,' says Jonathan, summing up both books, ' but when the same circumstances arise' the substitute protagonists show history now taking a different turn and thus show the present redeeming the past and, for the more mystically minded rabbis, prepares the way for the Messiah.

As this shows, Jonathan's instinct is always to explore echoes and parallels, both in the language and in the larger narrative structures. He is particularly sensitive to how a grasp of the ramifications across space and time of family relationships is often a key to understanding. The fact, easily overlooked, that Korah and Moses, for example, are cousins, or that Amalek is the grandson of Esau helps bring into focus much of the Book of Numbers and of *Esther*. At the same time the lack of direct family ties can also be the key to understanding: both Ruth and Tamar, Judah's daughter-in-law, are 'outsiders who take action to ensure the continuity of the family line'.

Central to Jonathan's thinking and to this book is the emphasis on hard-headed politics. 'We are never far from political issues in these biblical narratives' he says in one of his essays on Moses, who, of all the biblical characters, seems to be the one closest to his heart. His Moses is tough, ready to take difficult decisions, decisions which in the nature of things, will not please everyone, not even God. His almost impossible task was that of 'mediating between a seemingly unpredictable God and a people seemingly bent on self-destruction.' Like Abraham he is prepared to argue with God when the need arises, and Jonathan makes the fascinating suggestion that God clearly respects this, 'as if God is learning from them and through them what is needed if human history is to live up to God's hopes and expectations.' Only in this way was Moses 'successful in transforming a rabble of downtrodden, demoralised slaves into a strong, organised, legally constituted society'. By contrast Jonathan is quick to spot self-pity or the desire for self-aggrandisement among those figures more pious readers would not dream of criticising, such as Elijah and Jonah.

Jonathan has published a volume of stories and one of poetry and had an early reputation as a singer-songwriter. So though in one sense a pillar of the rabbinic establishment he is in fact much more quirky than that suggests and all too ready to challenge pious orthodoxies. This is well in evidence in the essay on Joseph, whose childhood traumas, he suggests, lead him, when in power in Egypt to transform that country into a slave society in ways utterly condemned by the later law-givers of the Israelites. In other essays he floats the idea that Jacob in fact stole the wrong blessing from his brother and that Jephtha may never have sacrificed his daughter.

As this suggests, this is a challenging and invigorating book. What it does is to make you want to go back and re-read these well-known stories, and, when you do so it makes you read them more acutely and with a greater understanding of both their minutest linguistic details and their widest human implications. What we are left with is a renewed sense of wonder at the inexhaustible richness of the Hebrew Bible.

Gabriel Josipovici

A novelist and literary critic, he is a Research Professor at the University of Sussex and the author of *The Book of God: A Response to the Bible*.

1 Introduction

An earlier suggestion as the title for this study of familiar Biblical narratives, 'Bible Stories through Adult Eyes', was deliberately provocative. It sought to challenge certain features that affect the way people tend to understand the nature, significance and literary quality of Biblical writings. Incidentally, by 'Bible', I am referring to what Christians regard as the 'Old Testament', but for which Jews have a variety of designations. The books that we are considering are the same as those in the 'Old Testament', but they are organised in a different order, which also affects the way in which they are understood in Jewish tradition. Scholars may refer to it as the 'Hebrew Bible', which distinguishes it from Christian Bible with its New Testament that was written originally in Greek. Another option is the acronym 'TaNaKh', which refers to its three divisions: *Torah* (the five books of Moses); *'Nevi'im'* (Prophets – from Joshua through to the twelve 'minor' prophets) and *Ketuvim* (Writings – from Psalms to the Second Book of Chronicles). Another traditional term is *'miqra'*, 'that which is read', an indication of the regular public reading. The word 'Torah', which means 'teaching', 'pointing the way', though initially limited to the Five Books of Moses, has come to include the whole of the Bible and ultimately all the derived commentaries and traditions associated with it.

Perhaps the first experience that affects the popular understanding of the Bible is the versions of Biblical stories that we learn as children. Understandably they are simplified to meet the interest and ability of the child. They serve as an introduction to the heroes that are to populate the child's imagination as part of their religious education and acculturation. Noah rescues the animals, 'two by two', in his ark; Jonah survives a storm at sea and lives for three days in a 'whale'; Joseph rises from humble origins to become the powerful governor of Egypt under Pharaoh; Moses, as a baby, is rescued from the Nile by Pharaoh's daughter; little David defeats the mighty Goliath with his slingshot. The problem is that this imprinting is often the last time the child, and later adult, may encounter these figures and stories, so that the complexity of the narratives, the characters themselves and the situations in which they find themselves are rarely re-examined with an adult consciousness. They remain on the same plane as fairy stories and Santa Claus, to be dismissed and discarded in later life, or simply passed on to the next generation with the same childlike evaluation.

A second problem is that even if as adults we are encouraged to 'read the Bible' we encounter it within the pages of solemnly bound volumes that belong to the 'serious' world of religion. This means that we are likely to approach the same stories we knew as children predisposed to assume some kind of moral high ground for those same 'heroes', but also with the expectation that 'faith' will explain away any problems that we may encounter. However, our own adult values may well challenge the morality of what we read, both in terms of people's behaviour in the stories or that of the Biblical God. Moreover, our rational mind my object to the occasional miraculous intervention in human affairs, and our secular education may rebel against the role, often seemingly arbitrary, contradictory or simply unacceptable, ascribed to that same God. If, in addition, those who teach and preach the lessons to be drawn are reluctant to address such concerns, it is all too easy to dismiss the entire exercise as wrong-headed.

Whatever the problems that may be raised by the Biblical texts themselves, they are further affected by the simple fact that they are usually encountered in translation. Inevitably something is 'lost' because of this, but in many cases, it can lead to a serious misunderstanding of the intention of the original Hebrew, separated from us not only by language and history but by its very different cultural environment. While most translations attempt to be as true as possible to the Hebrew original, or the early Greek or Latin translations, there are some that aim at providing an idiomatic contemporary version in the new language and the simplifications involved can really distort the meaning.

Unless we have the help of a commentary or take the trouble to compare a variety of translations, as readers we are totally dependent on the version to hand.

To indicate another factor, I will sometimes ask my students to imagine that they are donkeys reading the Bible and tell me what kind of stories they would be interested in reading. Once they get over the shock, they recognize that they would look for stories about donkeys. Most immediately pick on the talking donkey of Balaam, clearly a legitimate focus for attention and a significant donkey hero. But further thought suggests other, perhaps equally celebrated Biblical donkeys, like those ridden by Moses on his journey to Egypt to rescue the Israelites from slavery, or the prophet Samuel's donkey on which he did the rounds of the country as a judge. Some may even recall the donkeys of Saul's father which were 'lost' and thus led the young man on a futile journey to find them, which instead culminated in his being anointed as the first king of Israel. (I also note the anthropocentric bias in the telling of this story that assumes the donkeys were 'lost' and not simply enjoying a brief vacation.) Of course, what this exercise establishes is that the frame of reference under which we approach the Biblical text will determine what we are looking for and what we find; and similarly, that the perspective with which we ask the text questions, be they historical-critical, feminist, post-colonial or any other current ideological or scholarly set of approaches, will determine the answers that we get. We are inevitably subjective readers.

So, I must also address my own subjectivity insofar as I am able to recognize it. My approach is one that is sometimes called a 'close reading' of the Hebrew text, one that tries to be sensitive to identifiable literary or rhetorical techniques that give the narrative its coherence: like the use of 'key words', whose repetition suggests links within and across different narrative passages; 'type scenes' where variations on a conventional pattern of behaviour help indicate the particular character of the protagonists; concentric structures,

17

within and across entire chapters, that link seemingly diverse material together into a recognizable pattern; evaluations of the respective perspectives of the author/editor and the characters within the story; the significance of the immediate and wider context of any given passage within the Hebrew Bible as a whole. For all these approaches and more we can now find support, comparison, correction and debate, from several decades of scholarly literary studies. Moreover, Jewish tradition furnishes us with the extraordinary wealth of two thousand years of rabbinic Biblical commentary which offers detailed examinations of these texts, speculations on the cause of particular behaviour, as well as attempts to fill in apparent gaps in the narrative, sometimes out of intellectual curiosity, sometimes for broader homiletic purposes.

As a prelude to my own approach, I would like to give an example where a significant clue to the story of a particular Biblical figure remains almost completely invisible in translation, and, even goes largely unnoticed in the Hebrew original itself. One strand of traditional Jewish reading of the Bible was concerned with cases where the name of a character undergoes a minor change. In some examples the change is clearly pointed out by the Bible itself, most obviously the change of name of the patriarch Jacob to Israel. Another example is the change of name of Abram and his wife Sarai, to the names Abraham and Sarah. The Biblical text interprets the change in Abram's name, the addition of the Hebrew letter '*heh*', to mean that he will become the 'father of a multitude of peoples', a kind of wordplay in the Hebrew (*Genesis 17:5*).

I became sensitised to one such name change for obvious reasons. The name in question is that of Jonathan, the son of Saul, and the close friend of (later King) David. Since my own names are Jonathan David I may have some sympathy for the story of the Biblical Jonathan and his tragic fate, dying in battle against the Philistines. On one occasion during a visit to Israel I had a conversation with a young Orthodox Jew who asked me my name. I answered in modern Hebrew '*yonatan*'. He teased me that I had used that form of the name, and had not used the alternative version, '*yehonatan*'. 'That is typical of a Reform Jew' he said, 'to leave out the name of God!' What he was referring to is my omission of the Hebrew letter '*heh*' in the name. That letter '*heh*', being one of the four letters of the special divine name, the so-called 'Tetragrammaton', is often used, particularly in traditional circles, as a substitute for the full name in written texts to ensure that the name is not destroyed if the document is damaged. So by omitting the letter from my name I was showing how irreligious a Reform Jew really was. It was only a joke, as far as I could tell, but reflects that kind of 'one-up-man-ship' that is often to be found in intra-Jewish debates.

Scroll forward some thirty years and I am teaching the First and Second Book of Samuel to an evening class in London. Jonathan is introduced in *1 Samuel 13:2, 3, 16*, as the son of King Saul, a great warrior. His name here is written as '*yonatan*'. He reappears in chapter *14:1* with his name in this same form which is repeated in verses 3 and 4. However, at that point Jonathan decides to attack a Philistine outpost, accompanied only by his armour-bearer. Despite the enormous risk, he assures his companion:

> Come, let us go over to the outpost of those uncircumcised ones, perhaps the Lord will support us, for nothing can prevent the Lord from being victorious, whether through many or few! (*1 Samuel 14:7*)

In this sentence he is introduced as '*yehonatan*', and this version of his name is used in the following verse 8, which introduces his scheme. When the attack actually begins, in verses *12-14*, the name is repeated 5 times, but in the shorter form '*yonatan*', and then in the same way throughout the rest of the chapter from verses *27-49*. So why has the narrator introduced the addition of the letter '*heh*' when '*yehonatan*' evokes the name of God for his plan, only to revert to the shorter form subsequently. It is worth noting that in all but one of the many English translations I looked at the change goes completely unnoticed. This sort of change may appear to be inconsequential, perhaps the result of a copying error by an early scribe. But having seen this once I became curious about how the name is spelled in the subsequent stories. To be more thorough and see how often such differences occurred, I turned to a Hebrew concordance of the Bible to see if the same change occurs elsewhere in the stories about 'Jonathan'. Sure enough, the change happens again, but in a different context.

After David has killed Goliath, he is introduced to Saul, and immediately afterwards we learn that 'Jonathan's very self[1] cleaved to David's, and Jonathan loved him as himself' (*1 Samuel 18:1*). After our previous explanation, it will come as no surprise that in this verse, and in the following verses, *3-4*) the name is spelled *yehonatan*. The shortened version of the name only appears one further time in an extraordinary verse that seems to introduce at least one level of explanation to the change of name. The verse in question is *1 Samuel 19:1*. At the height of Saul's fears that David seeks his throne, he is now determined to kill David and issues instructions:

> Saul spoke to *Yonatan* his son and to all his servants to kill David, but *Yehonatan*, the son of Saul was devoted to David (*1 Samuel 19:1*)

Jonathan, who until then had been trying to reconcile Saul and David, now recognizes Saul's murderous intent and immediately warns David so that various agreements and covenants are made between them. But throughout all the further references to Jonathan in 1 Samuel, in the lament that David composes on the death of Saul and Jonathan in *2 Samuel 1:17-27*, and in chapters relating to David's responsibilities to Jonathan's children, the name is always spelled fully with the additional letter '*heh*'. This verse dramatically marks the transition in the loyalty of Jonathan from his father to David – from

---

[1] The translation is by Robert Alter. The word translated here as 'self', '*nefesh*', is customarily translated as 'soul', but the word is closer in meaning to the life-force, that which distinguishes a living person from a dead body. It is sometimes a way of expressing the 'self', or to emphasise the individual identity.

being 'his (Saul's) son' to the more distant 'son of Saul', reinforced by the change in name between the beginning of the verse and the end.

The point that I am making in this case, is that the text is offering a significant hint at an aspect of Jonathan's life that is reflected in the almost invisible change of the name, a change completely lost in translation. Speculations about what the change might mean is the secondary task – one possibility seems to be in association with his trust in God whose name he is ready to invoke; the other his love and loyalty to David which is uniquely celebrated in the Hebrew Bible. But one can only speculate on the possible meaning if the change has been noted and the context considered. Without the careful attention that notices the change we have done a disservice to the Biblical narrator.

In this book I will share my readings of some well-known stories to illustrate dimensions that are sometimes overlooked or misunderstood. I hope that this approach will indicate some of the subtleties in the Hebrew text, the wit and even humour, that is often overlooked, and the extraordinary skill with which the thoughts, emotions and inner development of the Biblical characters is conveyed through such minimal indications. At the very least I want to suggest a way of exploring these texts and allowing them, in turn, to speak to us afresh.

2 Language and the Tower of Babel

The passage in Genesis 11 about the Tower of Babel is generally recognized as an aetiological story, through which the Bible seeks to explain how it is that the descendants of a single human being, Adam, came to be scattered throughout the entire known world and why they ended up speaking so many different languages. Today we are inclined to regard the Biblical explanation as just another early mythological story, and in no way a reliable account of the origins of different languages. However, as with so much of the Hebrew Bible, it is not only the story itself to which we must pay attention, but also to the way in which it is told, for Biblical narrative is very concise, with hardly a word wasted.

When studying any Biblical passage it is important to direct attention to the Hebrew text of the Bible itself. So much of what the Bible has to offer is lost in translation. We leap far too quickly to generalisations about the meaning of the narrative as a whole without seeing the details and nuances that belong to the language itself. Since the theme of the Tower of Babel story is language and communication it is important to take this aspect of the text very seriously.

Though the general outline of the story is familiar it is helpful to have the actual text in mind when discussing it. What follows is a modified version of the translation produced by the Jewish Publication Society of America in 1917 which attempted to be close to the Hebrew original.

1 The whole earth was one language and one speech.

2 It came to pass, as they journeyed east, that they found a plain in the land of Shinar; and they settled there.

3 They said to one another, 'Come let us make bricks, and burn them thoroughly.' And they had the brick for stone and slime they had for mortar.

4 They said, 'Come, let us build us a city, and a tower, with its top in heaven, and let us make us a name, lest we be scattered abroad upon the face of the whole earth.

5 The Lord came down to see the city and the tower which the children of men had built.

6 The Lord said, 'Behold, they are one people and they all have one language; and this is what they begin to do; and now nothing will be withheld from them, which they intend to do.

7 Come, let us go down and there confound their language that they may not understand one another's speech.

8 So the Lord scattered them abroad from there upon the face of all the earth, and they left off building the city.

9 So its name was called Babel, because the Lord confounded the language of all the earth; and the Lord scattered them abroad from there upon the face of all the earth. (*Genesis 11:1-9*)

The reference to Babel alerts us to the great ancient Babylonian civilisation in central Mesopotamia (present day Iraq). Moreover the image of the Tower rising up to heaven probably derives from the Ziggurats, large artificial square mountains, built of brick, the Mesopotamian equivalent of the Egyptian pyramids. Their incomplete form would have suggested the disruption of some enormous building project.

I owe much of my initial understanding of the narrative about the Tower of Babel not to rabbinic exegesis, but to the important literary study of the text by the Dutch scholar Jan Fokkelman in his ground-breaking book *Narrative Art in Genesis*[2]. He notes the extraordinary compactness of the text; the story is contained within eleven verses. It is built in a concentric pattern: key words and phrases link the first half of the narrative, which details the actions of human

---

[2] J.P.Fokkelman *Narrative Art in Genesis: Specimens of Stylistic and Structural Analysis* (Van Gorcum, Assen/Amsterdam 1975) 11-45.

beings, with the second half, which details the exactly corresponding actions of God, measure for measure. The precision of this construction is shown in the ironic response of God to the activities of those building the tower. They say '*hava nilb'nah…*' '**come**, let us make (bricks) (v 3)', to which God responds with '*hava … v'navla..*' '**come**, let us … confound (their language)'. What is lost in translation is the word play between '*nilb'nah*' 'let us make (bricks)' (v 3) and '*navlah*' 'let us confound', because the letters of '*navlah*' (n-v-l) are the reverse of the letters of the root of the word used here for 'make', l-v-n'. God will literally turn their words back to front: the process of inverting the words actually inverts the physical actions at the same time. As we shall see again in this mythical world, 'words' and 'actions' are actually one and the same thing. (In English this reversal of language could be expressed as: what they 'do', becomes 'let us make odd'.) However, someone with an ear for the Hebrew language will already hear in the word '*navlah*' the name of '*bavel*', the Biblical Hebrew term for Babylon.

There are further word plays to consider. The author asks us to imagine a time in pre-history when the entire world had only a single language. Moreover, as we have just indicated, there seems to have been a close identity between objects and the words used to describe them. Thus by playing on words, transforming one word into another, the same transformation could take place in physical reality. In the Hebrew we can hear this in the numerous word plays that describe the actions undertaken by the people who built the tower. '*hava nilb'nah le'veinim v'nisr'pha lis'reipha vat'hi lahem ha-le'veinah le'aven v'ha-cheimar hayah lahem la-chomer.*' 'Come, let us make bricks, and burn them thoroughly.' And they had the brick for stone, and slime had they for mortar.'

The word for 'brick', *le'veinah*, will serve '*le'aven*', 'as stone'; this grammatical form, '*le'aven*', offers a wordplay and alliteration that exactly reflects the replacement of the one physical entity with the other, '*le'veinah* (brick) replacing *le'aven*' (stone). Similar is the play on '*cheimar*', 'slime', with '*chomer*', 'mortar'.   The Martin Buber-Franz Rosenzweig German translation of the Bible attempts to capture the word play: 'backen wir Backsteine… brennen wir sie zu Brande! So war ihnen der Backstein statt Bausteins'.

This equivalence of words and objects is echoed in the fact that the Hebrew word '*davar*', means both 'word' and 'thing'.   In this mythical pre-historic Hebrew-speaking world, to speak a word is to perform an act which brings about a physical change in reality.   This creative power of language echoes the actions of God in the opening words of the Creation story in Genesis. No translation can capture the precise repetition of the Hebrew.   'God said, "Let there be light", and there was light.' (*Genesis 1:3*). 'Y*'hi or va-y'hi or*'. Nothing changes between the word of creation '*Y'hi*' and the event itself '*va-y'hi*' – only the conjunction '*vav*', 'and', stands between them. Even the Buber-Rosenzweig '"Licht werde!" Und Licht ward.' requires a change of verbal form that is not needed in the Hebrew. Yet this intimate relationship between speech and action is not confined to God. One of the first gifts that God gives to Adam, the first man, is the ability to give names to the animals, and as he named them so they were (*Genesis 2:19-20*).   And when none of the animals is suitable to be a mate for Adam, God creates a woman from his rib. When Adam sees her and recognizes that she is 'bone of his bone and flesh of his flesh', he designates her as, '*ishah*', 'woman' because she is derived from the 'man', '*ish*'. The Hebrew grammar is actually quite complicated, but the word play and the sound play are very precise and suggestive. So giving a name, in this case *ish* and *ishah* can also indicate the relationship between things that are named. For the Hebrew Bible these abilities to name, to speak, to communicate, and to bring about change in the physical world, are divine gifts, and they bring with them great power and responsibility. That is why God scrutinises the actions of the builders of the Tower.

One language and one people

The world in which the Tower of Babel was created was a world of 'oneness'. The narrative is contained within a fourfold repetition of variations of the Hebrew word for 'one' '*echad*' (*Genesis 11:1,6*). The narrative begins by setting the scene: '*vayehi chol ha-aretz safah echat ud'varim achadim*'. The first words are easy to translate: 'all the earth was one language', but the last phrase '*ud'varim achadim*' raises problems. '*d'varim*' is the plural of '*davar*', 'word' or 'thing', but the form '*achadim*', a plural of the word for 'one', defies easy explanation or translation. In other contexts it may mean 'few', for example 'a few years'. This would suggest that they had a small vocabulary, few words. However it might also reinforce the idea of the 'oneness' of words and the objects they describe.

When coming down to observe the tower and the people, God notes that they are '*hen am echad u'safah achat l'chulam*', 'one people with one language for all of them' (v 6), again repeating forms of the Hebrew word for 'one'. Surely this 'oneness' is an enviable state, a unity of purpose and identity which we yearn for today and strive to achieve. Yet it is perceived by God as problematic. It is possible to dismiss God's concern as a kind of jealousy. The creatures God has created are simply celebrating their independence from God and their innate gifts. After all, if they are made in the image of God, as the Bible describes, then surely they should be free to explore the divine qualities such as creativity. There is even a further word play that hints at this in the phrase: '*asher banu be'nei ha-adam*', 'which the children of men built'. '*ben*', means 'son', '*banu* is the plural form of the verb '*banah*', 'to build'; the 'boys' have merely fulfilled their intrinsic task to be 'builders'. Nevertheless, if we accept the Biblical view that God is right to be concerned, we are forced to explore the nature of their 'oneness' and its consequences.

Their success at inventing materials, leads in turn to greater ambitions. To build a city in which to live is one of the great achievements of human beings in harnessing skills and labour to create a place where all can find shelter and livelihood. But that city is to contain a tower. The Hebrew term '*migdal*', 'tower', is derived from '*gadol*' which means 'great'. Already we can see in the term the aspiration to something more than simply utilitarian. Its top is to reach to heaven and the purpose is to make themselves a name. The Hebrew word '*shem*', name, carries a weight of meanings from 'reputation' and 'fame' to 'identity' and personal qualities. Their pride in the tower is to become the defining characteristic of who they are, of how they perceive themselves. But '*shem*', 'name', is also a play on '*shamayim*', 'heaven', hinting at a conscious level of competition with God. Their tower is to rise up into God's domain. However, the tower also serves a second purpose: 'lest we be scattered throughout the earth'. Bible readers will know that this is in direct contradiction to God's blessing given to the first human beings: they are to be fruitful and multiply and fill the earth (*Genesis 1:28*). This blessing was then repeated to Noah and his sons when they emerged from the ark to repopulate the world after the great flood (*Genesis 9:1*). In massing together these descendants of Noah are consciously rebelling against God, but also seeking through their collective numbers and power a feeling of security. But here is a further hint at the problem underlying their unity, if this unity is created by fear. Such a unity demands solidarity and uniformity; such a unity usually defines itself against an external other, whether real or artificially created; in the name of such a unity we may seek out those within who do not conform and punish them; unity built on fear can easily lapse into a kind of totalitarianism. In Europe we are haunted by examples of the destruction wrought by that kind of 'unity', yet we still allow our politicians and media to foster a climate of fear, to stereotype those we consider to be alien, different or threatening. This kind of fear-driven unity has to be countered by the quest for something different: a unity that acknowledges that each of us contains many kinds of identity; a unity that accepts otherness and pluralism as a human gift, and ultimately a source of strength; a unity that respects and celebrates difference; a unity that seeks a harmony that comes from sharing the unique contribution that each of us offers.

27

To return to the text itself, another series of word plays underpins the story. As mentioned above, the word for heaven is '*shamayim*', commonly used in the Biblical phrase, '*shamayim va'arets*', 'heaven and earth'. That phrase effectively defines the two domains that, in the Biblical view, are to be kept strictly apart. The earth is the place for human beings to work out their destiny; heaven, for the Biblical authors, belongs to God alone. In the words of *Psalm 115:16* 'The heavens are the heavens of the Lord, but the earth He has given to the children of Adam, to human beings.' The tower reaching to heaven is an assault on the divine domain, or, at the very least, an assertion of the irrelevance of God in their actions.

The triumph of technology

We have seen how the builders discovered that bricks can be used to replace stone; something artificial, something they had made themselves, could replace the natural raw material. This is the essence of technology and a breakthrough in human mastery of the material world. Yet in the course of a single verse, their discovery changes from a practical necessity, to build a city, to becoming an end in itself, the building of the tower. The story of the tower becomes a paradigm of our ambivalent feelings about technology as an autonomous force in the world, capable of massive acts of construction and equally massive acts of destruction, independent of moral considerations. This hint in the Biblical text is picked up in a rabbinic midrash, a parable, about the building of the Tower. According to the rabbis: If a man fell to his death while working on the tower, no one paid attention. But when a brick fell down, they stopped work and wept, saying: Woe unto us! When will another be brought up to replace it?' (*Pirke d'Rabbi Eliezer 24*).

A different perception of the significance of the technology comes from a modern Jewish writer, himself a master of the parable. In one of his short stories Franz Kafka, considers the Tower. For the builders of the Tower, he writes:

The essential thing in the whole business is the idea of building a tower that will reach to heaven. In comparison with that idea everything else is secondary.

But, writes Kafka, since the idea would never be forgotten, the concern became instead about the process of building itself. The builders argued:

human knowledge is increasing, the art of building has made progress and will make further progress, a piece of work which takes us a year may perhaps be done in half the time in another hundred years, and better done, too, more enduringly.

It is ..... likely that the next generation with their perfected knowledge will find the work of their predecessors bad, and tear down what has been built so as to begin anew.

In Kafka's parable their attention now switches from the tower itself to the needs of the builders.

Such thoughts paralyzed people's powers, and so they troubled less about the tower than the construction of a city for the workmen. Every nationality wanted the finest quarters for itself, and this gave rise to disputes, which developed into bloody conflicts.[3]

Kafka takes us into a later theme we will discover in the Biblical narrative, but now we need to return to the text itself. Until this point in the story the ambition of the builders of the Tower has been told from their perspective. But now we switch to God's perspective, and the Bible provides an ironic joke at the expense of the hubris of the builders. This magnificent

---

[3] Franz Kafka 'The City Coat of Arms' Parables and Paradoxes: In German and English (Schocken Books, New York 1961) pp 36-39.

tower that mounts into the very heavens is actually so small that God has literally to come down in order to see it.

As well as the emphasis on their desire to make a 'name', Hebrew, '*shem*', there is a further word play through the often-repeated word for place, '*sham*', meaning 'there', both words offering a complex interaction with '*shamayim*', 'heaven'. In the end, because of God's actions, instead of reaching '*shamayim*', 'heaven', they are scattered '*misham*', 'away from there'. In a further irony, after their language has been confounded and they have been dispersed around the world, the one thing they had tried to prevent happening, they nevertheless succeed in achieving one of their aims. The city they built does indeed acquire a name and a reputation, but the name is '*bavel*', 'Babylon', because there God, in yet another Hebrew word-play, '*balal*', 'confounded', their language. Instead of the ultimate symbol of their unity the name becomes the symbol of their disunity as they are scattered throughout the earth.

The missing neighbour

I would like to draw attention to one further linguistic effect in the Hebrew text. At the beginning (v3) there comes a phrase '*vayom'ru ish el re'ehu*', that literally translates as 'they spoke, each man to his neighbour'. The phrase 'a man to his neighbour' is an idiomatic expression, common in the Bible when people interact, so it is often translated, as in our English version, simply as 'they said one to another'. The word 'neighbour' disappears in the familiarity of the expression, 'one to another'. But it is important to point out that the word here for neighbour is not one to be lightly set aside, because it is the same word in perhaps the most famous sentence in the Hebrew Bible: 'You shall love your neighbour as yourself' (Leviticus 19:18). At the end of the story of the Tower, when God decides to confound their language, the result will be '*asher lo yish'm'u ish s'fat re'ehu*', literally, 'so that no man will understand the language of his neighbour'. (Again our translation is too idiomatic: 'that they may not understand one another's speech'.) What the Biblical author has done is take the conventional idiom and break it open, so that the 'neighbour' becomes once again a real person, a 'neighbour' with a specific identity and someone with whom one has a real relationship. But the irony of the story is that the true meaning of 'neighbour' only becomes clear when the actual relationship between 'neighbours' has stopped because communication has broken down between them, 'so that no man will understand the language of his neighbour'. The 'one another' of the idiom has been radically transformed, and 'another' has become instead 'the other', a stranger with whom communication is no longer possible.

But there is an additional element here that is puzzling. The verb conventionally translated as 'understand', 'they could not understand one another' because of the confusion of language, is the Hebrew verb '*sh'ma*'. In almost all of the many occasions when it is used in the Bible it means 'hear' or 'listen'. I suspect that the translation 'understand' is an attempt to make sense of this unexpected word. Nevertheless if we stay with the Hebrew 'listen', this suggests that it is not simply that people could no longer 'understand' one another once their language was confounded, but rather that they were unable or unwilling to take the necessary effort to 'hear', to 'listen', to effect communication, in the absence of a common language. It is as if the initial idiom, 'they spoke to one another', concealed what was already a failure. The enthusiasm that went into their common building project, did not require them to know the neighbour with whom they were working, beyond the practical requirements for the task itself. Only now, when direct speech was no longer available, did the real gap in their relationship emerge, the alienation that existed because no effort had been needed to communicate. The breakdown in language revealed the fracture in human relations that had been implicit before. Their intoxication with exploring their power to transform and build, their orientation towards the task itself, made them insensitive to the requirements of their relationship to one another as neighbours.

How are we to understand this story? One way is simply to explain it as an aetiological tale. The previous chapter in Genesis has already described the way the descendants of Noah produced the seventy nations of the Biblical world. Now the story of the Tower sets out to explain the puzzling development of the multitude of languages. In typical Biblical fashion it expresses the issue within the framework of the divine-human encounter. The story belongs to a series of narratives depicting, with a certain degree of irony, the strange picture of a Creator struggling to control this set of fiercely independent human creations. Indeed, in this story, God is sufficiently disturbed by what they are doing to make a radical intervention; not again a physical destruction as with the flood, but a more profound challenge to the one feature that distinguishes human beings from the rest of creation, their ability to communicate ideas across time and space. For the Biblical author, this is not simply a mischievous intervention by God, but belongs to a broader divine plan, though one that is not yet fully revealed, beyond God's intention that human beings populate the earth. We must wait for the next chapter of Genesis, and the appearance of Abraham, to understand how God would like to see human interaction built on the basis of justice and righteousness.

But, as we have seen, through the subtleties of the writing of the narrative a number of other elements appear. God takes the words with which they begin their actions and literally turns them inside out. Perhaps it is a reminder that every action contains its own potential opposite. There are no neutral deeds, even if we cannot foresee all the possible consequences at the time of acting. This suggests that the willingness to be self-critical, to acknowledge mistakes, and be prepared to correct them, is not evidence of weakness or failure, but an essential component in human communication and survival. Certainly it will be a major feature in the teaching of the Biblical prophets, and a central element in Jewish religious self-understanding.

The physical reality of words and speech is another feature beneath the surface. Words too have consequences, and any number of proverbial statements remind us to be careful about what we say. A word once spoken cannot be taken back. Yet we know as well that words can become trivialised and meaningless. Words can also become poisoned, used as weapons to mislead and misinform, euphemistic substitutions that conceal the true purpose of those who seek to manipulate others. It is a paradox that we have never been so blessed as today with technical devices to improve communication, from mobile phones to the internet, yet we still have such difficulty communicating with one another across the simplest of barriers. Therefore the emphasis on the word '*sh'ma*', 'hear', 'listen', in the story of the Tower becomes very important. Learning how to listen to one another, and hence to restore the 'other' to his or her rightful place as our neighbour, is a great art. It requires the investment of time and much self-discipline, especially in situations of conflict, where the last thing we want to hear is how the other views us. Yet anything less than that investment only feeds the rhetoric of conflict and threat. The failure of the people of Babel to invest the time to listen is perfectly understandable, painfully so.

Language within and without

As I prepared this analysis of the text, I became more and more aware of yet one more level of complexity that it illustrates. The deeper we go into the intricacies of the Hebrew text, the internal plays and nuances of the language, the harder it becomes to summarise the meaning of the story. This is not only because of the problem of translating from one language and culture into another, though that is challenging enough. Rather once we become exposed to the richness and complexity of any speech, of any human expression, we realise how little we can grasp the many possibilities it contains. It is a commonplace that the many levels of meaning, conscious and unconscious, of the author, are compounded by the interpretative skills and assumptions of every single reader. Babel is not just about different languages, but about the many 'languages' within every single human being, and the limits of what can be understood even within ourselves, let alone conveyed in the encounter with someone else.   In any meeting with another person which we wish to take seriously, in any dialogue, we need to ask: are we really attempting to create a relationship or only trading information?

It is not surprising that globalisation, for example, brings so much conflict in its wake.   It too assumes an ultimate human unity, but all too often a unity that is artificial, and threatens a loss of individuality.   Today we extend and extend our polyglot cities.   We also build our towers to heaven, and tragically there are those who seek to smash them down, also in the name of God.   Yet what is surprising is the degree of shared understandings that does exist, across religious, cultural and linguistic barriers.   For better or worse, Babel is where we live.   Now we have to find out how to create a different kind of unity, despite all the barriers of language and faith and culture that stand in the way.

3 Did Abraham pass God's test? Reflections on Genesis 22

This is one of the most problematic narratives in the Hebrew Bible. God's command to Abraham to sacrifice his son is deeply disturbing. How can God make such a demand on a human being, even if in the end Isaac is not sacrificed?   And how are we to understand an Abraham who is willing to undertake this act, seemingly without protest?   Where is the Abraham who challenged God's justice in the case of Sodom and Gomorrah?   What was the effect on Isaac who had to endure the threat of death at the hands of his father until the very last moment?   The narrator informs us at the very beginning that this is a test, and that changes the way we read the story. Without that information we might have read it in the same way we have read the other stories of Abraham's journeys and adventures. But here we are challenged to discover the nature of the test itself, and indeed whether Abraham passes it or fails. Undoubtedly the mainstream Jewish, Christian and Muslim traditions give Abraham a 'pass-mark', labelling him as a hero of faith, obedient to everything that God requires of him, even willing to suppress the love he feels for his son. Admirable, perhaps, but a very dangerous theology, with its justification to kill in the name of God. Nevertheless there are a number of features of the Biblical narrative itself that raise questions about this mainstream understanding.

Although the story is often studied as an independent unit, it does have a very specific context within the Hebrew Bible.   The rabbis recognised this, seeing it as the tenth and last of a series of tests to which Abraham was put by God.   In order to make up the number ten they had to add some non-Biblical stories, but I believe they are following the Biblical pattern in seeing it as a climax to the series of challenges presented to Abraham.   The pattern shows itself through a number of doublets of stories that have drawn the attention of modern Bible scholarship. For example, there are two separate narratives in which Abraham claims that Sarah his wife is actually his sister.   There are two narratives describing the Covenant that God makes with Abraham.   Whatever the origin of these doublets, when we look at them within the range of stories as a whole between Genesis 12, the call to Abram, and Genesis 22, the call to sacrifice Isaac, we see that they are arranged to form a concentric pattern.

12a Lekh l'kha Blessing promised. Abram Sarai

12b   Egypt Wife/Sister

13/14   Lot in danger Sodom

15   Covenant

16   Hagar Ishmael

17   Covenant (Abraham Sarah)

18/19   Lot in danger Sodom (Incest)

20   Gerar Wife/Sister (Incest)

21   Isaac Hagar Ishmael depart

22   Lekh l'kha Blessing confirmed

The first thing to notice is something to which the rabbis drew attention. The opening words of God's first summons to Abraham in Genesis 12 are '*lekh l'kha*', from the verb '*halakh*' 'to go' and the particle '*l*' meaning 'to' or 'for'. The effect of this grammatical construction is to soften the force of the imperative '*lekh*', 'go' to a request or invitation. It can be read in a number of ways, for example homiletically, as 'go to yourself', or 'go for yourself'. But what is significant is that the identical phrase occurs at the beginning of Genesis 22, and nowhere else in the Hebrew Bible. Thus the two invitations by God to 'go' create an *inclusio* around the entire set of Abraham narratives. Furthermore the two wife/sister stories (Genesis 12b and 20) and the two covenant chapters (15 and 17) are located in the corresponding places within the concentric structure. In addition chapters 13/14 and 18/19, both of which deal with themes about Lot, the nephew of Abraham, being in danger, in relationship to the town of Sodom, similarly correspond. A glance at the overall pattern locates the centre in chapter 16 with the birth of Ishmael. Theoretically this should be the climax of the stories with the birth of a child to establish the line of descendants promised to Abraham. Ishmael came into existence as an attempt by Abraham and Sarah to guarantee God's promise of a large family for Abraham. But God's intention was that Sarah be the mother, so the birth of Ishmael is a kind of detour in the divine plan. As the Bible indicates, Ishmael is not the correct child. Instead it is to be Isaac. So now the stories repeat themselves in reverse order. They begin with the covenant which is accompanied by a change of name for both Abram and Sarai to Abraham and Sarah, suggesting a new beginning. In chapter 21 Isaac the promised son is finally born and Hagar and Ishmael are forced to leave.[4] The stage is now set for Isaac to inherit. And then, when everything seems to be settled, God asks Abraham to sacrifice Isaac. This seems to be a final test of Abraham's trust that God will fulfil the promise with which the set of narratives began, even if Isaac is now taken away.[5]

---

[4] Since Ishmael is Abraham's son he is also the child of the same divine blessing to have a large family. His twelve sons correspond to the 12 tribes that will descend from Jacob.

[5] There is one further feature that is worth noting about the sequence, namely the narrative about the incestuous relationship between Lot and his two daughters after the destruction of Sodom. The resulting sons, Ammon and Moab, provide a somewhat belittling tale of origins for the two neighbouring states, with whom, incidentally, a later tradition will forbid intermarriage. But what is less noted, despite the two wife/sister narratives, is that Sarah is indeed Abraham's half-sister through a different mother. The later Biblical laws will ban such a marriage as incestuous. One possible reason for this emphasis is to draw a parallel with Adam who married a woman physically taken from within himself. Abraham is to be the new Adam, beginning a new initiative to draw humanity to the worship of God. Unlike Noah, who already has children when he is chosen to save humanity from

Once we examine the text in detail there is a further feature of the story that must also be taken into account, namely the different names for God that appear. The commonest are *elohim* which may be used to indicate the general concept of God that is known, whereas YHWH is the intimate name by which Israel alone know that same universal God. We will examine different ways of understanding the use of these names in particular in different contexts. From a purely narrative perspective, God is also a 'character' in Biblical stories and the various names and combination of names by which God is known are clues to the way in which we are to regard God's role in any given story.

The later rabbinic tradition suggested that the name '*elohim*' in a story hinted at the operation of God's attribute of 'strict justice', whereas the name YHWH reflected the attribute of God's 'love' or 'compassion'. Whatever the particular interpretation, in this narrative in Genesis 22 it is noteworthy that whereas the command to sacrifice his son, and the first half of chapter 22 utilise the name '*elohim*', it is an angel of YHWH who prevents Abraham from killing Isaac, and YHWH is the divine name used throughout the rest of the story, with one exception we will discuss later. Presumably, this is a factor to be taken into account in interpreting the meaning of the story.

The narrator has previously given us an insight into God's purposes with an internal dialogue when God debates as to whether or not to tell Abraham about the plan to destroy Sodom. Now we are told that the forthcoming event is to be viewed as a test set by God.

Having established something of this background, let us look at the actual narrative itself. We have noted already the rabbinic awareness of the repetition of the phrase '*lekh l'kha*' that links the narrative to that in chapter 12. There is a further narrative device that links the two chapters. In Genesis 12 the opening sequence in the Hebrew reads: 'Go, from your land, from your birthplace (or

---

the flood, Abraham and Sarah are childless, so that the chosen son will only be born after they have undergone a variety of tests by God. Moreover their incestuous relationship is the nearest possible way for Abraham to reproduce himself.

kinsfolk), and from your father's house'. The sequence runs from the general to the specific, or, in terms of the challenge it presents to Abraham, from the least to the most difficult choice. To abandon his homeland may be difficult, to cut himself off from his family is harder, but the hardest of all to separate from his own father. The same kind of sequence occurs at the start of Chapter 22, something often lost in the translations which truncate the Hebrew sequence to fit an English syntax. Literally the Hebrew reads: Take please your son, your only one, whom you love, Isaac. In his commentary to this verse the great mediaeval Jewish commentator Rashi reads God's words here as only one half of a conversation with Abraham. Rashi provides Abraham's evasive response as follows:

God: Take please your son.

Abraham: But I have two sons.

God: Your only one.

Abraham: But each is the only son of his mother, Isaac is the only son of Sarah and Ishmael the only son of Hagar.

God: Whom you love.

Abraham: But I love both of them!

God: Isaac!

Thus both chapters begin with a similar call which moves from the general to the specific, from the least to the most challenging and painful.

If we now turn to the specifics of the apparent command to Abraham we find another aspect that is often lost in translation. God says to Abraham: '*kach na*'. '*Kach*' is the imperative of the verb '*lakach*', 'to take', but the problem of interpretation arises with the addition of the particle '*na*'. If it is noted at all it leads to phrases like 'take now', which may even be seen as reinforcing the authority and urgency of the command. But the commonest use of '*na*' with an imperative form of the verb is to change the imperative demand to a request, 'please'. When Moses pleads with God to heal his sister Miriam of her leprosy, he says '*el na r'fa na lah*', 'please God, please heal her'. (*Numbers 12:13*).

39

When Elijah the prophet asks the Shunamite woman for water he says 'k'chi na', 'please take for me', using a feminine imperative of the same verb *lakach*, 'to take', with the additional '*na*'. (*I Kings 17:10*). When Jonah asks God to take his life from him he uses the same phrase as God in our chapter: '*kach na et nafshi mimmeni*', 'please take my life from me'. (*Jonah 4:4*). There is therefore every reason to assume that the same construction carries the same kind of meaning here in Genesis 22.[6] That is, God's words to Abraham are not a command but a request – please take your son. This means that Abraham is free to accept or refuse this call. If Abraham simply has to obey a divine command there is no longer any test involved. To reduce Abraham to a mere obedient slave of an autocratic master would undermine the entire thrust of the choice of Abraham in the first place as a responsible human being, with freedom of choice. How can Abraham raise his household to follow 'justice and righteousness', a major theme of God's choosing him, as expressed in *Genesis18:19*. The debate about the destruction of Sodom and Gomorrah, provides an opportunity for Abraham to reflect and strengthen these qualities, by actually challenging God. Something he could never do if he had no independent will of his own. The truly disturbing aspect of this call to sacrifice his son is that Abraham, given the choice, accepts obedience to God even when it calls for such an appalling act.

Abraham's silence is deafening. He rises early in the morning, a Biblical idiom suggesting a commitment to action. He personally saddles his ass, despite having two lads to serve him. The narrator passes over the three days of the journey without comment, and it is for the rabbis to fill them with

---

[6] This is also a rabbinic view of the event: Rabbi Simeon bar Abba said: The word '*na*' is only used to mean 'a request'. It is like a king of flesh and blood who had to withstand many wars and who had a particular warrior and won victories. One day a powerful war confronted him. He said to him (the warrior), please stand with me in this war lest they say that the former ones (wars) meant nothing. Similarly the blessed Holy One said to Abraham: I have tested you with many tests and you have withstood all of them. Now, stand with me in this test lest they say that the former ones meant nothing. (*Sanhedrin 89b*)

indications of Abraham's inner turmoil. On arrival at the place we have the brief instructions to the servants to remain with the ass. Abraham says that after the sacrifice 'we will return'. Perhaps here is his hope that somehow Isaac will be saved, or else a final act to deceive Isaac and the servants. After that all we are given is the enigmatic conversation between Isaac and Abraham.

They went on, the two of them together.

Isaac said to Abraham, his father, 'Father.'

He replied, 'Here I am, my son.'

He said, 'Here is the fire and the wood, but where is the lamb for the burnt offering?'

Abraham said, 'God will provide for Himself the lamb for the burnt offering, my son.'

They went on, the two of them together.

Isaac points to the strangeness of what they are doing. Where atop the mountain will they find a lamb suitable to offer to God? Abraham's answer leaves the solution to God. He uses the same name *elohim* who had given him the test. The conversation is made particularly painful by the repeated use of the terms 'my father', 'my son', so that the love that binds them, and the betrayal of this love, is stressed. The answer seems to satisfy Isaac who says nothing further and will later submit himself to being bound upon the altar. Does Isaac know and accept what is going on? The narrator suggests this is the case by bracketing the conversation before and after with the phrase '*vayel'khu sheneihem yachdav*', 'they went on, the two of them, together'. This repetition supports the rabbinic view that Isaac was aware of what was to come and voluntarily offered his life as a martyr for the sake of Abraham's God. Both Abraham and Isaac underwent this divine test.

This raises the question of the age of Isaac when this event occurred. Most artistic representations of the story make him a child. The only direct clue the text offers is the reference to him by both Abraham and later the angel as a '*na'ar*'. The term can mean a young man from childhood to adolescence

41

or even older, and additionally is used to refer to someone who is a servant. The young men who accompany Abraham are '*n'arim*'. The prophet Jeremiah tried to refuse God's call on the basis that he was only a '*na'ar*', (*Jeremiah 1:6*) yet he was clearly old enough to be called and to have the courage to try to refuse. Isaac is also strong enough to carry the wood for the sacrifice up the mountain. The Biblical chronology may also help. Sarah is 90 years old when Isaac is born (*Genesis 17:17*). Her death, at the age of 127 is recorded immediately after this episode, and at least the rabbinic tradition ascribes her death to hearing the news about what Abraham had tried to do to her son. Isaac is forty years old when he marries Rebecca. The text explains that he brings her into Sarah's tent and Isaac was comforted for his mother, presumably after her death shortly before. All the above would conform with the rabbinic view that Isaac was thirty-seven years old at the time and thus fully aware and accepting of what was happening.[7]

In contrast to the speed with which the three day journey passed, the last minutes before the sacrifice are described in agonisingly slow detail. Time seems to stand still as Abraham builds the altar, lays out the wood, binds his son, places him on the altar above the wood and stretches out his hand to take the knife to slay his son. Suddenly the angel calls.

The rabbis noted that at the beginning of the chapter God only had to call his name once for Abraham to respond. This time the angel has to call twice before Abraham responds. They saw in this Abraham's total concentration on the act so that he did not hear the first call. They also noted that the angel gives him two instructions: 'do not send your hand against the lad and do not do anything to him'. They assumed that at this moment Abraham was quite mad. When the angel told him not to slay his son, he pleaded: 'let me at least cut him to show my willingness', to which the angel replied, 'nor do anything to him'!

---

[7] Josephus makes him 25 (Antiquities I 227; Jubilees 17:15 makes him 16.

So the test is over. But what does it mean? I was once told that the writer Eli Wiesel had asked: If it was a test, who gave up first? And the answer, of course, is God. Was the intention from the very beginning to show Abraham's uncritical obedience? Did Abraham have to be put to such a test, to be driven almost mad, in order to prove his faithfulness? There is another way to read the story, since the God (*ha-elohim*) who invited Abraham to sacrifice his son is not the angel of YHWH who stopped him. This leaves open the possibility that this entire episode was something that began in the mind of Abraham himself, as represented by the name *elohim*. But if it was God, and, as we suggested at the beginning, it was an invitation and not a command, then God must have expected Abraham to refuse or at least argue. In fact, in this interpretation, God waited till the very last moment in the hope that Abraham would refuse. When it was clear that it would not happen and Isaac was likely to be killed, God had to send very quickly an angel to stop him. In this reading God did indeed test Abraham but was shocked to discover just how far human beings were prepared to go, even to the point of committing murder of a beloved child, if they were convinced that by doing so they were somehow serving their God. Abraham showed the limits beyond which even an Abraham should not be pushed. By this reading Abraham failed the test, but nevertheless thereby established a boundary that should not be crossed in terms of how God is to be served. Tragically, because the story has been read as Abraham's success, generations of sons have been condemned to death by their fathers in the name of some God or idol.

But this interpretation stands or falls on how we understand the conclusion drawn by the angel on behalf of God, because it seems to praise Abraham's willingness to sacrifice Isaac. The angel spells out what God has learnt from the episode.

> For now I know that you fear God and have not withheld your son, your only one from me. (*Genesis 22:12*)

43

The angel even repeats the latter part of this in his second speech to Abraham after the sacrifice of the lamb.

> By myself I have sworn, an oracle of YHWH, that because you have done this thing and not withheld your son, your only one, that I will surely bless you and multiply your seed as the stars of the heaven and like the sand which is upon the sea shore....' (22:16)

Nevertheless there are still questions to be addressed to the wording of the first response of the angel. The phrase 'that you fear God', *ki y'rei elohim attah*, echoes something said by Abraham himself a few chapters earlier when he had to justify to King Avimelech why he had claimed that Sarah, his wife, was actually his sister. It was because: *ein yir'at elohim ba-makom ha-zeh'* 'there is no fear of God in this place'. (*Genesis 20:11*) When we look at other examples of the phrase combining the verb *yara*, to fear or be in awe of, with the name of God E*lohim*, a consistent pattern emerges. The same accusation, 'that they did not fear God', is levelled against the Amalekites for their cowardly attack on the weakest people at the rear of the Israelites as they wandered through the wilderness. (*Deuteronomy 25:17-19*) More positively, it was the 'fear of God' greater than their fear of Pharaoh, that led the Hebrew midwives to resist killing the male children of the Israelites. (*Exodus 1:17*)[8] In all these cases the issue is not directly about faith or belief in God, but rather the presence or absence of a moral or ethical sense, a conscience that governed their behaviour.[9] Thus there is a deep irony in the appearance of this phrase as a

---

[8] Another example is probably Moses' father-in-law Jethro's set of criteria of people to appoint as judges, where 'fear of heaven' is located alongside men of wealth, of truthfulness and those who reject bribes. (*Exodus 18:21*)

[9] Where the combination of words is used with a more obviously religious sense a slightly different formulation may be used or the context makes it clear that God is specifically intended (*Deut 10:12; Kohelet 3:14; 7:18; 8:12-13; 12;13*). In *Leviticus 19:14* where the case is precisely about taking advantage of the weakness of others: 'You shall not curse the death nor put a stumbling block before the blind, but you shall fear your God.', the formulation is '*v'yareta me'elohecha*', the addition of the particle '*mem*' and the personal pronoun 'your God' distinguish the religious demand here from the generalised moral issue in the other cases. Elsewhere those who 'fear God' in the purely religious sense are called '*yir'ei adona*i' (*Psalm 115:11; 118:4*) where it is possible that those who hear that title are non-Israelites who have come to serve Israel's God.

word of praise for an Abraham who has actually suppressed his conscience and moral sense. In fact he has fallen into the way of behaviour about which he criticised King Avimelech. Nevertheless it is also possible to read the sentence as actually expressing the contradictory nature of Abraham's act. The Hebrew would allow us to read the 'vav' that links the two statements not as a conjunctive, 'and', but rather as an adversative 'but'. 'You fear God, have a moral conscience, but nevertheless you have not withheld your son.' Some support for such a reading comes from the omission of the phrase 'you fear God' when the angel speaks a second time.

The opening words of the angel need further examination. The phrase 'attah yadati', 'now I know', suggests that this is a confirmation of what God has been trying to discover about Abraham by the test. Yet this is the second time we are told what God knows about Abraham, using the same verbal form 'yadati'. Once again it takes us back to the story of Sodom and Gomorrah which is prefaced by God's internal monologue.

YHWH said: Shall I conceal from Abraham what I am doing? Abraham will become a great and powerful nation, and in him will all the nations of the earth be blessed. For I have known him (y'dativ) in order that he will command his sons and his household after him to keep the way of the Lord to do righteousness and justice so that the Lord may bring upon Abraham what he said to him (18:17-19).

Then comes the information about the destruction to come to Sodom and Gomorrah. Abraham challenges God, how can God slay the righteous with the wicked, shall the judge of all the earth not do justly? (18:25) In Abraham's accusation he uses the two terms God has previously highlighted, 'righteousness' and 'justice'. God allows Himself to appear to be in the wrong so that Abraham can practise these two values by challenging God. God knew that Abraham would respond in this way, and through that test helped Abraham grow into these values as his own. So what is the new information that God 'knows' as a result of the episode before us? One possible answer is Abraham's

45

limits. How far can he stretch his human readiness to serve God and yet maintain his independence and moral autonomy? Abraham's submission to such an immoral act, precisely because he believes it is to be carried out in the name of God, shows how, in the right circumstances, he will betray his conscience and moral compass. In this reading of the story Abraham is not a 'knight of faith' who suspends the ethical in order to serve his God, but a human being who breaks down when confronted with an impossible choice, who sacrifices his humanity in the name of an outer ideology. By not rebelling he fails the test. Nevertheless, through that failure God learns the limits of what may be demanded of the faithful.

Finally, the angel's confirmation of the blessing with which Abraham's journey began is puzzling. The original blessing was given by God without any conditions attached, so no action by Abraham was required to ensure that it would be fulfilled by God. Furthermore it is also curious that this final summation of Abraham's career should be left to an angel to say when the Biblical text is quite comfortable with God addressing Abraham directly from the very beginning of his call. If it is possible to read the story as Abraham's failure to pass the test by not protesting against God, then what the angel is saying is a kind of reassurance that despite the outcome, all will be well.

However we read the story, for the rabbis Abraham's actions should not be taken as a model for subsequent behaviour by his descendants. In fact the merit gained by Abraham by this once and for all action is something we can evoke to support us whenever we turn to God in times of need. The Abraham we are to imitate in the rabbinic tradition is a much more domestic figure – the model of hospitality, and an example of someone who led people to the belief in the true God, converting them to Judaism. But even these comforting thoughts do not take away the drama and problematic of this passage. It was chosen by the rabbis as the Torah reading for the second day of Rosh Hashanah. So the story returns to haunt us and challenge us on the day which is the birthday of the world, the day on which the behaviour of every person and every creature stands in judgment before God.

At the end of the story, Abraham returns to his young men and Isaac is notably absent. The text even repeats the sentence 'they went together', but omits the phrase 'the two of them'. Where is Isaac? The midrash offers a number of explanations. That Isaac was indeed killed and only later was resurrected by God. Or that he went to study in the Bet ha-midrash, the school, of Shem his grandfather. Even Isaac's later blindness is traced back to this episode. The angels wept when they saw him tied to the altar and their tears fell into his eyes. But if Isaac is the victim of this story, so also is Abraham, whether the God he obeys is a creation of his own dark imagining or indeed the same God to whom he said on so many occasions, '*hinneni*', 'here I am'. Like the young men told to remain at the foot of the mountain, we can only stand at a distance and wonder and speculate about the events that took place at the mountain peak. We can only watch spellbound and bewildered at the challenge faced by those two heroes confronting the meeting of life and death, of faith and conscience, and the eternal human struggle to understand, but also struggle with, the always unexpected demands of God.

4 Did Jacob Steal the Wrong Blessing (Genesis 27)?

The stories about the families of the patriarchs in the Book of Genesis are sometimes shocking and painful to read. They are not the kind of stories we would like or expect to see about figures who we assume are meant to be role models for good behaviour and religious faith. So, we may find our religious tradition, or we ourselves, making excuses for them, or trying to justify actions that are not morally acceptable. If we take a longer view of what happens to them, we may see that they do not escape from the consequences of their actions and that a price is exacted for wrong things that they do, or else that they learn and change and grow from the experience. In short, they are presented to us as normal human beings like any of us with strengths and weaknesses, ambitions and loyalties, responsibilities and failures. Like us they are trying, despite the sometimes-complicated entanglements of family life, to find their way in the world and act out as best they can their personal destiny.

Perhaps no one of the Biblical patriarchs is more complex than Jacob. From his very birth, holding onto the heel of his twin brother Esau, he carries a name that will remind him of their troubled relationship. The Hebrew word for 'heel' is 'akav', which forms the basis of Jacob's name 'ya'akov', initially because of the incident of his birth. But as a verb, and clearly in relationship to their story, it means to 'supplant', to take something that belongs to another[10]. Later Jacob will acquire a new name, Yisrael, meaning 'one who struggles with, or on behalf of God' But even when he gains this significant characterisation, the stories about him switch between the two names as an index of the inner struggles that continue to affect his state of mind or behaviour.

I want to examine the story that presents Jacob's most shameful act while still a young man, an act that led to his having to leave his family home in disgrace. In that period, during his exile, he himself experienced betrayal and

---

[10] Genesis 27:36; Hosea 12:4; Jeremiah 9:3

48

exploitation, nevertheless his character developed for the better. Moreover, he raised the family that made him the physical ancestor of the nation that came to be known as the people of Israel.

The Esau Blessing

As so often in the Biblical narratives, the significance of events lies in the small details that are revealed, and it is up to the reader to try to discover them and thread them together in a coherent way. There is inevitably a great deal of subjectivity in our choice of what to include in this exercise. What follows is a reading of what led to Jacob's stealing of the blessing that his father Isaac intended to give to Esau, his oldest son, and what followed from this action until the conflict with Esau was resolved or at least a way of living together was achieved.

The first important indication of trouble ahead arises with the pregnancy of Rebecca, the wife of Isaac, and what seemed to be a struggle in her womb between the two unborn children. She went to enquire of God and received the following response:

Two nations are in your womb

and two peoples shall emerge from your loins.

The one shall be stronger than the other,

the elder shall serve the younger. (*Genesis 25:23*)

As is often the case in such oracles, the Hebrew of the conclusion is ambiguous so that the final statement could equally mean that 'the younger shall serve the older'. The reader is already warned here that the conflict within the womb is to continue throughout the lifetimes of the twins and even beyond.

The traditions within the Biblical world expect that the firstborn son will succeed the father as head of the family. But over against this is the repeated Biblical pattern that God chooses the second-born son over the first, or the most unlikely person for a task, as if God is deliberately breaking conventional rules. Presumably God sees something in the individual that is necessary to fulfil some divine plan. This oracle leaves us with at least two questions. The first is simply what does it mean in terms of the future relationship between the twins and their respective families? Who will be the dominant figure, and is this something permanent or changeable? Secondly, and this is more speculative, how did Rebecca understand the oracle, and did she communicate it to her husband Isaac? Isaac had already entreated God on her behalf because she was barren. Why was he not involved in Rebecca's journey to enquire of God about what was happening within her? Perhaps she went alone because such intimate matters were kept within the inner world of women.

The first child is born, covered in red hair, and '*they*', presumably both parents, named him 'Esau'. Then the second one emerged, clutching the heel of Esau, and *he*, presumably Isaac alone, called him Jacob. The difference in who gave the names is an interesting distinction made by the narrator. It is the kind of thing that one notes without knowing whether it has significance or not. But immediately we are told that, despite being twins, the two boys were very different in temperament. 'Esau was a man skilled in hunting, a man of the field, but Jacob was a simple man, a dweller in tents,' (Genesis 25:27) The word '*tam*' which describes Jacob can mean 'wholeness', perhaps innocence or integrity. But it is not clear how far this truly represents his character.

If the twin brothers are very different, the parents each choose their favourite, and in this way, however understandable, heighten the potential conflict between them. It is the same kind of mistake, of favouring one child over the other, that will lead to the tragic experience of Joseph in the next generation.

Isaac loved Esau because of the game that he brought him, but Rebecca loved Jacob. (*Genesis 25:28*)[11]

It is a fascinating distinction here between the reason given by the father and the absence of a reason from the mother. In terms of the narrative, it is setting up the circumstances which will lead to Jacob's trick to obtain the blessing meant for Esau. But it is a reminder of the craft of the Biblical narrator to suggest the motivations and possible interactions of four different characters, in a couple of short sentences. Everything that is potentially there is left to the imagination of the reader to uncover because of this concise style of writing that, in Erich Auerbach's famous phrase, is 'fraught with background'[12]

The text leaps forward an unknown number of years. Jacob is preparing a vegetable soup, perhaps trying to obtain his father's love by means of his own cooking. Esau returns from the field tired and hungry. The rivalry between their two lifestyles is on display but also further evidence of their respective characters. Esau is polite in asking for some of the red soup but uses an unusual word for eating usually restricted to the way animals gobble their food. Jacob takes advantage of Esau's hunger to ask that he sell him his birthright, his legal status as the firstborn, for the price of the small pot of soup. Esau's response can be read as simple exaggeration or as a sarcastic put down but displays his indifference to it – 'I am dying! what does the birthright mean to me?!' (*Genesis 25:32*) Are they adolescents squabbling over something minor as they may have done on a daily basis? Are they adults, the one calculating how to improve his future, the other living in the immediate moment with its basic needs? All we

---

[11] The phrase about Isaac loving Esau reads literally 'because of the game in his mouth', which is generally understood to mean the food that he had hunted which he brought to his father's mouth to feed him. I mentioned the tendency in religious traditions to justify the problematic behaviour of exemplary figures, and conversely to criticise those perceived to be their opponents. In this case a rabbinic tradition understands the phrase that Esau 'was skilled in hunting', to mean that he was a cunning hunter. When the same word for 'hunt', '*tzayid*' is used for the 'game' he brought to his father, the rabbis assume that he came to him deceitfully to ingratiate himself with his father.

[12] Erich Auerbach 'Odysseus' Scar' in *Mimesis* (Princeton Paperback Edition, 1968 pp 3-23.

know is that the narrator has included this story as another important clue to the distinctive nature of the twins. Esau agrees and sells his birthright. The text offers five brief verbs describing what happens next, a literary equivalent of the jerky movements in a speeded-up movie sequence:

vayochal vayeisht vayakom vayeilech, vayivez eisav et ha-bechorah.

Esau ate, drank, rose, went, despised his birthright. (*Genesis 25:34*)

The next information we have about either of the twins is that Esau, aged forty, married two Hittite women and their behaviour disturbed both Isaac and Rebecca (*Genesis 26:35*). Chapter 27, which follows immediately, begins with the information that Isaac is old and his eyesight is failing. He asks Esau to prepare his favourite food for him to eat 'so that I may bless you before I die.' (*Genesis 27:4*) Isaac's closing words are literally 'so that my *nefesh* may bless you'. '*nefesh*', the 'life force' is conventionally translated as 'soul', but it is also used to express the 'self'. Robert Alter in his commentary on Genesis explains the word as 'life-breath' and adds that it is an intensive synonym for 'I' so adding emphasis to the importance of what Isaac is saying, 'so that I may solemnly bless you'.[13] There is no doubt about the seriousness of Isaac's intention. Esau departs for the field to trap an animal in order to prepare his father's special food.

Before turning to Rebecca's response let us fill in what we know about Isaac. His birth to his mother Sarah in her old age, long after she was past childbearing, was a miraculous event. The only reference we have to his childhood, is Sarah's concern about the way his half-brother Ishmael had 'played'[14] with him, and her insistence that Ishmael and his mother Hagar be sent away so that there would be no rival to Isaac as Abraham's successor. But

---

[13] Robert Alter Genesis: Translation and Commentary (W.W.Norton and company, New York, London, 1996) page 137.

[14] The word for 'play' here in *Genesis 21:9* '*m'tzachek*' is one of a number of wordplays on the name of Isaac, '*yitzchak*' based on a verb, '*tzachak*', whose meaning varies between 'laughter' (*Genesis 18:12*) and 'play', to 'combat '(*2 Samuel 2:14*) or 'sexual activity' (*Genesis 26:8*).

Isaac's fame lies not in his activities, but in his seemingly passive acceptance of God's request to Abraham to sacrifice him. At the last moment Isaac's life is spared, but though still alive, he somehow disappears from our consciousness. It is as if his existence and purpose in life have been somehow achieved by his role in Abraham's drama. In one sense he does quite literally disappear. The final verse of the story of his near sacrifice describes how Abraham and his two young men returned home, but Isaac's name is simply omitted. (*Genesis 22:19*) He next appears in chapter twenty-five when Abraham makes him his sole inheritor and sends away his other children. When Abraham dies in a good old age, Isaac together with Ishmael bury him in the cave of Machpelah in Hebron alongside Sarah (*Genesis 25:9-10*). After that a single verse mentions that just as God had visited Abraham in person and blessed him, so God also visited Isaac, though no details of the blessing's contents are given here:

> After the death of Abraham, God blessed Isaac his son, and Isaac dwelt by the well called *Beer-lahai-roi*. (*Genesis 25:11*)[15]

We learn that Isaac was forty years old when he marries Rebecca (*Genesis 25:20*) and that he pleads to God on her behalf because she was barren which leads to the birth of the twins with which we began. In a time of famine, on God's command, Isaac moves to Gerar in the land of the Philistines. There, like his father, he pretends that Rebecca is his sister out of fear that because the local men are interested in her beauty he might be killed. Abimelech, the king of Gerar, spots the couple making love[16], challenges Isaac on his lie, but accepts the legitimacy of his fear and ends up protecting him. Blessed by God Isaac prospers with produce, sheep, cattle and servants, so much so that the local Philistines become jealous of him. Abimelech tells Isaac to move because he has become too powerful, and Isaac departs and encamps in the wadi of Gerar.

---

[15] *Beer-lahai-roi* is the name of the well that saved the life of Hagar and Ishmael (*Genesis 16:14*) and where Isaac had previously lived before meeting with Rebecca (*Genesis 24:62*).
[16] The verb used here is *m'tzachek*, another of many plays on the name Isaac. See note 5.

The main activity of his life after this has to do with re-opening the wells dug by his father which had been stopped up by the Philistines, and opening new wells, even though it brought controversy with the local population. In the end Abimelech makes the journey to Isaac and concludes a peace treaty between them.

Unlike the many chapters describing the life of Abraham and of Jacob, virtually the whole of Isaac's life is covered in chapter 26 alone, and what follows is the story of his children (chapters 27-36). His death is briefly recorded in *Genesis 35:28*. Seemingly he was a quiet, yet highly successful and prosperous man, who was able to make his contribution to the society around him and create a peaceful relationship with its leadership. So, although he is now old, is there a good reason to question his decision about the blessing he wishes to give to his son Esau?

Clearly Rebecca has her doubts about it. She has heard Isaac's words to Esau '*his* son', and feels the urgent need to intercede, so recounts them to Jacob, '*her*' son. Since we have reminded ourselves about Isaac's history and character, we should similarly consider the life of Rebecca. She is introduced dramatically in Genesis chapter 24, when Abraham has sent his unnamed servant to his homeland to find a wife for Isaac. The servant sets a test and it is undertaken at once by Rebecca who is introduced to the reader as the daughter of Bethuel, the son of Milcah, the wife of Nahor, Abraham's brother (*Genesis 24:15*). She is described as very beautiful, a virgin whom no man had known. When asked by the servant for water, she agrees and when he had finished drinking offers to give water to his camels. This fulfils exactly the servant's proposal to God of a test designed to indicate an appropriate wife for Isaac. There seems to be, at least in western art, a conventional picture of Rebecca as a dainty girl happily trotting to the well, filling her jug and then emptying the water into the trough for the servant's camels, perhaps indicating her concern for the welfare of animals. But we have to remember that a thirsty camel, after a long trip, can drink up to thirty gallons of water. The servant has travelled with ten camels.[17] So whatever other qualities she may have, she is physically strong, has stamina and determination.

When the wedding is agreed, the family try to delay her departure for a year, but when Rebecca is asked if she is willing to go at once, she agrees. So, we see evidence of her independence. As we have already noted, when the twins struggle within her she is prepared to go by herself to seek an oracle from God to explain what this means.

Why was Rebecca listening to the conversation between Isaac and Esau? We remember that in the previous generation, Sarah also listened in to a conversation between Abraham and his three visitors (*Genesis 18:10*). It suggests that this is simply part of the dynamics of the Biblical patriarchal domestic life. Legal and political power lay with the patriarch, but what happened in the household was the responsibility of the wife, and it was up to her to ensure that she knew what was going on. Since Isaac was old and his eyesight was failing, Rebecca might have felt the need to protect him from himself if necessary. We have already learnt that Esau's marriages have caused distress to his parents. Because Isaac's words to Esau have a direct impact on Jacob, Rebecca feels the need to act on his behalf. But more than her maternal feelings may be at stake here. She may well have been influenced by the ambiguous oracle from God that spoke about some kind of struggle in their later life between the two sons, with one in servitude to the other. She might have argued to herself that to intervene might well be what God would have expected of her.

---

[17] It is quite possible that the servant set this massive task in the hope that no one would fulfil it. Though he is unnamed there is reference to a servant called Eliezer who might inherit from Abraham if he had no children (*Genesis 15:2-4*). That would explain why the servant stares with astonishment as Rebecca sets about doing the task, and has reluctantly to acknowledge that God is indeed looking after the needs of his master.

When we come to examine Rebecca's actual words, we are faced with an important exegetical choice. How much significance are we to place on minor differences of expression between what has been recorded by the narrator and the version of it that is reported by one of the participants in the narrative? Are such differences to be ignored as mere stylistic variations on the same words or do they point to a significant change of emphasis or meaning? We noted that in the narrator's version, Isaac says to Esau: 'so that my *nefesh* may bless you before I die,' or 'solemnly bless you before I die.' Rebecca, however, says to Jacob:

> Look, I have heard your father speaking to Esau your brother saying: 'Bring me game and make me a tasty dish so that I may bless you *before the Lord* before I die'. (*Genesis 27:6b-7*)

There is no doubting the importance and solemnity of Isaac's words when he says that he wishes to bless Esau, but in her version, Rebecca adds the words '*lifnei adona*i', 'before' or 'in the presence of' 'the Lord'. Does this give an additional meaning to Isaac's actual words that was not previously there? What significance does Rebecca place upon Isaac's proposed blessing?

In great detail we learn about how she persuades a reluctant Jacob to exploit the blindness of his father. Frightened, Jacob worries, that if Isaac discovers the deception, 'I will receive a curse, not a blessing.' To which Rebecca reassures him. 'On me shall be your curse, my son. Just obey my voice.' (*Genesis 27:12-13*) So Jacob disguises himself in such a way as to convince Isaac, despite Isaac's obvious doubts that it is Esau who is before him. The trick works and Jacob receives the blessing intended for Esau:

> See, the scent of my son is as the scent of the field which the Lord has blessed.
>
> May God give you from the dew of the heavens and of the fatness of the earth, and plenty of grain and wine.

Let peoples serve you and nations bow down before you.

Be lord over your brothers and may your mother's sons bow down before you.

Cursed be everyone who curses you and blessed be everyone who blesses you.[18] (*Genesis 27:27b-29*)

No sooner has Jacob left than Esau returns from the hunt and sets about preparing the food for his father. When he brings it to Isaac the truth is revealed and the betrayed Esau lets out 'a great and bitter cry'. (*Genesis 27:34*)[19] He asks of his father a blessing but Isaac can only offer:

Look, from the fatness of the earth shall be your dwelling and from the dew of the heavens above.

By your sword shall you live, and you shall serve your brother;

But when you break loose, you shall break off his yoke from your neck. (*Genesis 27:39-40*)

The first sentence is almost identical to that given to Jacob. It is possible to read it as if meaning '*far* from the fatness of the earth' thus establishing a difference, but it could simply mean that both will benefit from the produce of the earth. Absent from Esau's version, however, is the invocation of God as the source of this bounty. But it does emphasise for Esau a living earned by the

---

[18] This is the only part of the blessing that echoes the blessing given by God to Abraham at the time of his call – *Genesis 12:3*.

[19] Though it is not immediately relevant to our paper, that cry of Esau will echo throughout the rest of Biblical history. Esau's son Eliphaz has a son, through his concubine Timna, called Amalek (*Genesis 36:10-12*), who is presumably the ancestor of the Amalekites. Because the Amalekites attacked the weakest of the Israelites when they left Egypt, God asks that their memory be blotted out on the earth (*Exodus 17:14-16*; *Deuteronomy 25:17-19*). However, when King Saul has the opportunity to do so, he spares their King Agag (*1 Samuel 15:8*). Centuries later, in the Book of Esther, an enemy arises who wishes to destroy the Jewish people, his name is Haman the Agagite, presumably for the narrator the descendant of the Amalekite king. On learning of Haman's plan to exterminate the Jews, Mordechai, in the identical words of Esau lets out 'a great and bitter cry' (*Esther 4:1*).

sword, though with the promise of an eventual change of the power balance between them.

We are told that Esau hated Jacob and threatened to kill him but only after the eventual death of Isaac. In those circumstances, Jacob's only choice was to run away. His mother, for a second time, tells him to obey her voice (*Genesis 27:8, 43*) and flee to her brother Laban in Haran and stay there till Esau's anger turns away. Her farewell words to him are 'Why should I be bereft of both of you on one day!' (v 45)[20] But that time of exile is to last for twenty years, and she will indeed carry the burden of the curse she promised to take on for Jacob. Rebecca will never again see her beloved son.

She explains to Isaac that because of their difficulty with the Hittite wives of Esau it is better if Jacob goes to stay with her family in the expectation of finding there a suitable wife.

There the story of the stolen blessing might have ended, but for a final conversation between Isaac and Jacob. Picking up Rebecca's suggestion, Isaac formally instructs Jacob to go to the family of his mother and there find a wife from the daughters of her brother Laban. But before he leaves Isaac offers Jacob a parting blessing. With this blessing a reader of Genesis will by now be very familiar, because variations of it have been given already to Abraham and Isaac.

The Abrahamic Blessing

.   God's call to Abraham to leave his homeland on a journey to an unknown place includes a promise about his future, expressed as a blessing. It is the

---

[20] Rebecca has a dramatic way of expressing herself. When the twins struggle within her she cries: 'If so, then why me?!' (*Genesis 25:22*) Here she asks another rhetorical question. 'If Jacob marries a wife from the daughters of Het, like these daughters of the land, what good to me is life?!' (*Genesis 27:46*)

simplest form of what will be repeated and further amplified a number of times throughout the story of the Biblical patriarchs.

> I will make of you a great nation and I will bless you and make your name great and you shall be a blessing. I will bless those who bless you and those who damn you I will curse, and all the families of the earth shall be blessed through you. (*Genesis 12:2-3*)

It is almost absurd in its grandeur – from one individual will arise a great nation, and his fame will spread throughout the known world. With that fame will come both blessing and hatred from others. But as part of some ultimate divine purpose Abraham is to bring blessing to all the inhabitants of the world.

The next appearance of this blessing is in *Genesis 17:1-8* where God introduces Himself as *El Shaddai*, a name that will recur later.[21] In this passage God establishes a formal covenant with Abraham. Part of the process is to change his name from Abram to Abraham, explained as meaning 'the father of many nations'. It is reinforced by introducing two words that take us back to the first chapter of Genesis (*1:28*) and the first command to Noah after the flood (*Genesis 9:1*), '*p'ru u'r'vu*', 'be fruitful and multiply'. Here the words are divided across two verses: verse 2 reads 'I will multiply you greatly' and verse 6 'I will make you greatly fruitful'. Variations of these two sentences will appear in the versions of the blessing in *Genesis 22:17; 26:4; 28:3* and *35:11*.

As if to resolve the initial question about which land God intended to show to Abraham, the closing of this covenant includes the sentence:

> 'I will give to you and to your seed after you the land in which you sojourn, all the land of Canaan as an eternal holding. (*Genesis 17:8*)

Famously the next appearance of this blessing follows God's testing of Abraham in Genesis 22. This version expands the 'multiplying' of Abraham's

---

[21] *Genesis 28:3; 35:11; 43:14; 48:3; 49:25; Exodus 6:3*

descendants: 'I will greatly multiply your seed as the stars of the heaven and as the sand on the seashore'. The imagery of the stars will recur in the version of the blessing in *Genesis 26:4*. The passage ends with the emphatic 'because you obeyed my voice' (*22:18*) and this is echoed in *26:5* when God tells Isaac that all these blessing will happen 'because Abraham obeyed my voice.'

We have noted that after the death of Abraham God blessed Isaac (*Genesis 25:11*) but the content of that blessing is not given there. However, when there is a famine, God instructs Isaac not to go down to Egypt but to go to Gerar, the land of the Philistines. There follows the direct transmission by God to Isaac of Abraham's blessing.

> Settle in this land and I will be with you, and I will bless you, because to you and to your seed I will give all these lands, and I will fulfil My oath which I swore to Abraham your father. I will multiply your seed as the stars of the heavens and I will give to your seed all these lands, and in your seed shall be blessed all the nations of the earth. Because Abraham obeyed my voice and kept my charge, my commandments, my statutes and my teachings. (*Genesis 26:3-5*)

Perhaps the responsibility of owning and assessing these territories explains Isaac's persistence in re-opening his father's wells and finding new ones throughout the land, because these would determine the viability of human settlement there.

All of this background is necessary to explain the significance of the blessing that Isaac knowingly bestowed upon Jacob before sending him away to Padan-Aram, the household of Bethuel, his mother's father.

> May *El Shaddai* bless you and make you fruitful and multiply you so that you become an assembly of peoples. May He give you the blessing of Abraham to you and your seed after you to inherit the land where you sojourn which God has given to Abraham. (*Genesis 28:3-4*)

Just to complete the further continuity of this chain of tradition of blessing from Abraham to Isaac and then to Jacob, each of them received the blessing directly from God as well and it will also be Jacob's turn. Long after his return to his homeland and reconciliation with Esau, God confirms the change of his name from Jacob to Israel that had happened after his night-time struggle with the mysterious man, and continues:

> God said to Jacob 'I am *El Shaddai*. Be fruitful and multiply, a nation and an assembly of nations will stem from you, and kings shall come forth from your loins. The land which I gave to Abraham and to Isaac I will give to you, and to your seed after you I will give the land. (*Genesis 35:11-12*)

Though there are many issues about the possible origins, differences and purposes of these blessings, it is clear that for the Book of Genesis an Abrahamic blessing, is successfully transmitted across these three generations despite all sorts of hindrances that have stood in the way. Who is to be the right person to inherit it is challenged in each generation: Ishmael or Isaac, Jacob or Esau? What happens when people try to force their own decision on this – Sarah insisting that Abraham take Hagar so as to conceive a son because she is barren; Rebecca trying to make Jacob acquire the blessing that Isaac wanted to bestow on Esau? In every case, despite these digressions on the way, God's plan is fulfilled. This leaves us with the obvious answer to the question posed by this paper. If it is the Abrahamic blessing that is the crucial one for the divine plan, then Jacob, at Rebecca's insistence, stole the wrong blessing. In fact, almost incidentally, he received the right blessing from Isaac just as he was leaving home. That Isaac deliberately passed it on to Jacob, suggests that the blessing he intended for Esau was something completely different.

If we look at the Esau blessing, there is virtually nothing in it of the Abrahamic blessing except the concluding sentence 'Cursed be everyone who curses you and blessed be everyone who blesses you' (compare *Genesis 27:29* and *Genesis 12:3*). So, what is it intended to be? It seems to have been a simple parental blessing bestowed upon the firstborn son as part of the indication of his right to inherit his father's property. But Rebecca, presumably fully aware of the Abrahamic tradition, misunderstood Isaac's intention. Which is why she reported to Jacob a version of Isaac's words that added the phrase '*lifnei adona*i', 'before' or 'in the presence of the Lord'. That set in train a whole series of events that led to Jacob's exile, his years of suffering at the hands of Laban, his acquiring of a family and a considerable wealth in livestock. But because Jacob stole the blessing from Esau, there is something he has to do to repair the harm he caused to Esau before reconciliation is possible.

Jacob attempts to do it when he finally returns to his home by means of a series of gifts of livestock for Esau that he sends on ahead of himself. The Hebrew word for this gift is *minchah*, and it is repeated several times, making it a key word that grabs our attention. When Esau asks about each group of animals, Jacob instructs his servants to respond:

> They belong to Jacob your servant. They are a *minchah*, a gift, sent for my lord Esau, and he [Jacob] is following…. For Jacob said to himself 'I will appease him with the *minchah* that goes before me, and afterwards I will see his face and perhaps he will show me a kindly face.' And the *minchah* went on before him. (*Genesis 32:19-22*)

That night Jacob wrestles with the mysterious man and acquires his new name. The next morning, he sees Esau approaching with four hundred men. When he finally confronts him, Esau asks: 'What do you mean by all this camp that I have met?' Clearly, he is referring to the groups of animals. Presumably it is intentional either on the part of the narrator, or even of Esau, that he uses the word 'camp', *machaneh*, to describe the teams of animals as it is a direct word play on the word *minchah*, 'gift'. Jacob responds to the question with, 'To find favour in the eyes of my lord'. To which Esau replies 'I have much, my brother, let yours be what is yours.' (*Genesis 33:8-9*) The narrator has introduced us to a very different Esau than the rather crude hunter that Jacob knew. He seems to be quite deliberately, and possibly ironically, refusing to accept Jacob's obvious bribe for his favour. The reference to 'let yours be what is yours', speaks to the stolen blessing, as if Esau is waiting for something more from Jacob. Jacob tries to recover by begging Esau:

> Please, if I have found favour in your eyes, take my *minchah* from my hand for I have seen your face as one sees the face of God, and you have accepted me.' *(33:10)*

There is no obvious evidence from the textual tradition of a pause at this moment. Nevertheless, I have a suspicion that Jacob finally realised that this flowery language, though appropriate, is not what Esau is looking for. So, Jacob continues but with the change of a single word. He replaces the much-repeated '*minchah*', 'gift', with the word '*b'rachah*', 'blessing'.

> 'Please take '*birchati*', 'my blessing', which has been brought to you, because God has been gracious to me and I have everything.' And he pressed him and he took it. *(Genesis 33:11)*[22]

Jacob has returned the material blessing that he stole, and by using the word 'blessing' acknowledged the wrong that he had done, and Esau has accepted it. The brothers can now begin the process of attempting to heal the rift between them. How far this is successful we do not know, but just as in the previous generation, Isaac and Ishmael together buried their father Abraham, so, too, Esau and Jacob together buried their father Isaac *(Genesis 35:29)*.

---

[22] Thanks to a suggestion from Hiroshi Hihara, the significance of this term to Esau is reinforced by its only other appearance in Genesis *(27:36)* where Esau bewails that Jacob has stolen not only my 'birthright', '*b'chorati*', but also, in a word play, '*birchati*', 'my blessing'.

Conclusion

The question posed by the title of the paper still remains. It is true that in terms of Biblical conventions about the transfer of patriarchal authority across the family generations, Jacob stole the wrong blessing. He took the one that was due to Esau, even if he returned it, symbolically, at the end. On the other hand, because of the transformation he underwent during his experience in exile, culminating in the change of his name to Israel, on that level, at least, it turned out that he stole the right blessing. But all of this is almost irrelevant in terms of the Biblical understanding of God's plan for humanity mediated through Abraham and his descendants. Jacob received the correct blessing from Isaac anyway, irrespective of his initial misbehaviour. Isaac, it seems, was quite clear about what was legally required for Esau, but also which blessing was destined for Jacob.

So, a pattern is established in the Hebrew Bible that frequently sets the intentions of God in conflict with the wilful independence of human beings. But our desire for independence is built into us as part of our creation itself, for are we not made in the image of God? The rabbinic tradition acknowledged this paradox, that must be played out in our individual lives and in the collective history of humanity. It was formulated by Rabbi Akiva:

> He used to say: Beloved are human beings for they were created in the image of God. Yet with even greater love it was revealed to them that they were so created in the image of God.

He concluded:

> *Hakol tsafui v'har'shut n'tunah.*

Everything is foreseen, yet freedom of choice is granted. (*Pirke Avot 3:19)*

5 Joseph's Revenge

The narrative about Joseph in the Book of Genesis is unlike the stories that have gone before it on a number of levels. The previous ones about Noah, Abraham, Isaac and Jacob tend to be episodic, snapshots of particular events in their lives. In contrast the story of Joseph is a continuous narrative with only one brief interruption, the story of Judah and Tamar (*Genesis 38*), and even that has verbal links with the surrounding Joseph story.

Secondly, while God appears in those earlier stories of the patriarchs in person, in the Joseph stories the divine immediacy becomes muted. The transition comes after Genesis 39 where the author credits Joseph's success in the house of Potiphar, (*v 2-5*) and subsequently in prison (*v 21-23*) to YHWH's presence and blessing. However, when Joseph offers to interpret the dreams of Pharaoh's Chief Butler and Chief Baker, in prison with him, he points out that the interpretation of dreams belongs to 'God', *Elohim*, and from then on God's presence is viewed indirectly through Joseph's interpretation of dreams and of the events in his life using that divine name exclusively.

The Joseph story is a masterfully crafted narrative filled with dramatic events and with scenes switching between the experience of Joseph in Egypt and that of his family back in Canaan. The author allows us to follow not only the physical journey of Joseph but also the way in which he changes and matures from being the spoilt favourite son, through his enslavement in Egypt and imprisonment to his final elevation to power. These stages are signalled by repeated elements: the loss or acquiring of clothing and the shock of being thrown into a pit or dungeon. He is first stripped of his 'long-sleeve coat' (or 'coat of many colours') by his brothers and cast into the empty 'pit' or 'cistern', Hebrew '*bor*'. Enslaved in Egypt he acquires a new set of clothing from his master, Potiphar, only to have them stripped off him by his master's wife in an act of frustrated passion. He is accused of having sexually assaulted her, and as a result is cast into prison, another descent into the 'pit'. Finally, when he interprets Pharaoh's dreams, he acquires new clothing, the trappings of power, even a new name and his own wife and sons (*Genesis 41:42, 45, 50*).

In a similar way, dreams play a part in showing the stages of his life. As a child he has dreams about his own special destiny. In the prison he becomes the interpreter of the dreams of his fellow prisoners, correctly describing their subsequent fate. These dreams are not about himself, but he does try to use them to his own advantage, hoping that Pharaoh's Chief Butler will remember him. Finally, he becomes the interpreter of Pharaoh's dreams, rising to a position of power having hinted that he is the one person who can save the crisis that Pharaoh's dreams have foretold. The beautiful, gifted but spoilt child has grown into the attractive and capable young man and subsequently the wise statesman. But all of these stages have happened because of the initial murderous betrayal by his brothers. Since the author has given us so much information to work with can we trace the effects of this violent act on Joseph's later behaviour? I want to point to two elements of his actions that might be considered examples of Joseph's revenge on others for the suffering he had to undergo.

In passing we have to note one example of the potential for cruelty in Joseph's character. It can be seen in his responses to the dreams of Pharaoh's Chief Butler and Chief Baker. Both of them are in prison with Joseph and both dream a dream but do not know how to interpret it. Joseph, the dreamer, now becomes the interpreter of dreams. The Chief Butler dreams that he will fill Pharaoh's cup and pass it to him again as in the past. Joseph interprets this positively saying literally: 'In three more days Pharaoh will lift up your head and restore you to your post.' (*Genesis 40:13*) The Chief Baker's dream is clearly more sinister, but given Joseph's positive interpretation of the dream of his colleague, the Chief Baker hopes for something similar. And indeed, that is what Joseph seems to offer. He responds with the identical opening words in the Hebrew text, thus raising the Baker's hopes: 'In three more days Pharaoh will lift up your head…' However it is with the next word that Joseph destroys these hopes: '..Pharaoh will lift up your head – *from off you*, and hang you from a tree…' (*Genesis 40:19*) Just one word in the Hebrew, '*from off you*', marks the difference, but this raising of the Chief Baker's expectations and then destroying them in this elegant but cynical way is an indication of Joseph's darker side.

In the same exchange with the chief Butler we get a hint of the desperation and bitterness that Joseph must feel at his fate until now. He asks the Chief Butler to remember him after he has been restored to his post.

'Please show kindness to me and mention me to Pharaoh and bring me out from this house. For I was forcibly abducted from the land of the Hebrews. Moreover, I did nothing here that they should put me into the *pit*' (*Genesis 40:14-15*).

By referring to the prison as 'the pit', '*bor*', Joseph is echoing that first assault by his brothers when they took him and threw him into the '*bor*', pit or cistern (*Gen 37:24*), which suggests how deeply that experience is ingrained in his mind. But his plea has no immediate result and it will be two more years in prison before the Butler has occasion to remember him.

Joseph rises to power on the basis of his ability to interpret Pharaoh's two dreams, forecasting seven years of plenty followed by seven years of famine. There is a certain ambiguity in the Hebrew text when it describes the reaction of the court magicians and wise men to Pharaoh's request to interpret his dreams (*Genesis 41:8*). The Hebrew uses a participle form to express, literally, that 'no one interprets' them to Pharaoh. This could mean, as it is often translated, that 'no one was *able* to interpret', but equally that 'no one was *willing* to interpret'. After all it is always dangerous to be the messenger of bad news to a powerful king. Clearly Joseph had no such qualms, adding to his interpretation a potential solution and giving a broad hint that he might be the 'clever and wise' man who could take on the task.

Pharaoh's instant appointment of Joseph reads like a fairy tale solution. But here too it is possible to see certain ambiguities, in particular the need to safeguard the position of Pharaoh and his court. Joseph is proposing to impose a major tax on the entire population to the extent of one fifth of their produce. The grain he acquires is to become Pharaoh's property, locked away and guarded in special cities. It is to be made available to the population during the years of famine, though it is only later that the price for obtaining the food will become evident together with its consequences. To act as a major tax collector and then the arbiter of how and to whom the food is to be distributed is actually a very dangerous and vulnerable role. Joseph becomes the 'middle man' between the starving population and the court, the potential target for the anger of the people should things go wrong. Moreover, from the perspective of the regime, Joseph is a convenient dispensable foreigner should the need for a scapegoat arise so as to protect their own position. In this sense Joseph is the first of a number of similarly promoted and sometimes destroyed, '*Hofjuden*', 'Court Jews', in later European society. On a slightly less serious note, this makes Joseph the first recorded person to invest in the 'futures market', with all the risks this also implies.

Yet, just as with everything else that Joseph undertakes in Potiphar's household and in the prison, Joseph is remarkably successful. The grain is gathered and stored in the years of good harvests, ready for distribution in the years of famine.

In his behaviour Joseph performs as the ideal servant, working diligently to further the interests of his master. He served so successfully in Potiphar's household that Potiphar could literally leave everything in Joseph's capable hands, excepting only, as Joseph points out, his wife! Likewise, as Pharaoh's servant he acts in the same way, as is evident from what happens when it comes to the distribution of the food when the years of famine begin. The sequence of events is described in detail in the Bible (*Genesis 47:13-27*). It stands in stark contrast to the situation Joseph arranges for his family which is described in the verses immediately before.

Joseph settled his father and his brothers and gave them property in the land of Egypt in the best of the land, in the land of Ramses, as Pharaoh had commanded. And Joseph supported his father and his brothers and all the household of his father with '*lechem*', bread, according to the needs of the children. (*Genesis 47:11-12*)

But in the next verse, there was no 'bread' (the same word *lechem* as in the previous sentence) in all the land, for the famine was very severe and the land of Egypt and the land of Canaan languished because of the famine. (*Genesis 47:13*)

In the first year people from both countries paid for the grain with money, which Joseph paid into Pharaoh's house – *v 14*.

When the money was exhausted the Egyptians came to Joseph. 'Why should we die before you, for there is no money left?'

Joseph's solution is to buy all their livestock as payment which suffices to provide food for that year – *v 17*.

But when this year passes and the famine continues, the Egyptians tell Joseph that all they can offer now are their bodies and their land – v 18. They offer to become Pharaoh's slaves (*avadim*) in exchange for seed so that they do not perish and the land is not desolate – *v 19*. Joseph buys up each person's field so that the entire land comes into Pharaoh's possession. As a consequence, Joseph initiates a major population transfer from the land into the cities – *v 21*. (This practice of buying up land and depopulating it of its previous owners is condemned by the prophet Isaiah (*5:8*)). At this point the Bible notes an exception to this sale of land. Joseph is unable to purchase the land belonging to the priests because they have a special status, granted to them by Pharaoh – *v 22*.

Now that the Egyptians have become Pharaoh's slaves they can receive seed with which to work the land, but a fifth of the produce will become Pharaoh's, leaving four fifths which will be theirs for seed for the field, for food for their households and for food for their 'children' (*v 24*). (The last phrase, literally 'for your little ones to eat', 'children', echoes the provision Joseph made for his own family (*47:12*)). As far as the Egyptians are concerned Joseph has saved them, and they are seemingly happy with their new status as Pharaoh's slaves (*v 25*). The Bible finally notes that this becomes a permanent law until today, established by Joseph, that Egyptians pay a fifth of their land's produce to Pharaoh, but that the priests remain exceptional as sole owners of their land (*v 26*). The next verse of this chapter reverts to the situation of Jacob, here referred to as Israel, and the fact that the family acquired possessions and were fruitful and multiplied, hinting towards the problem noted by a later Pharaoh about their growing numbers.

In terms of the subsequent Biblical history, the scene has been set for the way in which a later Pharaoh, 'who knew not Joseph', will single out the Israelites for a worse kind of slavery – forced labour and ultimately a policy of genocide. But there is another dimension. The concept of a society built on enslavement to a Pharaoh is completely unacceptable to the Israelites, at least as reflected in their laws. Following the Ten Commandments, the Book of Exodus lists the '*mishpatim*', the laws that are to make up the basis of the covenant with God, the constitution of the new nation. The very first one sets strict limits on the concept of slavery, on the ownership of one Israelite by another. The law deals with the situation of someone who falls into debt and in order to discharge it becomes a slave to another Israelite to earn enough to repay it.

> If you acquire a Hebrew slave, six years he will work for you but in the seventh he shall go free for nothing. *(Exodus 21:2)*

There are subsequent details and conditions attached, and such a release is not possible for foreign slaves, but the essential point is that the new Israelite nation is not to reproduce the Egyptian system of permanent enslavement to one another, but rather to assert the independence of each individual Israelite. As such the willingness of the Egyptians to accept the surrender of their land and their individual freedom must have seemed to later generations of Israelites to be a massive failure of personal dignity. Moreover, the status of the priests within Israel is established as the exact opposite of that in Egypt, for the Israelite priests do not own land as a special law of the king, but are dependent on the gifts of the people for their sustenance.

Even if this element in the Joseph story is part of the broader Biblical theme, it nevertheless raises questions about Joseph's actions. Clearly, he saves the lives of the Egyptian people while at the same time furthering the interests of his master Pharaoh. As a reward Pharaoh offers him a choice piece of land on which to settle his family and seems to treat him with great friendliness. Nevertheless, Pharaoh keeps a close watch on everything that happens in Joseph's household (*45:2*). When Jacob dies Pharaoh gives Joseph permission to take the body home to Canaan for burial, but the children stay behind in Egypt, perhaps a deliberate hint of what will happen later when the Pharaoh of the Exodus refuses to allow the Israelite to leave for a three-day journey into the wilderness to make a sacrifice to their God 'with their children' (*Exodus 10:10*). A military escort accompanies the funeral procession (*Genesis 50:8-9*), perhaps to protect them but possibly also to ensure that Joseph returns.

Joseph's actions represent a brilliant and magnificent solution to a major catastrophe and nothing can take away from his achievement. Nevertheless, at the personal level, one wonders if the end-result, reducing the nation to the status of slaves, is somehow a projection onto the entire population of Joseph's own experience of being sold as a slave. Such an end-result may have been the unforeseen consequence of a strategy designed to solve a particular problem, and the result of improvisation year by year in response to the changing financial circumstances. However, an alternative solution would have been simply to distribute the food for free – after all it was food donated by the Egyptians in the first place, and that may even have been Joseph's original intention. But the accumulation of such capital leads to its own logical consequences and the urge to acquire yet more capital. The suspicion remains that, even if only on an unconscious level, Joseph had transformed the Egyptian nation as a whole into a version of the slavery that he himself had experienced. That would be one possible example of Joseph's revenge.

If this can only be a conjecture, there is another example of Joseph's behaviour which is much less ambiguous. The narrative has indicated in a number of ways that Joseph is a strategic thinker. He tried, eventually successfully, to get the Chief Butler to support his cause. He could plan ahead through the seven years of plenty to have sufficient food for the years of famine. So it is no surprise to read his elaborate plans to deal with his brothers when they arrive in Egypt looking for food.

Genesis 42-44 describes in great detail how Joseph manipulated and toyed with them. Because of the famine, Jacob sends his sons down to Egypt to obtain food, stipulating only that Benjamin is to remain behind. Jacob is still affected by memories of Joseph's disappearance, and fears that some accident might befall Benjamin as well, the last child of his beloved Rachel (*Genesis 42:4*). Joseph recognises his brothers, though they do not recognise him, and he remembers the dreams in which they had bowed before him, something which was now being fulfilled (*Genesis 42:9*). His first move is to act in an aggressive manner, accusing them of being spies. In defending themselves, they reveal that they are twelve brothers, one is still with their father and one is dead, literally 'is not' (*Genesis 42:13*). This information seems to be the trigger that leads Joseph to tell them to bring Benjamin down to Egypt to prove their story. He promptly places them under guard for three days, thus experiencing themselves, however briefly, part of Joseph's fate. When releasing them Joseph insists that he is a 'god-fearing man'. The Hebrew phrase, using the word '*elohim*' for God, is less a religious designation than one which means a 'moral person'.[23] So, to make the point, Joseph tells them that they can return and take

---

[23] As we have noted in Chapter Three, when Abraham justifies to Abimelech, the king of Gerar, why he claimed that Sarah was his sister, he says that he thought there was no '*yir'at elohim*', 'fear of God', in that place and they would kill him for his wife (*Genesis 20:11*). Conversely, the Egyptian midwives spared the Hebrew male children because they 'feared God' (*Exodus 1:21*)

with them food for their households. But one brother is to remain as a hostage till the younger brother comes.

The brothers talking amongst themselves see this experience as some kind of punishment for their uncaring treatment of Joseph, not listening to his distress and ignoring his pleas. Unbeknownst to them Joseph understands their conversation and has to excuse himself when he is overwhelmed with emotion and weeps in private. At this point, if his only concern was to learn how the brothers had changed, he could have ended the entire charade. But instead, as he has threatened, he has Simeon bound in front of them. He then orders their sacks to be filled and provision given for their return journey, but secretly he has the money they brought for food returned in their sacks, which they discover to their horror on the way home. When they return, they tell their father Jacob the story, but he is adamant that Benjamin will not go down with them to Egypt. The famine gets worse, and in this life or death situation Judah takes the lead in trying to persuade his father to let them take Benjamin. Only when he offers to stand as a surety for Benjamin does Jacob reluctantly agree. But Jacob is enough of a practical man to suggest that they give back the money found in their sacks, bring twice as much to pay for the food and also bring some choice gifts for this difficult Egyptian man (*Genesis 43:11*).

When Joseph sees them with Benjamin he has them invited to his house. The brothers are afraid that this is going to be a punishment for the money in their sacks, so explain themselves to Joseph's steward, who reassures them and releases Simeon. When the formal greetings are over, Joseph becomes overwhelmed at the sight of Benjamin, the son of his mother, and again weeps privately in his room. This is also the moment at which he could have revealed himself, but clearly, he has something more in mind. At the meal he seats them according to their age, something that worries the brothers, and he gives very special treatment to Benjamin.

When they leave Joseph again instructs his steward to fill their sacks with money and to add the silver goblet in which he performs his divination to the sack of the youngest brother. The brothers are stopped after they leave the town and accused of stealing the divining goblet. In desperation, and sure of their innocence they say: whoever took it will die and we will become slaves to your master. The steward counters: 'Whoever has it will be a slave, but you will be innocent.' This is the second example of Joseph putting his brothers through his own experience – that of being falsely accused of a serious crime, as in the case of Potiphar's wife. The goblet is discovered in Benjamin's sack, and the brothers are horrified, tearing their garments. They have to return to Joseph who accuses them of betraying his kindness to them. Again Judah, now clearly the spokesman for the brothers, desperately asks how they can prove their innocence. He offers that all of them become slaves, but Joseph once again protests his moral concerns – only the one in whose sack the goblet was found will be his slave, the rest can return in peace to their father.

Perhaps we should stop at this moment and examine Joseph's strategy, and its cruelty. The brothers are on a mission in a foreign country to obtain food for their families back home. They are confronted with the most powerful figure in the land, the one who controls the distribution of food, who accuses them of being spies, with terrifying possible consequences. On the second visit they are concerned to note that his investigators have even learned enough about the family to be able to sit them at the table according to their respective ages. Added to the fear of possible arrest is the worry about what will happen to their families back home if they cannot get food. When Simeon is taken away they face the reality of their impotence in this situation and the shame of losing their brother. Worse still, they will have to explain to their aged father Jacob what has happened and face his anger and distress. But even more serious is the threat posed by the demand that they bring Benjamin with them, knowing what a massive blow that will be to Jacob. Joseph puts them under relentless pressure. He causes additional fear and confusion by returning the money in their sacks. Finally, after his steward has reassured them about the money in the sacks and released Simeon, Joseph offers an apparently courteous invitation to a meal. However, once they are underway, Joseph sends the new accusation about stealing the goblet, leading to the public exposure of Benjamin as the thief. These actions orchestrated by Joseph seem aimed at cutting off all hope. Moreover, Joseph has also overheard how they believe that all of their present misfortune is a punishment for their treatment of Joseph and observed the inner conflicts that now break out amongst the brothers as to who is to blame. Perhaps as a conscious final blow, Joseph, cynically, twice takes the moral high ground by insisting that he is a man who 'fears God', emphasising his strong moral sense. So twice *(42:18-19; 44:17)* he expresses his concern that they take food home to their families until the matter of Benjamin is resolved. Lastly, he asserts that only the guilty party, Benjamin, will become his slave, and his last words to them are phrased with bitter irony: 'and you go back *in peace* to your father.' (*Genesis 44:17*) It is utterly brutal.

What lies behind Joseph's behaviour? On one level he is exposing them collectively to some of the pain he himself suffered at their hands all those years ago. There is a commonly held view that Joseph is testing them to see whether they have really changed since that incident, and so his actions are justified. The brothers' admission of guilt to one another about their treatment of Joseph is part of that change and also the attempts to protect Simeon and later to stand surety for Benjamin. On this reading, thus satisfied, Joseph is able to reveal himself to them. However, the actual resolution to the entire episode comes immediately after Judah's personal plea to Joseph in *Genesis 44:18-34*, and it is to this that we need to turn for some final clarifications.

Judah recounts what has happened. You asked your servants, 'do you have a father or brother?' We said we have an elderly father and a young brother, a child of his old age, whose brother died, so that he alone remains of his mother, and his father loves him. You told us to bring him down to Egypt and we told you that the lad cannot leave his father as this would kill him. But you insisted and when our father told us to come here again for food we said we cannot come without our younger brother. Then Judah quotes Jacob's words:

'You know that my wife bore me two sons, and one left me and I said, "He has surely been torn to pieces", and I have not seen him till now. And if you take Benjamin from me and something happens I will go grieving to my grave.' (*Genesis 44:27-29*)

Judah then adds that he is a surety for the safety of Benjamin. So, Judah offers himself to become a slave as a substitute for Benjamin.

These closing words reinforce the view that this was the final information that Joseph needed to see how the brothers had changed, and so it was at that point that he finally broke down and revealed himself to them. That may well be one factor, but I do not think it answers a deeper question that lies behind Joseph's behaviour. Clearly, he is both testing and taking revenge on his brothers, but who is he really targeting with this entire charade? Who is the one who is bound to suffer the most if Benjamin will be lost, a possibility that is so frequently mentioned? Clearly the answer is Jacob.

The one thing Joseph does not know is the way in which the brothers produced evidence to Jacob that Joseph had been killed by a wild animal. His deepest question throughout the period of his exile must have been, why did his father who loved him so much simply abandon him? Why did Jacob not come down to Egypt to look for him and ransom him Perhaps it was his anger at that apparent betrayal by his father that sustained him through all the long years of his exile in Egypt. It is even hinted at in the name he gave to his firstborn son Manasseh – 'for God has made me forget all my toil and all my father's house'. (*Genesis 41:51*) That would explain his repeated insistence on taking Benjamin away from his father as a punishment, precisely because he knew the pain it would cause Jacob. That would also explain why despite all his power in Egypt he never took the opportunity to contact at least his father, even if he had little interest in seeing his brothers.

So, it was not only Judah's statement that he was willing to offer himself as a substitute for Benjamin that affected Joseph so deeply. Rather it was the one piece of vital information that turned inside out Joseph's entire

76

understanding of what had happened – that Jacob his father had not abandoned him, because Jacob thought that Joseph was already dead, that 'he has surely been torn to pieces'. So, all the explanations he might have made to himself about his father's failure to find him, all the anger he must have nursed to give him the strength to continue, are shattered in this one moment. Now Joseph has to weep and expose himself to his brothers and go in search of the father that for all these years he thought he had lost forever.

The Joseph who emerges from this analysis is a complex and conflicted figure. He is a masterful administrator and strategist, able to plan and execute complex programmes. At the same time, he is revealed as someone whose emotions are very close to the surface when his private life is affected. Seven times we are told of his weeping: when he overhears his brothers' confession about how they had mistreated him (*42:22*); when first he sees Benjamin (*43:30*); when he learns from Judah that his father had thought him dead and he finally reveals himself to his brothers (*45:1*); when he embraces Benjamin and his brothers (*45:14*); later when he meets his father Jacob (*46:29*); again when Jacob dies (*50:1*); and finally after the brothers tell him that Jacob has left instructions that Joseph should forgive them (*50:17*). It is as if all the bottled-up emotion of his years of exile come pouring out.

It is tempting to see in his loyalty to his various masters, Potiphar, the overseer of the prison and Pharaoh himself, substitutes for the father he thought had abandoned him. Perhaps part of his lost childhood is also expressed in the pride with which he sends messages to Jacob via his brothers about his extraordinary success in Egypt (*45:9,13*), the little boy showing off to his father. But behind this is also the memory of his early dreams and the conviction that God lay behind his journey to power. This gave him the strength in the end to forgive his brothers and reassure them that all that happened was the divine will (*45:5-7; 50:19-21*).

Those who are used to the prettified version of the Joseph story from their children's Bible may be shocked by this reading, But the Biblical version locates Joseph in a real world of fear, pain and suffering. Joseph is a victim of abuse, violated and abandoned by those he should have been able to rely on, surviving as best he could in difficult circumstances until his successful rise to power. His anger and bitterness had to be expressed when his brothers unexpectedly fell into his hands. The pain and suffering through which he put them and, indirectly, his father Jacob, reflect his own emotions. The Psalmist who told Joseph's story in his version of the early history of Israel was not afraid to depict the suffering that shaped his character and actions.

God sent a man before them; Joseph was sold as a slave,

his feet they hurt with fetters, iron entered his soul, (*Psalm 105:17-18*) Yet when the truth was revealed the other side of Joseph could emerge, including the faith that had sustained him. Like so many major Biblical characters he is depicted with all his strengths and flaws. Joseph emerges from the pages of the Hebrew Bible as a full, complex human being.

6 How Did Moses Know He Was A Hebrew?[24]

A Close Reading of Exodus 2:11

My title arises from the brief sentence in the Book of Exodus. It tells the reader that Moses grew up in Egypt and one day went out to see his 'brothers'. He intervened on behalf of one of the Hebrew slaves who was being beaten by an Egyptian. Having lived his entire life as an Egyptian Prince how did Moses know that the Hebrews were his brothers?

Moreover, how did the Hebrews regard this Egyptian prince who claimed to belong to them?

For the former question the Hebrew Bible offers no direct information. As a baby, in the famous story, Moses was rescued from the Nile by Pharaoh's daughter. Through the intervention of his sister Miriam, he was suckled by his birth mother. But from the time he was weaned he was raised in the royal palace as the son of Pharaoh's daughter, to all intents and purposes an Egyptian. Two sentences in Exodus chapter 2 cover the whole of his early life, each repeating the verb '*vayigdal*', 'he grew up'. The first (*Exodus 2:10*) says '*vayigdal ha-yeled*', 'the child grew up', meaning until the age that he was weaned when his mother brought him to Pharaoh's daughter. The following verse begins '*vayigdal Moshe*', 'and Moses grew up'. Presumably it means that he grew into the adult person with the identity and qualities that will distinguish him as Moses. The same sentence continues 'he went out to his brothers and looked upon their burdens'. We are accustomed to assume that what is meant here are his Hebrew brothers, especially given his subsequent intervention on their behalf, so somehow he must have known the truth about his identity. But how and when did he learn it?

---

[24] An earlier version of this paper was given as the Leon Yudkin Memorial Lecture (10 November 2015)

In order to answer this question I want to begin in a rather unusual place, and I need to spend a few moments explaining why. We are accustomed in scholarly circles to work within the confines of the textual tradition itself, evaluating the witness of historical versions of the Biblical text and the classical commentaries, as well as debating the opinions of contemporary academic exegesis. Nevertheless, there are other modes of interpretation that can often offer valuable insights, and today these 'intertextual studies' are increasingly being considered. One obvious example is the area of the historical novel, where authors, having steeped themselves in the relevant historical background, seek to fill in the gaps in the often very brief Biblical record, using their own imaginative and literary skills. Sometimes coming from such a different perspective they can offer insights into the text that more conventional approaches may overlook.

But in the case of such a significant, compelling and popular narrative as that of the life and achievement of Moses, the medium that most suits retelling his story, is that of the epic movie. So before I turn to a more conventional study of the relevant Hebrew verses, I would like to introduce you to a number of popular films and television series that have tried to depict the drama of Moses' story. One of the reasons for doing so is that all the examples I examined felt the same need to explain how Moses knew that he was a Hebrew, so they help set the scene for our enquiry. I should add that those who made these films, just like us as Biblical scholars, had a professional interest in this topic, so they approached it with the same seriousness and commitment as ourselves, however different their purpose.

My first port of call, metaphorically, was to ask Charlton Heston, who starred as Moses in Cecil B DeMille's epic 1956 movie 'The Ten Commandments'. (Incidentally, DeMille first tackled the same subject with a famous, spectacular silent version in 1923.) In the later version, a handmaid of Pharaoh's daughter called Memnet was present when Moses was found in the bulrushes, and she was sworn to secrecy about his origins. But when Moses was about to marry Nefretiri, an Egyptian princess, and was in line to inherit Pharaoh's throne, Memnet could not tolerate that this Hebrew should become the possible successor to Pharaoh. Mistakenly, she informs Nefretiri about Moses' origins hoping to stop the marriage, and displays the Levite cloth in which the baby had been wrapped. But out of love for Moses, Nefretiri does not want the secret to be known and makes Memnet fall to her death from the balcony. However, when Moses visits Nefretiri immediately afterwards he sees the cloth. He forces Nefretiri to tell him the truth and thus learns about his origin. It is a good Hollywood-style version, and as feasible as any other explanation.

Along the same lines, I wanted to ask that other great Hollywood film star Burt Lancaster who played Moses in an Italian television series, called 'Moses the Lawgiver', made in the nineteen-seventies. Actually, the young Moses was played not by Lancaster himself but by his son. In this version, Moses' Egyptian mother as she is about to cross the symbolic river into death tells Moses that he was himself drawn from the river. Dissatisfied with what he considers the limitations of Egyptian wisdom, Moses, the intellectual seeker, finds himself drawn to the Hebrew slaves. That is where he tries to prevent an Egyptian overseer from beating a Hebrew slave and accidentally kills him. Betrayed by one of the Hebrews he meets his sister Miriam and brother Aaron. The voiceover tells us that Moses was empty of all knowledge of his people and Miriam had to fill this emptiness. Miriam is depicted as the one who keeps alive the memory of Moses' birth and the tradition that a saviour will come to end their slavery. The same role for Miriam occurs in Steven Spielberg's animated musical 'Prince of Egypt'. This time Moses has no prior knowledge of his background, but while chasing an attractive slave girl, ends up by chance at the house of Miriam and Aaron. Again, it is Miriam who blurts out the information about his birth.

Just to make sure I was up to date with more recent film 'scholarship' I watched the 2005 remake of 'The Ten Commandments' starring Dougray Scott, playing a somewhat wimpish and reluctant Moses. Here Moses' mother only agrees to breastfeed the child for Pharaoh's daughter if she swears to tell him of his origins. This she does, though Moses' first visit as a child to his real Hebrew family turns out to be pretty disastrous. Nevertheless, the seeds are sown.

Finally, at the cutting edge of film scholarship, I checked out the spectacular 'Exodus: Gods and Kings' with a more heroic Christian Bale in the role of Moses. Here Moses knows that his background is suspect, his mother was Pharaoh's daughter, but his father was an unknown soldier. On a visit to the city of Pithom he learns the truth of his birth from the leader of the Hebrew elders, played by Ben Kingsley. Moses dismisses the information as a poor example of Hebrew storytelling, though, clearly, he is in denial. When he leaves in anger and is mistaken for a Hebrew by some guards who try to arrest him, he kills them. The rest, as they say, is history and computer-generated special effects.

All the above merely shows that this gap in the Biblical narrative begs to be filled.

Perhaps the most obvious place to look for a Biblical answer is in the verse in Exodus chapter two that has already been mentioned, the one which says that when Moses grew up he went out to his brothers. Let us see if a close reading of this verse yields any more information. In full the verse reads as follows:

> *vayehi ba-yamim ha-hem vayigdal Moshe vayetze el echav vayar b'sivlotam vayar ish mitzri makkeh ish-ivri me-echav.*
>
> It was in those days that Moses grew up and went out to his brothers and looked upon their burdens; he saw an Egyptian man strike a Hebrew man of his brothers. (*Exodus 2:11*)

Some things about the verse require attention. The conventional translations often omit the word '*ish*', 'man' that appears twice, and simply have an 'Egyptian' smiting a 'Hebrew', whereas the Hebrew text specifies, 'an Egyptian man' and 'a Hebrew man'. The repetition of the word '*echav*' 'his brothers', at the beginning and the end of the verse, is also noteworthy. If we are sensitive to rabbinic, and a similar contemporary scholarly, focus on the 'close-reading' of Biblical texts, we will want to enquire about the significance of this apparent redundancy. Finally, the phrase 'on their burdens' raises the question about to whom the suffix 'their' belongs as there is no obvious information earlier in the chapter.

The Hebrew term for 'on their burdens' is '*b'sivlotam*', and if we have been reading from the beginning of Exodus we will recognize it from the previous chapter. It appears in exactly the same form in *Exodus 1:11*. In a previous verse in chapter one, Pharaoh has referred to Israel as '*am b'nei yisrael*', 'the people, the children of Israel'. From then on in chapter one the Israelites are referred to by the collective term *am*, people, which is treated in Hebrew as a singular noun. Hence in his infamous statement Pharaoh says '*havah nitchachmah lo*', 'Come let us deal wisely with "him"' (*Exodus 1:10*) meaning, of course, the people, Israel. Understandably, most translations are forced to use the word 'them', 'come let us deal wisely with them', for the sake of clarity. Having established this system, in verse eleven, wherever the plural is used in these opening chapters it refers to the 'Egyptians', but the singular always refers to the people of Israel. *Exodus 1:11* reads:

> *vayasimu alav sare missim l'ma'an annoto b'sivlotam vayiven are misk'not l'faroh et pitom v'et-ramses.*
>
> *They* [the Egyptians] placed upon *him* [Israel] taskmasters in order to oppress *him* [Israel] with *their* [the Egyptians'] burdens, and *he* [Israel] built store cities for Pharaoh, Pithom and Ramses.

So, if Israel is referred to in the singular throughout chapter one verse 11, it is also clear that the word 'their' of 'their burdens' can only refer to the burdens of the Egyptians, presumably the task of building these cities for which the Hebrews provide the slave labour. Since there is no intervening indication in the following verses that might change this usage of the word, it must presumably have the same meaning when it reappears in *2:11*. So when Moses goes out to his brothers and looks upon '*their*' burdens, the reference can only be to the burdens of the Egyptians, those whom Moses considers to be 'his brothers'. So, the verse effectively reinforces the idea that Moses does not know anything about his origins.

But what does Moses actually see, what does he witness the first time he leaves the closed, secure world of the palace? He sees 'an Egyptian man striking a Hebrew man *of his brothers*'. Perhaps you can already see where I am going with this. What seems to be intended here is that Moses now identifies as 'his brothers' the victim of the blows. He may well be fully aware that the person is a Hebrew, but it is possible that the ethnic identity of the victim is largely irrelevant, or at least of only secondary importance. What causes Moses shock and distress is the act of violence against a helpless slave that he is witnessing. It is the first-hand experience of this injustice that affects Moses, causing him, if only for a moment, to step out of his role as an Egyptian prince, and it is his consequent act of intervening that will transform his destiny. The seeming redundancy of the repetition of the phrase 'his brothers', appearing at the beginning and the end of the same sentence, is resolved if the second reference is actually to a different set of people with whom he now identifies as his brothers; no longer the Egyptians but the Hebrew slaves.

I would like to take some credit for this observation, but it was already noted by the twelfth century Spanish Jewish Bible scholar, Abraham Ibn Ezra. In his commentary on Exodus 2:11, on the phrase 'he went out to his brothers' he explains the word 'brothers' to mean 'the Egyptians', adding, 'for he was in the palace of the king'. He goes on to explain the meaning of the second appearance of the phrase 'of his brothers' as 'of his family', as in the phrase '*anashim achim*' in *Genesis 13:8*, where it does not mean literally 'brothers', but 'relatives'.[25]

---

[25] Incidentally I was amused to read a footnote on this comment of Ibn Ezra in the Torat Chaim Chumash, a scholarly, beautifully laid out, edition of the rabbinic bible published by the Orthodox publishing house Mossad HaRav Kuk. To Ibn Ezra's identification of the first 'his brothers' as 'the Egyptians', the editor has added a footnote correcting him: 'It seems that he meant to say "the

Moses has seen something but not yet decided to act. So, the next sentence is crucial for what happens and also requires careful attention.

Vayifen koh vakhoh vayar ki ein ish vayakh et ha-mitzri vayitm'nehu ba-hol.

He looked here and there and saw that there was no man and he struck the Egyptian and buried him in the sand. (*Exodus 2:12*)

Unless they translate it literally, many versions imply that Moses looked around to see if anyone was watching and when it seemed to be all clear he hit the Egyptian. Some translations almost brand Moses as a coward at this moment. But clearly there were people about since the matter was known the following day. But a literal translation should note that Moses saw that there was no '*ish*', no 'man'. The word *ish*, as opposed to *adam,* 'a human being', carries with it a sense of individuality, even authority, a significant personality. If we now remember how the word was used in the previous verse, there was no '*ish*' present independent of a label, either as an *ish mitzri* 'a man, an Egyptian' or an *ish ivri* 'a man, a Hebrew'. This would suggest that both of them were acting out the role designated for them by their qualifying titles as Egyptian and Hebrew, master and slave, oppressor and victim. On this reading Moses looks around for an '*ish*', someone sufficiently independent of these labels to intervene and stop what is happening.

But there was no 'man', and Moses finds himself forced to act. If this seems too clever an interpretation, I can at least support it from within the Hebrew Bible itself. It would seem that precisely this is what the author of the section of the Book of Isaiah known as the Third Isaiah had in mind with this phrase. *Isaiah 59:15-16* reads:

Truth is lacking and he who departs from evil makes himself a prey. The Lord saw and it was bad in His eyes that there was no justice. *Vayar ki*

Hebrews"'! Given Ibn Ezra's track record for sarcastic comments at the expense of those he disagreed with, I would have enjoyed seeing his response to this attempt to improve his own commentary.

ein ish vayishtomem ki ein maphgia, He (God) saw that there was no man and wondered that there was no intercessor, therefore His arm brought salvation to Him and His justice, it sustained Him.

The parallel phrase 'and wondered that there was no intercessor' confirms the significance of the word '*ish*' as someone willing to intercede, to act. At a time of injustice God saw that there was no man prepared to take a stand. This would seem to be an example of inner exegesis within the Hebrew Bible itself, the later Isaiah text interpreting the earlier Exodus one. Perhaps this is even the source of Hillel's famous, first century, saying:

In a place where there are no men (*anashim*), strive to be a man (*ish*) (*Pirqe Avot* 2:6).[26]

On this reading, Moses moves from mere observation to action with all the consequences that will follow. Some late rabbinic commentaries also focused on this interpretation, wondering what prevented one of the 'men' who were present from doing something. Professor Nehama Leibowitz quotes two opposing suggestions, the first from Rabbi Naphtali Zvi Yehuda Berlin, the head of the Volozhin Yeshiva in the 19th century, in his commentary *Ha'amek Davar*. In this view there was no man amongst the Egyptians:

Moses sought to find a way to bring the Egyptian to justice for his criminal and inexcusable conduct. 'He saw that there was no man' – he saw there was no one to whom he could appeal for justice since they were all enemies of Israel.

But Nehama also quotes the author of the 18th century work *Ha-katav veha-kabalah*, who points to the Israelites, who were so intimidated by their slavery that they could not take a stand even when one of their own was being killed.[27]

---

[26] The same sentiment is expressed in Rudyard Kipling's 'If': 'And –which is more – you'll be a Man, my son!'

[27] Nehama Leibowitz Studies in *Shemot*: The Book of Exodus (Translated and Adapted by Aryeh Newman) (The World Zionist Organization, Department for Torah Education and Culture in the Diaspora, Jerusalem 1976) Volume 1, pp 43-44.

So, Moses decides and Moses acts and strikes the Egyptian man. The same verb is used for Moses act of striking as was used for the actions of the Egyptian man when striking the Hebrew man. The blow kills him. Presumably even for a Prince of Egypt, this act is unacceptable and Moses buries the man in the sand.

This should have been the end of the matter, but the following verse, thirteen, also deserves careful attention.

Vayetse ba-yom ha-sheni v'hinneh sh'ne-anashim ivrim nitzim vayomer la-rasha lammah takkeh re'ekha.

He went out on the following day, and behold, two men, Hebrews, were fighting and he said to the guilty one, why are you striking your neighbour? (*Exodus 2:13*)

(Again, we should note in passing that Moses uses the same verb from the root '*nakah*', 'to strike' that was used of the two blows (by the Egyptian and by Moses) in the previous sentences.) What is Moses doing involving himself with a dispute between two Hebrews, even to the extent of determining who is the guilty party in the conflict? It seems to suggest that overnight Moses has considered the action he had taken and has moved beyond identifying with the victim to a certain curiosity about this people with whom he has become involved, and hence the desire to learn more. If we want to find a moment at which Moses might have discovered the truth about his own identity it would have been during that night when reflecting on what he had done.

But his attempt to engage with the Israelites will have an immediate and shocking consequence as the words of the Hebrew man whom Moses has pronounced to be the guilty party reveal in the next verse:

Vayomer mi sam'kha l'ish sar v'shofet alenu. hal'horgeni attah omer ka'asher haragta et ha-mitzri. Vayir'a moshe vayomer akhen noda ha-davar.

And he said: 'Who placed you as a man who is a lord and judge over us. Do you intend to kill me just as you killed the Egyptian?'

And Moses was afraid and said, 'Surely the matter is known.' (*Exodus 2:14*).

Firstly, this confirms that Moses was not alone when he killed the Egyptian. Rather it would suggest that the act was witnessed by the Hebrew slaves who were present. Moses may have assumed that out of gratitude and solidarity they would keep the matter secret. That is why he is shocked and afraid when he learns that the action has become common knowledge at least amongst the Hebrews. That suggests that it will soon come to the attention of the Egyptians, as indeed the following verse indicates. But this also means that Moses' intervention on behalf of the Hebrews has actually been betrayed by the very people he thought he was helping. This is what he experiences in his first actual engagement with the people whom, now or later, he will have to recognize and accept to be his own. Secondly in the harsh words of the guilty person we have the first evidence of resentment against Moses; that this prince of Egypt has condescended to engage with them. Again the word '*ish*' has a prominent place: 'who placed you as an *ish*, a man who is lord and judge over us?!'.

We will return to this verse later. But the answer to my first question: 'How did Moses know that he was a Hebrew and thus get involved?' is simply that he did not know at the time. The discovery was secondary to his intervention in what he observed as an act of injustice, and everything flowed from this. It was not a case of family loyalty, but a profound commitment to justice that affected him. It was this quality that singled out Moses as God's choice as the future redeemer of an enslaved nation.

While we are studying the words of the attack on Moses it is worth noting a significant change of language. As we have already noted, the blow that Moses struck against the Egyptian uses the same verb *nakah*, 'to strike', as was used by the Egyptian man against the Hebrew man. This would suggest that Moses' action was a measured response to the earlier act. Since the verb does not have to indicate a fatal outcome, Moses might even have pleaded manslaughter for his action. He uses the same verb in his accusation of the guilty Hebrew man, *lammah takkeh re'ekha*, 'why do you strike your neighbour'. The reason for noting this is to point up the different word used by the Hebrew man whom Moses has just accused,

hal'horgeni attah omer ka'asher haragta et ha-mitzri,

Do you intend to *kill* me just as you *killed* the Egyptian?

The verb *harag* carries with it the definite intent to kill, something missing in the verb *nakah*. It redefines Moses' act and presumably this is how it came to be understood in public when Pharaoh, in the next verse, seeks *l'harog*, 'to kill', Moses.

This is the second of three episodes that tell of Moses' actions that led him from Pharaoh's palace to exile in Midian. But they also show the particular qualities of Moses which will suit him for his later task, and lead God to choose him for it. First is his concern for justice to the point of taking action himself. Moreover, despite the dismissive way in which the Hebrew describes his role, Moses' qualities as a judge and leader have been established.

But now Moses has to flee from Pharaoh. Perhaps even an Egyptian prince is not above the law, though some leniency might have been shown. But Pharaoh seeks '*l'harog*', to kill, Moses. Perhaps we can see here already some deeper political implications. In Pharaoh's reckoning, potentially more dangerous than Moses' action in striking the Egyptian may have been his new-found engagement with the Hebrew slaves. After all, this is the Pharaoh who had expressed his fears at the growing numbers of the Hebrews and their potential to act as a fifth column and assist Egypt's enemies. Hence his attempt at genocide by killing the male children by means of the midwives. Perhaps Pharaoh also made enquiries about Moses' origins and realised the potential threat he posed to the regime as someone with status and authority in Egypt. We are never far from real political issues in these Biblical narratives. Moses has no choice but to flee and arrives in Midian at the well.

In the third episode in this chapter Moses intervenes on behalf of the daughters of Jethro, the priest of Midian, against the other shepherds, a situation of injustice where no personal, ethnic dimensions are involved. It is a disinterested act, though perhaps influenced by the fact that the victims are women.[28] Actually, this episode is also a variant on the Biblical 'type scene' whereby a man meets a woman by a well and they marry. Jacob met Rachel at the well; Abraham's servant, as a substitute for Isaac, finds Rebecca. So, we are prepared for the comic sequel when Jethro, with seven unmarried daughters, is shocked that they have not invited this helpful Egyptian man for a meal! In the event Moses is invited to stay and marries Jethro's daughter Zipporah. When a son is born, Moses calls him Gershom, giving as the reason

ger hayyiti b'eretz nokhriyyah,

I was a stranger in a foreign land (*Exodus 2:22*).

Clearly this could refer to his present exile from Egypt, but the form of the verb allows for another explanation. If his Hebrew origin is now a conscious part of his new existence, then the 'foreign land' could equally apply to his upbringing in Egypt, in exile through most of his life from his Hebrew origins. But perhaps the naming of the son effectively draws a line for Moses between that period of his life and his new settled existence and identity.

Moses exists in a kind of double exile, from both of his two former identities, and his two former peoples, and is probably happy to leave the whole unfortunate business behind. And so he might have remained as a shepherd in Midian, till an episode with a burning bush was to bring back the whole of his past, and together with it a disturbing new challenge.

Until now we have been studying a coherent piece of narrative with a consistent view of Moses' initial ignorance of his origins. For his attitude towards this people with whose fate he is now inextricably bound, we will have to pick a few passages from the long and complex story of the wilderness

---

[28] Perhaps this also prefigures Moses' support for the daughters of Zelophehad in their claim to inherit from their father despite being women.

experience. His comments about the Israelites tend to be influenced by the particular crisis with which he is confronted at the time. Moreover, the context is his conversations with God where sometimes Moses is complaining about the burden of the people, whereas at other times he is negotiating on their behalf to save them. For example at the beginning of the journey when the people, in panic, complain about the lack of water, Moses cries to God: 'What shall I do for this people, a little more and they will stone me!' (*Exodus 17:4*) 'This people', not 'my people'. Even more forceful is his reaction when the people complain that they are sick of eating Manna every day in the wilderness and want meat! Moses is clearly at the end of his tether:

> Did I conceive this people? Did I give birth to them that You say to me carry them in your bosom, like a male nurse carries a suckling, to the land which You swore to their forefathers? (*Numbers 11:12*)

The birth language is extremely powerful here. In a post-Freudian age, it is tempting to hear in Moses' words a rejection of his own conception, birth and earliest nourishing by this very people whom he now has to carry. God's response is to provide Moses with the help of seventy elders who will share the burden with him. But on another occasion the debate between Moses and God carries a comic overtone despite the seriousness of the issue. It follows the episode of the golden calf when seemingly both God and Moses want to dump responsibility for the actions of the people on each other.

> The Lord said to Moses, 'go, descend, for *your* people whom *you* brought up from the land of Egypt have acted perversely.' (*Exodus 32:7*)

To which Moses responds:

> Why, Lord, should *You* be angry with *Your* people whom *You* brought out from the land of Egypt...? (*Exodus 32:11*).

As the rabbis pointed out it is like two parents blaming one another when their child has done something wrong.

The above examples are a reminder of the breadth and complexity of the Biblical narratives about Moses. But there is one passage that I would argue is directly linked to the stories of Moses' first encounter with the Israelites that we have already considered. It illustrates not only Moses' ambivalence about that choice he made so long ago, but also the residual resentment amongst some of the Israelites about the role that he seemingly took upon himself. After a series of disasters, including sending the spies into the land and their negative report, a number of groups come together in a rebellion led by a man called Korah (*Numbers 16*), a text we will study in greater detail. In a remarkably statesmanlike manner Moses manages to separate out the different factions and address successfully their individual grievances. The one exception is the complaint of the leaders of the tribe of Reuben, led by Dathan and Abiram, the tribe that represents the former political leadership of the people while still in Egypt. Their opening words are a scathing attack on Moses' political manifesto, the promise to bring them into a land 'flowing with milk and honey'. Instead they accuse him of taking them *out* of a land flowing with milk and honey, Egypt, in order to kill them in the wilderness! This is clearly an absurd description of their former state as slaves, but it works well as an example of negative political campaigning.

But then they taunt Moses with another accusation,

ki tistarer alenu gam histarer,

'Will you also like a lord, lord it over us?' (*Numbers 16:13*).

The emphatic repeated use here of the verb '*sarar*', 'to act as a prince or ruler', reminds us of the accusation of the Hebrew back in Egypt whom Moses had found guilty of striking his neighbour. He had used the same Hebrew verbal root, '*sarar*', but that time as a noun, '*sar*',

mi sam'kha l'ish sar v'shofet alenu,

Who placed you as a man who is a *lord* and judge over us? (2:14)

It is no surprise that it is only at this point when dealing with the Korah rebellion that Moses actually loses his temper. So much so that he feels obliged to make a public oath before God about his integrity:

No single donkey of theirs did I take, nor did I do harm to any one of them. (*Numbers 16:15*)

It is as if all his suppressed resentment about that first attack and betrayal that he experienced at the hands of the Hebrews back in Egypt now expresses itself, and he must defend the twin functions that he has fulfilled as political leader (*sar*) and judge (*shofet*). I am sure that it is this juxtaposition that led the rabbis to assume that the two Hebrews who were fighting back in Egypt were actually the same two men, Dathan and Abiram mentioned here, and link them to other events. For example, after the disastrous report of the spies who warned against trying to enter the Promised Land, we are told that 'a man said to his brother: "Let us set up a head and return to Egypt!"' (*Numbers 14:4*). Who were 'the man and his brother' according to the rabbis? Obviously Dathan and Abiram (*Nedarim 64b*)! One may or may not go along with these identifications, but what is interesting is that they suggest that rather than treat each rebellion in the wilderness in isolation, there was an organised opposition to Moses throughout the period of his leadership, the same people who spoke out at each crisis.

The rabbis made another observation about the way that Moses was actually viewed by the people. When Aaron died, the Bible records that

> *vayivku et aharon sh'loshim yom kol beit Yisrael.*

> the whole house of Israel wept for Aaron thirty days' (*Numbers 20:29*).

Yet when Moses died the mourners are differently identified,

> *vayivku v'nei yisrael et moshe....sh'loshim yom,*

> the children, (literally: sons) of Israel, wept for Moses thirty days (*Deuteronomy 34:8*).

For the rabbis, the use of the phrase *kol beit yisrael*, 'the whole house of Israel', puts special emphasis on the word 'house' to focus on families, and particularly on the mourning of the women. Aaron, in the rabbinic view, did much to defend the rights and welfare of the women. But for Moses it was a more formal period of mourning, and it was only the men, the *b'nei yisrael*, 'the sons of Israel', who participated. (*Rashi quoting Pirke d'Rabbi Eliezer 17*)

Whether or not we wish to accept this interpretation, it does serve to remind us that as a leader Moses had been supportive of the people but at times utterly ruthless in punishing those who were presumed to act against the teachings of God. Such leadership may be feared, honoured and respected, but it hardly evokes the sort of love and affection that a more populist figure like Aaron could evoke.

I have tried to stay within the confines of our received Biblical text. On this basis, the fact that Moses did not grow up as an enslaved Hebrew gave him the strength and independence to take on the task of freeing the people. His Egyptian education towards a leadership role in that society would have given him some of the necessary legal and administrative skills to develop a constitution and infrastructure for an experimental new society. The rabbis also noted that, as in the case of King David, Moses' experience as a shepherd gave him other essential leadership skills, those of caring and compassion for his flock, animal and human. Moses was successful in transforming a rabble of downtrodden, demoralised slaves into a strong, organised, legally constituted society. In a way he managed, at least personally, to bridge two cultures, and in the process created a workable synthesis for himself and for the nation that he led. It was Moses' 'outsider/insider' status, the variety of his identities and the questions each of them raised for him, that made him the extraordinary leader that he became. Without Moses, there would be no Jewish people, no Israel. But, without the ambiguities and challenges posed by his own mixed identity, there might never have been a Moses!

7 What really happened at the 'burning bush'?[29]

Having fled from Egypt, Moses has found his new home in the land of Midian. He has married one of the daughters of Jethro, the priest of Midian, started a family, and now leads the life of a shepherd. Chapter three of Exodus finds him exploring territory 'beyond' the wilderness and coming to the 'mountain of God', to Horeb. The opening suggests that he has gone outside the usual area of pasturing. It leaves open the question as to whether his arrival at a place known as the 'mountain of God' is merely a chance matter, or in some ways reflects a desire on his part to satisfy some kind of spiritual need. Like Moses we are startled by the sudden appearance of a visual phenomenon that is completely out of place in this landscape. The Hebrew names it a '*malach adonai*', an 'angel' or 'agent' of the Lord, which signals the beginning of yet another transformation in Moses' life.

The word written here as '*adonai*' refers to the so-called 'tetragrammaton', the four-letter name for God, written with the letters '*yod – hey – vav- hey*', transliterated as YHWH. Jewish tradition has safeguarded this name to the extent that it was only to be pronounced in its actual written form by the High Priest on the holiest day of the Jewish calendar, Yom Kippur, the Day of Atonement, and that in the innermost sanctuary of the Jerusalem Temple. When the name is to be read aloud in liturgical contexts, it was substituted with the word '*adonai*', which is a variation on the Hebrew word, '*adon*', meaning 'lord'. However in the text which follows in Exodus 3, another name for God is also introduced – '*elohim*'. The ending '-im' is the conventional masculine plural ending of Hebrew nouns, and in some contexts, when accompanied by a verb in the plural form, it can represent the 'gods' worshipped by other peoples and in some cases 'judges'. However when accompanied by a verb in the singular, as in the opening of the Book of Genesis, 'In the beginning God

---

[29] A *version* of this paper 'The bush that never burnt' (Narrative techniques in Exodus 3 and 6) appeared in *The Heythrop Journal* Vol 16 No 3 July 1975 pages 304-311.

created....' it can stand for the One God of all. In general terms for the Hebrew Bible, if *'elohim'* suggests a universally known concept of the divine, the name YHWH represents the name of that One God that is known uniquely by Israel. However from a narrative point of view, the precise meaning or usage of these names in any given case, particularly when they appear together, may depend upon the particular context.

In the following verses in Exodus 3, it is noteworthy that the two names interchange. As a result this been an important text for the attempt by the historical-critical school of Biblical scholarship to distinguish two original sources of the narrative, one that used the name *'elohim'*, the so-called 'Elohist' source, and the other that used the name YHWH, the so-called Yahwist source. On this basis it is possible to separate out these strands by a judicious selection of which verses appear to belong to which divine name. Thus verses 3-4a and 7-10 explicitly use the tetragrammaton which also reappears in verse 15 with the final revelation of the divine name YHWH. Conversely, perhaps including verse 1, where the mountain of *'elohim'*, may simply be a place name, verses 4b-6, 11-14 explicitly use the designation *'elohim'* or with the definite article *'ha-elohim'*. It is possible using this separation to compile two fairly coherent accounts of what happened and the message that the voice from the bush delivered to Moses.

Moreover, a further clue to help separate presumed sources within a given text can be found in apparent redundancies, where the same idea is repeated for no apparent reason. One such example is the obvious repetitions in verses 7 to 10, where angel twice explains why God wishes to intervene to rescue Israel, having seen and heard their suffering in Egypt. Since this explanation is essential information for both 'sources', it is easy to attach verses 7 and 8 to the original 'Yahwist' source and the repetition of the same information in 9 and 10 to the original 'Elohist' source.

However if we pay attention to the way the two names of God are introduced in this particular chapter it is possible to recognize here a Hebrew literary convention that is at play, one that offers a more coherent way of reading the narrative.

> The angel of YHWH appeared to him in a flame of fire out of the midst of the bush; and he saw and behold, the bush burned with fire but the bush was not consumed. (*Exodus 3:2*)

The literary convention lies in the repetition of the verb '*ra'ah*' to see within the verse – at first in the '*niphal*' passive form,'*vayera*', 'there was seen', 'appeared', followed by the active form of the same verb '*vayar*' and he, Moses, saw. Effectively the convention creates two different perspectives on the same scene before us. One is the 'objective' view of the narrator, who informs the reader that the angel of YHWH 'appeared' in the midst of the bush. The narration then switches to the subjective perspective of the character Moses, and what he actually 'sees'. The emphasis on this new perspective is further spelled out by introducing the word '*hinneh*', 'behold', which effectively puts us, the reader, into Moses place, we see through his eyes. We, the reader, know that there is an angel manifesting in this bush in a light that resembles a fire; Moses sees what appears to be a fire in the bush which nevertheless is not consumed. The emphasis on 'seeing' is reinforced in verse three when Moses decides 'I will turn aside and 'see' this great 'sight' (*mar'eh* – again the verb *ra'ah*) – why is the bush not consumed. Verse four marks the transition between these two perspectives.

> YHWH saw that he turned aside to see, and '*elohim*' called to him from the midst of the bush and said 'Moses Moses' and he said 'Here I am'.

That is to say, from Moses point of view this is clearly some kind of 'divine manifestation' for which the general term '*elohim*' is being used. From now on the narrator will consistently switch between the two perspectives, the

97

objective and subjective, by use of the appropriate name of God. We, the reader, enjoy the knowledge that is concealed from Moses.

Before seeing how this works out, it is important to recognize that this narrative convention can be found elsewhere. A previous example is the appearance of three 'men' to Abraham in Genesis 18:1-2.

> YHWH *appeared* to him by the oaks of Mamre, as he sat at the door of his tent in the heat of the day. He *lifted up his eyes* and *saw* and *behold*, three men stood in front of him. When he saw them, he ran from the tent door to meet them, and bowed himself to the earth.

Here the convention is even more explicitly expressed: YHWH 'appeared' to him (the same *niphal* form of the verb *ra'ah*) followed by the threefold indication, 'he lifted up his eyes and saw and behold' – which introduces his subjective experience of seeing and greeting three men.

Once the two-sided perspective on the encounter has been introduced by this literary convention, the narrator can switch between 'objective' statements about YHWH and the 'subjective' experience of Abraham (or Moses) without having to make further explicit reference to this technique. The reader, aware of the method, simply recognizes and enjoys the contrasting views.

The convention is not limited to these two passages but is used explicitly in two other such moments of divine revelation: An angel of YHWH appears to Gideon (*Judges 6:12*); and similarly to the future mother of Samson (*Judges 13:3*). In both cases the recipients of the experience require reassurance that what they have encountered is truly of divine origin, and the reader enjoys the comic element in their struggle to make sense of what is happening to them.

To return to Moses:

And (God) said: 'I am the God of your father, the God of Abraham, the God of Isaac, and the God of Jacob.' And Moses hid his face, for he was afraid to look at (the) God. (*Exodus 3:6*)

With this sentence we are reminded of something that underlies the dramatic development of the text. It is also something we have covered in the chapter on Moses' ignorance of his family background. From his infancy he was raised in the household of Pharaoh, growing up within the culture and society of the Egyptian court. His first adult experience of his Hebrew origin has come in two brief occurrences, the rescuing of the Hebrew slave from the taskmaster, and the attempt to separate the quarrelling Hebrews. Although his sense of identity as a Hebrew is re-established, his formal knowledge of his background and its traditions remains limited. Hence, we can recognize in the introduction 'I am the God of your father' the necessary personal prelude to the subsequent identification of this God with that of the patriarchs. Later, when God instructs Moses in the words he must say to the Israelites (*v 15*) he is to open the formula listing the names of the patriarchs with the equally formulaic 'the God of your fathers', the plural form which is replaced here with the more intimate reference to his own unknown father. The device of the 'ignorance' of Moses allows the narrator to explain the 'name', 'history' and plans of the God who encounters him to Moses and to the reader.

It is now appropriate to address the apparent redundancy of the 'duplication' in verses seven to eleven. This requires us recognizing here another well documented Biblical literary convention, namely the use of chiastic or concentric structures. They are a feature of biblical poetry. For example, the opening of Psalm 19:

The heavens	declare	the glory of God,
a	b	c
	X	
c'	b'	a'
the works of His hand	tells	the firmament.

'The heavens' and 'firmament' (a, a'), 'declare' and 'tell' (b b' are synonymous, The other corresponding terms 'the glory of God' and 'the works of His hand' (c c') force us to seek the connection between them. The pattern can also be expressed as:

a

   b

      c

      c'

   b'

a'

While this pattern appears here within a verse, using the same pattern, a and a', b and b' etc. might consist of entire sentences, and can even encompass entire chapters as in the case of Genesis 12-22 describing key elements in the life of Abraham. (See the beginning of chapter 3). In this form, the corresponding elements may be shown by the strategic repetition of 'key words'. What happens if we examine Exodus 3:7-10 according to this pattern?

7. YHWH said:

> I have surely seen (*ra'oh ra'iti*) the suffering of **My people** who are in Egypt,
>
> and I have heard their cry (*tza'akatam*) because of their taskmasters
>
> for I know their pain.

8.
> I will come down to rescue them from the hand of Egypt
>
> and bring them up from that land (*eretz*)
>
> to a land *(eretz)* good and broad, a land (*eretz*) flowing with milk and
>
> honey, to the place of the Canaanites, Hittites, Amorites, Perizites,
>
> Hivites and Jebusites.

9.
> And now, the cry (*tza'akat*) of the **Children of Israel** has come up to Me
>
> and also I have seen (*ra'iti*) the oppression with which the Egyptians oppress them.

10. And now, please go and I will send you to Pharaoh and bring out **My people, the Children of Israel**, from Egypt.

The 'key words' that establish the pattern are:

> a *ra'oh ra'iti* (see)
>
> > b *tza'akatam* (cry)
> >
> > > c *eretz* (land).
> > >
> > > c *eretz* (land)
> >
> > b *tza'akat* (cry)
>
> a *ra'iti* (see)

It is a formally constructed rhetorical passage, designed to reassure the people that God sympathises with their plight and suffering, and has determined to take them out of 'that land' of slavery and oppression to another land, one that is broad and prosperous. In the context of the Book of Exodus, this is the

101

first word from God to the people after a silence of some hundreds of years, so it requires this great rhetorical flourish!

One other factor should also be noted, one that is similar to the equating of 'the glory of God' and 'the work of His hands' in the opening to Psalm 19. In the opening of the structure, verse 7, God refers to Israel as 'My people'. In the closing part, verse 9, they are referred to as 'the Children of Israel'. At the close, with the appointing of Moses to the task, verse 10, and with a final flourish, the two terms are united as: 'My people, the Children of Israel', thus tying together their identity and their relationship with God.

There is an additional dimension to this 'two-perspective' revelation narrative, which is common to the others indicated above (with Abraham, Gideon and Samson's mother), namely the special position given to the reader. We are in the privileged position of knowing both the 'reality' of what is going on and the limited understanding and experience of character involved. In this case it dramatizes the 'otherness' of revelation – that even a Moses did not truly understand or recognize it at first, so how much more should we be aware of our limitations when it comes to such experiences. But it also adds to the humanity of Moses, despite all his authority and power and extraordinary achievements, he is not a superhuman figure.

Moses' humanity is immediately evident in his reaction to this task. In verse 10 God has actually 'invited' Moses to accept it. Hebrew allows for three ways of 'softening' the force of an imperative.[30] When 'commissioning' Moses God says: '*l'cha v'eshlach'cha*', the form '*l'cha*' 'please go (and I will send you)' being such a softening of the imperative '*lech*' 'go!'. It is only later, when

---

[30] We have seen two examples of changing imperatives into requests in God's instructions to Abraham in Genesis 22 to *kach-na* 'please take' his son and *lech l'cha* 'please go' to sacrifice him.

God becomes impatient with Moses' hesitations, that the request becomes an imperative e.g. v 17 *lech*, 'go and gather the elders of Israel!'

One can sympathise with Moses who thought that he had put his difficult experience with the Hebrews behind him in his new life in Midian. Whatever power and knowledge he once had in Pharaoh's palace must have seemed remote, and how absurd the task for one man alone to bring out the mass of enslaved people. So his first reaction is to emphasise his inadequacy, both personally and for the task. He is still addressing the '*elohim*'. He receives the assurance that God will accompany him and that at a later stage Moses will bring the freed Israelites to this very mountain as a sign that the long-term promise of entry into their own land will be fulfilled. Now he expresses his curiosity about this God. If we take seriously the narrative about Moses' background, what he asks now about learning the name of this God is not a rhetorical question, but a genuine expression of his ignorance of so much of his origins and identity. How he sets about learning the name of this mysterious God and in the process gains the kind of insight needed to address and even negotiate with God, will be the subject of the next chapter.

8 Negotiating with God: A Masterclass with Moses

There are a number of examples in the Hebrew Bible where individuals enter into a negotiation with God about an issue that is important to them – either personally or on behalf of others. We think immediately of Abraham confronting God on the threat to destroy Sodom and Gomorrah as an example of the latter. But there are also attempts to persuade God to fulfil some personal need – for example the case of Jephthah's promise to offer something to God if he is victorious in a battle. At many times in the stories of the journey of the Israelites through the wilderness, Moses was called upon to persuade God to forgive the actions of the people and restore what seemed to be a potentially catastrophic breakdown in the covenant. Two examples show how Moses learnt to do this and then apply it. We will examine these two encounters between Moses and God which can be seen as successful negotiations, in that they satisfy both parties, a win-win outcome.

At the Burning Bush

We have already studied some aspects of that first encounter between God and Moses when he was guarding the flock of this father-in-law in the wilderness and his eyes were drawn to the phenomenon of a bush that is burning but not consumed. *(Exodus 3:2)* The first stage of any negotiation is to bring the two parties concerned into a conversation. Here it is God's initiative. Moses is drawn to the strange phenomenon when a voice calls to him by name 'Moses, Moses'. Whatever his feelings about this, Moses is able to reply, 'Here I am', the Hebrew word '*hinneni*' implying full attention and commitment to whatever is to follow. The next words from God serve to establish the seriousness of this event by designating the place where they are meeting as holy ground. Moses is to understand fully the significance of what he is encountering here. But the next statement by God establishes a more personal and intimate note. 'I am the

God of your father.' According to the Biblical account of Moses' origins, he has grown up as a prince in the land of Egypt, knowing only that his mother is a daughter of Pharaoh. The mystery of his origins is only partly revealed to him as an adult when he intervenes in the lives of the Israelite slaves and discovers, seemingly for the first time, that he belongs to them. But when he tries to intervene in a dispute between two Israelites, he is immediately rebuffed and faces public exposure that requires him to flee from the death penalty imposed on him by Pharaoh. So, what might it have meant to him personally when this divine voice invokes his father?

However, these words are followed by a formulaic phrase that fills in for Moses the Israelite history, 'the God of Abraham, the God of Isaac and the God of Jacob'. God tells Moses that when he speaks to the Israelite elders for the first time in Egypt, he is to introduce God's name with the phrase 'the God of your fathers', in its plural form, followed by the list of the patriarchs, thus evoking the collective memory and identity of the people (*Exodus 3:15*).

Perhaps this is a good moment to pause and ask what God has at stake in this encounter. It has been God's promise to each of the three patriarchs that one day they will inherit a special land. Behind this promise is God's attempt to create a model society, based on the choice of Abraham who is to command his descendants to keep the way of God, to do righteousness and justice (*Genesis 18:19*). In Moses God has the ideal figure to further this aim. Having grown up in Pharaoh's palace, Moses has not been reduced to the subservient status of slaves like the rest of his people who would be incapable of freeing themselves. He has been brought up in the Egyptian court with educational and, presumably, administrative and military skills that would fit him for the difficult task of nation-building. Moreover, despite his own complete identification as an Egyptian prince, at a crucial moment Moses chose to take the side of a victim of his own unjust society and had radically to reassess his values and perspective. So, to win Moses to the cause of freeing the Israelites God must

105

speak in terms that correspond to Moses' personal qualities and values. God opens with a powerful piece of rhetoric, concentric in structure, designed to appeal to Moses' proven compassion for victims of oppression and his wish to offer them a vision of a better future. We have examined it in the chapter on the 'burning bush' and noted the repetition of three key words (*seen*, *cry* and *land*) that are the building blocks of the concentric structure of the passage.

The opening and closing emphasis on what God has '*seen*' and '*heard*' of the suffering of the Israelites, illustrates God's sense of compassion for the people but also echoes Moses' own experience of witnessing and intervening in their suffering. These verses surround the central promise of the change of '*land*' from the slave state of Egypt to the rich and fertile '*land*' prepared for them, which, geographically, is the place where a number of different peoples currently live.

Having appealed to this experience and potential vision for Moses to share, God introduces the action that must now follow, with the opening phrase '*v'attah*', 'And now!' In this final appeal the last part of the rhetorical structure is sealed by combining the two terms God has used in the opening and close: 'My people' and 'the Children of Israel'.

> And now, I am asking you to go and I will send you to Pharaoh, and bring out My people, the Children of Israel from Egypt! (*Exodus 3:10*)

The word translated as 'I am asking you to go', is an attempt to indicate the form of the Hebrew verb 'to go' which is used here, *l'chah*, which is a softened imperative, intended to persuade, not to order. Moses has a choice.

Now it is Moses' turn. 'Who am I that I should go to Pharaoh and that I should bring out the Children of Israel from Egypt?' On the face of it his response is a modest disavowal of his competence, perhaps reinforced by the fear of the death penalty facing him should he return to Egypt. But if God has hit the right note with the opening remarks and Moses is interested, he may actually be hinting at his need to know what support and safeguards God will provide. God's response is to offer a personal engagement with Moses throughout with the word '*ehyeh*' (grammatically the 'imperfect' form of the verb *hayah*, 'to be') 'I will be (with you)'. It is a word that will keep recurring throughout this encounter, Moreover, God offers a future public event here on this same mountain that will be the sign that the long-term result, entering the land, will also be successful.

But now Moses' insecurity about his identity and his knowledge of the Israelites comes to the fore with his second objection. What if they ask me the name of their God, what shall I say? Given Moses' relative ignorance about his origins this is a legitimate request for knowledge. But it conceals a problem that God will address with the first of three replies. For to know the name of a god in the Ancient Near East implied a measure of secret knowledge and potential power over that god. So, this is to be Moses' first lesson in the uniqueness and otherness of the God of Israel. The answer that God offers is open to any number of translations. It includes the same Hebrew word '*ehyeh*' God has just used when promising Moses 'I will be with you'. Grammatically this form of the Hebrew verb can cover all the modalities: I am, I will be, I shall be, I can be, etc. Here it is joined by the 'particle of relation' '*asher*' to a repetition of the identical word, *ehyeh asher ehyeh*, which multiplies the number of possible meanings of the sentence. Perhaps the best translation is the simple 'I am what I am' which is effectively a refusal to provide any name at all. It is as if God is saying: 'I retain the right to keep My name secret from human knowledge'.

What follows depends very much on how much weight we put on the appearance of seemingly redundant words in a Hebrew Biblical text. Because once again God speaks, but instead of simply continuing the previous sentence, God's next words are introduced by the conventional formula 'And he said: So shall you speak to the Children of Israel…' The use of 'And he said' suggests that this further statement by God is not a direct continuation of the previous one, but a new beginning and implies that something has intervened, so that a new opening is required. What has intervened would appear to be a silence from Moses. This could mean bewilderment about what God's words mean or a dissatisfaction about them as a response to Moses' legitimate question. In either case, perhaps Moses has begun to recognize the value of a deliberate silence as a negotiating tactic. Effectively, he waits out God who is forced to offer this second explanation.

But this second statement, once again uses the same Hebrew word *ehyeh*, literally, *'ehyeh* sent me to you'. This suggests that the name of this God is *ehyeh*, 'I am' – though to those who hear Moses say it it must sound like: 'I myself sent me to you.' Clearly it is unsatisfactory and again it is met by Moses' silence. So finally, God is forced to reveal the actual name in verse 15. This agreement on God's part is introduced by 'and furthermore God said to Moses', reinforcing the apparent reluctance with which God gives this final answer.

Thus shall you say to the Children of Israel, YHWH, the God of your fathers, the God of Abraham, the God of Isaac and the God of Jacob sent me to you. This is My name for ever, and this is how I am to be remembered from generation to generation.' (*Exodus 3:15*)

In terms of our theme of negotiation, God's first approach has been successful in winning Moses to the cause, but Moses has managed to win a serious concession by God to reveal the special name, that will come to be the intimate name whereby Israel knows God.

God seems sufficiently pleased with the outcome so far that there follows immediately the command: 'Go and gather the elders…, (*Exodus 3:16*) using now the imperative form of the verb 'go', '*lech*'. But perhaps God's confidence in the outcome of the negotiation is a bit premature, for much of the next chapter in Exodus is about Moses' doubts and insistence on the precise support he will need in order to fulfil the task: including signs to convince the elders, someone to speak publicly on his behalf. God is beginning to learn that Moses is indeed a worthy agent, but one who will come to think of himself more as a partner in this enterprise whose views and opinions will also have to be considered. The stage is set for a fascinating but troubled relationship.

There is a rabbinic view that recognizes the significance of the silences we have noted above – hinted at by the insertion of the repeated 'and he said'. Rather than simply understanding this pause in the text as silence, one rabbinic commentator filled in a missing conversation. Moses understood God's 'I am that I am' to mean: 'Just as I am with the Israelites now in this their time of trouble, so will I be with them in the future when troubles arise.' To which Moses corrected what he considered to be a psychological mistake on God's part: 'Master of the universe, it is enough for them to endure the current enslavement, there is no need to mention future enslavements!' So God shortened the phrase by omitting the second 'I am' in his statement and used only the first 'I am (*ehyeh*) (who is with you now in this trouble) sent me to you.'(*Berachot 9b*) By reminding God of the need of the moment, Moses is displaying a rabbinic understanding of his negotiating and diplomatic skills.

But there is a broader question the rabbis have about the various encounters between God and the people God chooses to be leaders. It is exemplified by the case of Abraham. Why did God inform Abraham about the plan to destroy Sodom and Gomorrah? In a rabbinic view it was a test intended to help Abraham fully realise the long-term task given to him by God: to pass on to future generations God's 'way' (Hebrew *derech*), the qualities of righteousness and justice (*Genesis 18:19*). Although these qualities may be latent within Abraham, it was important that they become overt, active parts of his character and behaviour. God deliberately elicited Abraham's concern about the injustice of God's destroying the two cities without regard to the innocence or guilt of individuals. So Abraham was forced to challenge God's behaviour and argue the case for sparing the cities down to the smallest number of innocent people required to do so. In this reading God gives permission to Abraham and successive generations to question or challenge God's actions when moral issues arise. As we shall see, God behaves in a similar way with Moses, encouraging him at great personal risk to challenge what God is planning.

After the Golden Calf

For the purpose of this study I am accepting the chronology and the narrative coherence of the passages we will examine. Moses does indeed lead the Israelites out of Egypt to the same mountain where he had encountered God. Here, by means of another major negotiation mediated by Moses, the people enter into a covenant with God. But Moses delays returning from the mountain with the Ten Commandments carved into two stone tablets. As a result, the people, fearing his prolonged absence, demand that Aaron creates for them a tangible God that they can recognize as leading them for the rest of their journey. God informs Moses of this betrayal of the recently made covenant and threatens to destroy the people.

God announces to Moses what has happened:

> Go down (from the mountain) because *your* people whom *you* brought up from the land of Egypt have become corrupt. They have turned away very quickly from the way which I commanded them, have made themselves an idol cast in the shape of a calf and have bowed down and sacrificed to it and said: These are your gods, Israel, who brought you up from the land of Egypt. (*Exodus 32:7-8*)

Once again, God's next remarks are introduced by 'And God said' which, as I have suggested above, implies silence from Moses. Perhaps he is truly lost for words at the collapse of everything that had been achieved, or else Moses is already aware that in negotiations, perhaps especially with God, one should never react with the first thing that comes to mind. God speaks again:

The Lord said to Moses: I have seen this people, and, look, they are a stiff-necked people. And now, leave Me alone and My anger will rage against them and I will destroy them and make you into a great nation! (*Exodus 32:9-10*)

Moses has now had time to recover and mount his own response. It is introduced by the words that Moses 'entreated' or 'mollified' God, but his opening remarks are not exactly designed to be polite! He reacts to God's reference to '*your* people whom *you* brought up from Egypt'. Moses is not prepared to take the blame alone and responds:

Why is the Lord angry against *Your* people whom *You* brought out from Egypt with great strength and a powerful hand? (*32:11*)

The rabbis commented that this is like parents each blaming the other for the bad behaviour of their child. Moses does soften the attack by pointing to the extraordinary lengths to which God had gone to achieve this unique victory. But this also opens up the broader dimension of what is at stake here by reminding God of the universal significance of this event. What would be the consequence if the Egyptians saw the destruction of the people not merely as a disastrous failure by God but even a betrayal of the people by bringing them out merely in order to destroy them? That alone should be enough to make God relent of the threatened punishment.

But Moses feels the need to counter another threat from God, to begin the entire experiment again, this time founding the nation with Moses himself. If Moses might have been tempted by such an offer in the past, this was no longer the case. By now he so fully identified himself as belonging to Israel that he could invoke the patriarchs and God's repeated promises to them that their descendants would become as many as the stars of heaven, and that they would inherit the land that God had promised to them. However problematic the people may be, they were willed into existence by God (v *12-13*).

Again, we are left with questions concerning God's behaviour and responses. Is God simply furious and lashing out, or is this a calculated anger aimed at strengthening Moses in the face of this disaster? A hint of this possibility lies in God's extraordinary statement: 'Leave Me alone and My anger will rage against them', which has to be seen as an invitation to Moses to do the exact opposite and do everything possible to prevent God's threat. However we read the arguments of both sides, the immediate crisis is averted. God literally 'changes His mind about the punishment and does not do it.' (*Exodus 32:14*)[31]

Moses descends and seeks to undo the damage that has been done but by very drastic and violent means. The following day Moses returns to God on the mountain to deal with unfinished business. This is no longer the tentative Moses of the burning bush. Rather he is someone hardened by the initial disappointments and final triumph against Pharaoh, and the myriad struggles to turn this collection of slaves into a self-confident and responsible nation. Along the way he has also learned how to interpret and debate the will of God. He begins with a confession on behalf of the people:

> Alas, this people have sinned a great sin. They have made for themselves a god of gold (*Exodus 32:31*).

The truth requires this acknowledgment as a starting point for any attempt at reconciliation. But, as a partner with God in this enterprise, Moses is prepared to challenge God's response. He begins:

> 'And now, if You will forgive their sin....

But his speech suddenly stops here and goes no further because Moses has touched on a fundamental issue. Is God's only response to sin to punish and even destroy? That is the human response – and that is exactly what Moses has

---

[31] This sentence will be evoked by the author of the Book of Jonah who applies it to God's willingness to cancel the threatened punishment to the people of Nineveh, to Jonah's great anger! (Jonah 3:10)

just done in slaying a large part of the population as a punishment. Moses cannot complete the sentence in this form for there is no way of understanding how or with what end result God might forgive their sin. Instead he changes direction and asserts the consequences if such forgiveness is not available:

> but if not. blot me out of Your book which You have written.' (*Exodus 32:32*)

This is Moses' ultimate response to God's offer to make Moses the founding father of a new nation.[32] It is also Moses' acknowledgment of his complete identification with the people and their fate, and his willingness to do whatever is needed to save them. But behind this seeming ultimatum Moses is addressing the long-term problem of mediating between a seemingly unpredictable God and a people seemingly bent on self-destruction.

God seems to feel the need to respond to Moses' dramatic willingness to offer himself, and says:

> The one who has sinned against Me I will blot out from My book (*Exodus 32:33*)

God is not prepared to accept this gesture by Moses and turns instead to practical matters. But the questions of guilt and innocence, and what punishment is appropriate, have moved into a central place in their ongoing dialogue. For now, God reserves the full punishment for a later time and says:

> Now go, lead the people to the place of which I told you. Behold, my messenger will go before you. But on the day when I visit, I will visit their sin upon them. (*Exodus 32:34*)

---

[32] The rabbis characterised Moses' refusal as being on pragmatic grounds: If a stool based on three legs (the three patriarchs) cannot stand, how much less can a one-legged stool stand. (*Berachot 32a*)

In the following chapter, Moses takes the initiative and opens a new negotiation. He presents his concerns to God with all the formality of a legal submission before a judge. He begins with the Hebrew word '*r'eh*', 'see'. In this context the word is effectively a technical term that defines the issues that need to be addressed. In a legal document it would be translated as 'whereas', meaning 'taking into account the fact that'. We should bear this formality in mind when we read the verse:

> See, You say to me bring up this people, but You have not let me *know* who You will send with me. And You have said 'I *know* you by name and also you have found favour in My eyes.' So now, if I have found favour in Your eyes, please let me *know* Your way, so that I may *know* You and find favour in Your eyes. And see, this nation is Your people (*Exodus 33:12-13*).

In analysing Moses' somewhat repetitive statement three things stand out. Firstly, the Hebrew text regularly inserts the personal pronoun '*attah*', 'You' thus emphasising the three statements that Moses makes about God's initiative and therefore ongoing responsibility: '*You are the One* who says to me bring up this people', '*You are the One* who has not let me know who You will send with me'; and '*You are the One* who said "I have known you by name".'

Secondly, there is a clue to the underlying intention of Moses' statement in the use of the verb '*yada*', 'to know'. For it is God who both *knows* and withholds *knowledge*, and for Moses this withholding of knowledge is no longer acceptable. God has promised that a '*malach*', a divine messenger or agent, will accompany the Israelites on their journey, even though God will no longer be in their midst (*Exodus 32:34*) – but Moses does not *know* who this will be. God claims to *know* Moses by name, which implies both that Moses has been specially chosen by God and that they have an intimate relationship[33].

Thirdly, four times Moses uses the phrase 'I have found favour in Your eyes', a common and flexible Biblical phrase used of someone in a subservient or petitionary situation seeking to establish an appropriate relationship – Jacob trying to reconcile with Esau,(*Genesis 33:8*) Ruth trying to ingratiate herself with Boaz (*Ruth 2;10*). However, the word commonly translated as 'favour' is from the Biblical root '*chanan*', meaning 'to act with grace', to give without expecting anything in return. Although the phrase itself might be overlooked because of its idiomatic usage, the fourfold repetition suggests that the issue of God's 'graciousness' in dealing with Moses, and ultimately the people, is deliberately introduced here. It will become a key term in defining God's attributes at the end of this negotiation.

Almost as an afterthought Moses uses the word 'see' a second time to introduce the other 'given' reality that both Moses and God have to deal with:

And see, this nation is Your people! (*Exodus 33:13*)

The short sentence carries within it the weighty problems of the immediate disaster with the golden calf, and God's frequent description of the Israelites as 'a stiff-necked people'[34], implying that they are stubborn and incorrigible. God's long-term relationship with the Children of Israel is the issue at stake here.

But before addressing this, Moses has already introduced his request. Verse 13 begins with '*v'attah*', 'and now', which, as we noted in the burning bush negotiation, signals the action to be undertaken as a consequence or outcome of the circumstances that have just been described. At the burning

---

[33] For the use of the verb '*yada*' to mean 'choose', see God's 'knowing/choosing' of Abraham for the purpose of instructing his descendants in God's way. (*Genesis 18:19*)
[34] Exodus 32:9; 33:3, 5; 34:9

bush it was God who used it to introduce Moses' task. Now it is Moses' turn to set the terms for his further involvement. If Moses has truly found favour in God's eyes, that is to say, if they have a partnership in the task, then God must make known to Moses' 'God's way', so that Moses can anticipate what God desires in any given situation.

But what is God's 'way', the Hebrew word '*derech*', that Moses wishes to learn? We have already noted a precedent for God's 'way' being revealed when God informed Abraham the plan to destroy Sodom and Gomorrah. God's explicit purpose in choosing/knowing Abraham is that he will instruct his descendants in God's way, defined there as 'to do righteousness and justice' (*Genesis 18:19*). However, for Moses in this situation, justice alone is not sufficient or helpful when it comes to dealing with fallible human beings. If the relationship with God has been damaged, as in the case of the 'golden calf', are punishment and destruction the only options? Is there no way in which the break with God can be repaired? Is there not a divine quality or attribute that can lead to forgiveness and reconciliation? Moses becomes the new Abraham. He must confront God on behalf of the entire people with whom a solemn covenant has been made. Where is there some quality or value within the covenant to resolve the conflicts and betrayals that are bound to arise? That is Moses' question and challenge to God.

God's immediate answer is to avoid the larger issue and simply confirm: 'My presence will go with you and I will give you rest' (*Exodus 33:14*). But Moses is not satisfied because the issue is not simply one of Moses' comfort, but that of God's long-term relationship with the entire people. So, he continues to press God and, while repeating that he has found favour in God's eyes, he smuggles the people as well into this favour. Moreover, he repeats the universal significance of what is happening, that it is God's presence that distinguishes this people from all others in the world.:

Moses said: 'If Your presence does not go, do not take us up from here. How will it be known that I have found favour in Your eyes, I *and Your people*, surely it is through Your going with us, so that we are set apart, *I and Your people*, from all the people upon the face of the earth. (*Exodus 33:15-16*)

God's response seems to be aimed at bringing the negotiation to a formal conclusion and repeats the two major phrases about the intimacy of their relationship with which Moses began.

The Lord said to Moses: This thing too which you have said I will do. For you have found favour in My eyes and I have *known* you by name. (*Exodus 33:17*)

But Moses is not so easily satisfied and introduces one further request:

'Show me please Your glory.' (*Exodus 33:18*)

The word regularly translated as 'glory', is the Hebrew word '*kavod*', which is derived from a root meaning 'weight, heaviness'. So its basic sense would seem to be 'that which gives someone weight in the eyes of others'. But in the Bible it is also used to describe the supernatural effects that accompany God's 'presence'. Moses seems to be adding a new personal dimension to the experience of the encounter with God. God is prepared to allow this and offers to pass God's 'goodness' before Moses. But in explaining what this 'goodness' might mean, God again reverts to the same ambiguous grammatical form as in the case of: 'I am what I am'.

I will pass all My goodness before your face and call out in the name of the Lord before you, but I will be gracious to whom I will be gracious and have compassion on whom I will have compassion. *(Exodus 33:19)*

God has read behind Moses requests what he is actually hinting at, for God to reveal the grace and compassion that God also possesses. But at the same time God seeks to keep these a matter for God alone to administer. But, as in the case of the gradual revelation of the divine name to Moses, because of Moses' persistence, God is once again forced to concede to Moses' negotiating skill. In the next chapter, again to Moses alone, God will express the full extent of God's compassion, and quite specifically indicate how God is willing to forgive all the different kinds of sin that human beings may commit, if they are willing to acknowledge them.

> The Lord descended in a cloud, stood with him (Moses) and proclaimed in the name of the Lord. Then the Lord passed before his face and called:
>
> *Adonai, Adonai*, a God of mercy and compassion, slow to anger, generous in love and truth, showing love to thousands (of generations), forgiving sin, wrongdoing and failings but who does not entirely declare innocent, visiting the sins of the fathers upon the children and the children's children to the third and fourth generation. (*Exodus 34:5-7*)

It is important from the outset to clear up a fundamental misunderstanding about the warning that comes at the end of this passage. A similar warning is found in the Ten Commandments, and in both cases the one being directly addressed is the adult, Israelite man who is the direct legal partner in the covenant with God in this patriarchal society. To this man belong wife, children, slaves, animals and land as part of his total person. In his lifetime he can see children, grandchildren and great grandchildren, so that any wrong actions he does will have an immediate and direct consequence on all those who 'belong' to him. This text is not about punishment echoing through the generations in the future, it is about what happens to those alive now, at this moment in time, for whom he also bears complete responsibility. But nevertheless, as the early part of the text suggests, it is always possible to evoke God's forgiveness and compassion if the wrongdoer is willing to confess and repent.

It would be hard to overestimate the significance of this passage in the Hebrew Bible. Moses will use a version of it when negotiating with God after the other great crisis in the wilderness journey when the spies gave a negative report about the possibility of entering the land of Canaan (*Numbers 14:18*). Two Psalms, 103 and 145, are meditations on its theme of God's compassion, and *Psalm 86:15* quotes it as part of a personal appeal to God. Moreover, phrases and echoes appear in other Psalms. It plays a crucial role in the final chapter of the Book of Jonah where the angry prophet accuses God of being too compassionate to the wicked people of Nineveh *(Jonah 4:2)*. The same version of the text is found in *Joel 2:13-14*. Beyond the Hebrew Bible a shortened version becomes the central text in Jewish festival liturgies, with particular importance throughout the services on Yom Kippur, the Day of Atonement.

With this final revelation the negotiation is almost complete. There remains only Moses' final plea to God to remain with the people and forgive their iniquities as promised.

> If now I have found favour in Your eyes, Lord, let the Lord please go in our midst, for it is a stiff-necked people, and forgive our iniquities and our sins and take us as Your inheritance. (*Exodus 34:9*)

Some concluding remarks

Would God have revealed this aspect of the divine character without Moses' stubborn insistence? Or is this what God intended to reveal all the time, as in the case of Abraham, but God needed Moses to bring it out? What is clear in this and the Abraham negotiation, is the great respect God shows to these human partners[35], as if God is learning from them and through them what is

---

[35] For anyone curious as to how Moses' negotiation skills would be evaluated today, a paper on negotiation would suggest that he would earn high marks. Michael Mamas writes on Five Steps to Master the Art of Negotiation (https://www.entrepreneur.com/articlers/253074)

needed if human society is to live up to God's hopes and expectations. Abraham bequeathed to us one aspect of God's way, that of righteousness and justice. Moses earned for us access to God's way of graciousness and compassion. Both 'ways' are also models for human behaviour, for how we are to conduct our personal and collective lives. We exist in the tension between these two poles of divine and human experience, between justice and compassion. The survival of our world depends on how well we negotiate the complex relationship between them.

---

1. Establish the relationship. 2. Choose 'honey over vinegar' – but the honey must be genuine. 3. Focus on the win-win – understand what all parties need. 4. Embody your inner adult – be the stable anchor, the respectful adult at the table. 5. Respect the rhythm of the relationship. Never forget that silent pauses can be a very powerful tool.

9 Korah versus Moses

According to the sequence of stories in the Book of Numbers, the rebellion against Moses led by Korah (*Numbers 16*) comes in the wake of a major political disaster. Following the sending of a team of tribal leaders to spy out the land of Canaan, and their negative report about the chances of conquering it, the Israelites are condemned by God to remain in the wilderness for forty years till a new generation is born that will be willing to face the challenge (*Numbers 13-14*). In such a crisis, it is inevitable that individuals and groups with disagreements with the leadership will come together to express their dissatisfaction, and Korah becomes the figurehead and spokesman who draws them together.

The Motivation of the Rebels

The first two verses list the participants in the rebellion:

Now Korah, the son of Izhar, the son of Kohath, the son of Levi, with Dathan and Abiram, the sons of Eliab, and On, the son of Peleth, sons of Reuben, took … and they rose up before Moses with certain of the children of Israel, two hundred and fifty men, princes of the congregation, the elect men of the assembly, men of renown. (*Numbers 16:1-2*)

In the Hebrew, the opening verb *vayyiqah qorah*, 'and Korah took', lacks a direct object to identify what Korah 'took'. Translators and commentators are forced to supply one for it to make sense. The King James Bible and those that follow it provide the word 'men'; others read the verb as if reflexive, so that they 'took themselves', and this leads to a variety of options: 'took action', 'took charge' or even 'became insolent'. However, none of these are justified by the Hebrew text, which leaves the question of what Korah 'took' hanging in the air. So, unless we simply assume that the text is corrupt, from a literary point of view, this absence is a puzzle that will remain with the reader as we continue with the story. There is a possible literary explanation, but it will have to wait until we have much more of the story behind us.

There follows the long pedigree of Korah – son of Yitzhar, son of Kohath, son of Levi. As a rule, the longer the list of names, the more significant the individual. Whatever may become of Korah, and whatever value judgments we make on him, his importance as a leader of the people must not be overlooked. Yet who is he? Many commentators have drawn attention to the genealogy in *Exodus 6:14-26*, which provides a family tree for Moses. But in effect it also offers a cast list of characters who will play significant roles in events that take place during the wilderness period.

If we look at the actual family tree a couple of features become clear. First and foremost is the relation of Korah to Aaron and Moses. They are first cousins, of the same generation as each other and therefore of similar rank. Perhaps it was that proximity, and Korah's lack of a leadership role that led him to attempt his rebellion. That is the assumption of the rabbinic sages who noticed another feature of the family tree. In *Numbers Rabbah 18:2* we find the following explanation:

> Why did he rebel? Because Elizaphan, the son of his father's brother, was appointed prince over his family. For it says in Numbers 3:30 'and the prince of the fathers' house of the families of the Kohathites being Elizapahan, the son of Uzziel'. Korah argued: My father, Izhar, was one of four brothers, as it says in Exodus 6:18, And the sons of Kohath: Amram and Izhar and Hebron and Uzziel. As for Amram the first-born, his son Aaron attained to greatness and Moses to royalty. Who then should rightly take the next office? Is it not the next in age? It is said: 'And the sons of Kohath: Amram and Izhar'. Now I, being the son of Izhar, should by right be the prince of the families; yet Moses appointed the son of Uzziel! Shall the youngest of my father's brothers be superior

to me? Behold I shall dispute his decision and put to nought all that has been arranged by him!

The genealogy in Exodus traces the Levites so as to include Elizaphan, and lists the descendants of Aaron down to Pinchas. All of these were involved in important events connected with the functioning of the sanctuary. For example, it includes the two sons of Aaron, Nadab and Abihu, who are struck down by heavenly fire when attempting to serve in the sanctuary in the wrong way, the same fate that will befall the 250 men who join Korah's rebellion. Therefore, the genealogy in Exodus seems to belong to an overall editorial narrative concern, which will include our chapter. By giving a prominent position to Korah's family tree the Biblical text itself hints at a possible motivation for his rebellion without directly spelling it out.

Ambiguity also surrounds the motivations of Dathan and Abiram, the other major rebels, even when their overt criticism of Moses is given to us. They, too, are the characters singled out in a genealogy, at the expense of all other Reubenite families, in *Numbers 26:5-11*. According to *Psalm 106:16-17*,

> They were jealous of Moses in the camp, and of Aaron the holy one of the Lord. The earth opened and swallowed up Dathan and covered the company of Abiram.

This clearly belongs to a different strand of Biblical tradition and the omission of Korah here, as also in the reference in *Deuteronomy 11:6*, raises important questions about the connection between the various rebellions in our text in *Numbers 16*. Nevertheless, the assertion that they were jealous of Moses and Aaron for some reason is borne out by the form of their accusation and their singularly undiplomatic attitude when invited to discuss the matter with Moses. In the midrash (*Numbers Rabbah 18:5*) the interesting observation is made that the camp of Dathan and Abiram was on the south side of the Tabernacle (*Numbers 2:10*), as was that of the Kohathites (*Numbers 3:29*), so that the proximity of the two groups led to their feeding each other's discontent and ultimately uniting in rebellion. The midrash however goes even further in identifying Dathan and Abiram as troublemakers throughout the wilderness period and even back in Egypt itself!

After the spies brought back a bad report and the people despaired, we read (*Numbers 14:4*): 'and they said, each man to his brother, let us set up a leader and return to Egypt!' Which two brothers would have been speaking? Obviously, Dathan and Abiram. (*Exodus Rabbah 1:30*). They were the two who took the extra rations of manna on Shabbat (*Exodus 16:20*) (*Midrash Tanchuma T'tzaveh 11*). Back in Egypt they were the elders who criticised Moses after his first unsuccessful encounter with Pharaoh (*Exodus 5:20*) (*Exodus Rabbah ad loc.*). And they were the two Hebrews whom Moses had tried to stop fighting while he was still an Egyptian prince (*Exodus Rabbah 1:30*). In the end the rabbis were so exasperated with them that they said, 'Whatever you can hang on this wicked pair, hang it!' (*Yalkut Shimeoni, Exodus 167*).

In examining this aspect, we have run ahead of our story and must return to the rest of the conspirators. On ben Pelet, having been mentioned in this opening section, completely disappears from the rest of the narrative. Perhaps some textual problem lies behind his appearance or he was a well-known character to the immediate audience of this narrative. The Talmud offers an entertaining account of how he was saved from continuing to support the rebellion:

> Rab said: On, the son of Peleth, was saved by his wife. She said to him, 'What difference will it make to you? Whether Moses remains master or Korah becomes the master, you will still only be a follower!' He replied, 'But what can I do? I have taken part in their planning and sworn loyalty to Korah.' ... She said, 'Sit here, and I will save you.' She gave him wine to drink, made him drunk and laid him down in the tent. Then she sat

124

down in the entrance and loosened her hair so whoever came to summon On retreated [it being immodest for any man to look upon a married woman with her hair down]! (*Sanhedrin 109b-110a*)

Who were the two hundred and fifty men? The three terms used to describe them are not exactly matched elsewhere; nevertheless, there are enough similarities to other phrases used of the leaders to indicate the positions they might have held. *n'sie edah*, 'leaders of the congregation', reminds us of the leaders who brought their offerings at the dedication of the tabernacle described in chapter 7: 'the leaders of Israel, heads of their fathers' houses, the leaders of the tribes who were over those who were numbered, brought near their offerings' (*v 2*). From these Moses had chosen for his census one man as 'head of his father's house' *(Numbers 1:54)* and these were the *q'ru'e ha-edah*, 'the summoned ones to the congregational assembly' (*1:16*), a title which also applied to Dathan and Abiram (*26:9*). A variation on this term is *q'ri'e mo'ed* in our verse in Numbers. Given the third title as well, *anshe shem*, 'men of renown', i.e. men of significance and fame, we have a mixture of people with some degree of privilege and status within the community. But what led them to join the rebellion?

The mediaeval Jewish commentator Abraham ibn Ezra provides a plausible explanation, based on the fact that they carried censers. The firstborn males had been 'consecrated' to God (*Exodus 13:2*) and they had the privilege of bringing the sacrifices on behalf of the people. But later they were replaced in this role by the Levites, and it was the loss of this holy task that led them to join with Korah. We will examine the details of this below.

Moses' strategic response

The task confronting Moses as leader of the people is how to sort out legitimate complaints from illegitimate ones, how to defuse the situation as much as possible, but also to punish where necessary those who threaten the very fabric of the Israelite community and its structure. How does he achieve this?

In v 3 the rebels 'assemble' against Moses and Aaron. Once again, we need to be precise in our understanding about the meaning of a Hebrew verb. The impression here might be of an angry mob cornering them in a violent way. But the verb *qhl* suggests a more orderly assembly with legal authority. Such an 'assembly' is constituted in *Numbers 14:5* following the incident of the spies. In the former case both Moses and Aaron 'fall upon their faces' before the assembly, whereas in this case Moses alone does so. Assuming that this is indeed a formal gathering, the act of falling on their face would represent an acceptance of the authority of the assembly before which they have to justify their actions. This would explain the otherwise redundant 'and Moses heard' in verse 4, suggesting his willingness to hear the charge brought against him and submit to the judgment of the assembly.

The actual charge is not entirely clear. What do the conspirators mean when they say: '*kol ha-edah*', 'all the congregation are holy', and which is the *edah*, congregation, that is meant here? It could mean the Israelite population as a whole, an argument used to justify Korah as a kind of democratic advocate. But if we look at the use of the same Hebrew phrase, again in the episode of the spies, something else becomes evident. The Biblical text notes the reactions of different groups to the 'bad report' of the spies.

> And all the congregation (*kol ha-edah*) lifted up and gave voice; and the people (*ha-am*) wept that night; and all the children of Israel (*b'nei yisrael*) murmured against Moses and Aaron; and all the congregation (*kol ha-edah*) said: 'If only we had died in Egypt or if only we had died in this wilderness. Why does the Eternal bring us to this land to fall by the sword? Our wives and children will be prey. Would it not be better to return to Egypt?' (*Numbers 14:1-3*)

Three groupings are distinguished: the 'people' seem to represent a generalised despair, whereas the 'children of Israel', literally the 'sons of Israel', may have represented more politicised groups that felt freer to complain about the leadership. But 'all the congregation', which appears twice and brackets the more general reaction, seems to refer specifically to the leadership group or governing body who debate the situation vigorously and loudly all night and come to a policy conclusion that it would be better to return to Egypt. Presumably they are the ones who convoke the most formal legislative body of the people '*kol k'hal adat b'nei yisrael*', 'all the assembly of the congregation of the children of Israel', before whom Moses and Aaron are called to account and whose authority they accept by 'falling on their faces'. If this understanding of '*kol ha-edah*' is correct, Korah is not referring to the people as a whole, but rather to the leadership elite alone.

Given the subsequent developments, there would seem to be two charges that are being brought against Moses and Aaron. The reference to 'holiness' seems to be restricted to the specific role of the priesthood, under Aaron, and that of the Levites within the sanctuary. But the reference to 'lifting themselves above the *kahal*, assembly, of the Eternal' would imply abusing the political leadership, which Moses has countered by submitting to the authority of the '*kahal*' for a judgment.

To understand how Moses addresses the first issue, we need some background information, part of which is supplied in the earlier chapters of Numbers. Already during the time in Egypt God had 'sanctified' the first-born male Israelites as belonging to God. But following the episode when the Israelites worshipped the Golden Calf and the Levites showed their loyalty to God, the Levites were to replace the firstborn in the particular task of offering sacrifices to God.

Again, the Eternal spoke to Moses, saying, 'Now, behold, I have taken the Levites from among the children of Israel instead of every firstborn,

127

the first issue of the womb among the children of Israel. So, the Levites shall be Mine, for all the firstborn are Mine. On the day that I struck down all the firstborn in the land of Egypt, I sanctified to Myself all the firstborn in Israel, from man to beast. They shall be Mine; I am the Eternal. (*Numbers 3:11-13*)

The specific role of the Levites is spelled out at the beginning of the Book of Numbers:

But the Levites shall encamp around the tabernacle of the testimony that there may be no wrath (*ketzeph*) upon the congregation of the people of Israel, and the Levites shall keep charge of the tabernacle of the testimony.' (*Numbers 1:53*)

One part of their task is to be the intermediaries between the people and the sanctuary, for if the Israelites should enter it or come into contact with the holy vessels then God's anger would blaze out and destroy them. The three sons of Levi, Gershon, Kohath and Merari, are assigned different tasks as the tabernacle was dismantled and reassembled during the wandering of the Israelites through the wilderness. The Gershonites were in charge of the tabernacle, the tent with its covering, the screen for the door of the tent of meeting, the hangings of the court, the screen for the door of the court which is around the tabernacle and the altar, and its cords (*3:25f*). The Kohathites, under the leadership of Elizaphan the son of Uzziel, were in charge of the ark itself, the table, the lampstand, the altars, the vessels of the sanctuary with which the priests minister and the screen. That is to say they were in charge of the most sacred implements and vessels of the sanctuary, under the direction of Elazar the son of Aaron (*vv. 31ff*). The Merarites, the youngest of the Levite families, had responsibility for the frames of the tabernacle, the bars, the pillars, the bases, and all their accessories – that is to say the least significant parts of the structure.

And I have given the Levites as a gift to Aaron and his sons from among the children of Israel, to perform the service for the children of Israel at the tent of meeting, and to make atonement for the children of Israel, that there may be no plague (*negeph*) among the children of Israel in case the children of Israel should come near the sanctuary.' (*Numbers 8:19*)

Although the Kohathites were in charge of transporting the holiest objects within the tabernacle, the ultimate responsibility for handling and dismantling them lies with Aaron's sons, the priests. These latter are to cover them with cloths and put them on poles ready for transport by the Kohathites, only after the task of the sons of Aaron has been completed. (*Numbers 4:15*) In fact there is a specific warning that the Kohathites must not touch the holy things

The Eternal said to Moses and Aaron, 'Let not the tribe of the families of the Kohathites be destroyed from among the Levites; but deal thus with them, that they may live and not die when they come near to the most holy things: Aaron and his sons shall go in and appoint them each to his task and to his burden, but they shall not go in to look upon the holy things even for a moment, lest they die.' (*Numbers 4:17-20*)

We thus find the Kohathites placed tantalisingly near the holy vessels of the sanctuary, but set apart from them by the sons of Aaron. Within the hierarchy of gradations of holiness, and hence power and danger, they are at the very edge of the innermost ring – and yet not quite there, and subservient to Aaron's sons. The logic of this structure is clear, given its premises – but the possibilities for discontent are also evident even at this stage, and the fact that it is Korah, a significant figure among the Kohathites, who leads the rebellion, becomes somewhat clearer.

We have now been introduced to two terms that are given as a warning about what might happen if this hierarchical structure should be disturbed, '*ketzeph*', 'wrath' and '*negeph*', 'plague' might break out and destroy the people. Indeed, both terms will be used to describe the destruction that appears as part of the aftermath of the Korah rebellion (*Numbers 17:11*). A contemporary analogy would be to view the presence of God in the tabernacle in much the same was as we view an atomic reactor. Properly controlled, through appropriate safeguards and protocols, it can be a source of great power. But any mistake, and that same power can be unleashed and have devastating consequences. So, the issue about who is 'holy', that is to say, who has permission to serve in God's presence, and in what capacity, is an essential part of the cultic structure that Moses has created. It is this structure that is being attacked by some of those participating in the rebellion. Although Korah is addressed as the main ringleader, in what follows, Moses will actually speak through him to the Levites who, it would seem, are not satisfied with the task assigned to them.

Moses' first response is his address to Korah and all *his* congregation, presumably to differentiate this particular group from the other participants in the rebellion. He says that the Eternal will indicate who is the holy one, the chosen one – so that Moses moves the discussion away from their argument that all are holy to the point that only one person can stand at the centre of the sacred system. To prove this, he challenges the entire group to present themselves with their censers on the morrow, for this is the task that only the priests may perform. He closes with a direct address to the Levites, using the same words used against him and Aaron (*v 3*) *rav lachem b'nei Levi'*, 'You have gone too far, sons of Levi'. In verse 8 he continues to address Korah, according to the narrator, but again he is actually speaking to 'the sons of Levi' whom Korah represents. Moses' opening phrase *shim'u-na,* 'please listen', is softer than an imperative, and is instead a request to listen, so that his subsequent argument, that they have already a great task given to them by God, and should not desire the priesthood, is meant persuasively rather than as an attack. Hence also his conclusion and warning (*v 11*): 'it is against the Eternal that you and your brothers are gathering, and as for Aaron, what is he that you should complain against him?' Moses' ploy at this stage seems to be to separate out the various groups who have banded together, and define and address their specific concerns, the overt ones and the hidden ones. That he is successful in persuading the Levites to accept their special role and leave the rebellion is evident from their absence from the rest of the chapter.

Now Moses summons Dathan and Abiram as leaders of the 'political' faction, to come to him. This is his first tactical mistake, because in summoning them he appears to be imposing his leadership authority, which is precisely the issue that they are disputing. (He will correct this later by going to them – *verse 25*) They refuse to come to him, asserting their denial of his right to lead. There is, of course, an irony in their twice repeated *lo na'aleh* 'we shall not go up', for their fate is indeed to go down, when the earth will swallow them! Further it is worth recalling that their opening remark *hame'at* 'is it a small thing...', is a contemptuous echo of Moses' words to the Levites *(v 9)* – just as the play on *rav lachem* ,'you have gone too far', features in the speech of two different groups. On hearing their reply, Moses becomes angry.

Their response contains a vicious piece of political assassination, attacking Moses' and God's 'political manifesto' – to take the children of Israel out of slavery and bring them to a new land 'flowing with milk and honey' *(Exodus 3:8)*. 'You have taken us *out* of a land "flowing with milk and honey" to die in this wilderness!' – hardly a realistic description of their experience as slaves in Egypt. But their final knife thrust is to accuse him of 'acting like a *lord* over us', the Hebrew verb *'sarar'* evoking Moses' origins as a 'prince of Egypt' and, even more specifically, repeating the words of the Israelite man who had rebuked Moses back in Egypt when he intervened in a dispute: 'Who made you a *lord* and judge over us?!' *(Exodus 2:14)* No wonder it is only at this point that Moses loses his temper! His appeal to God that he has in no way abused his power – 'I have taken no single donkey from them, nor have I done harm to any one of them!' (*Numbers 16:15* is probably not a private prayer but, rather, a public oath that he makes before the assembly, challenging anyone to disprove what he says. (God would not need to know this, but the people would need to know whether Moses lied under oath!)[36]

With all these actions, Moses has allowed time for better judgments to be formed and people to have second thoughts. Perhaps this purpose lies behind his second speech to Korah.

Is this speech (vv. 16-18), merely a variation on his earlier one (vv. 5-7) coming out of a different version of the same story and edited in, rather clumsily, as a repetition of the same instructions, perhaps in slightly more detail? It should be noted that in fact no new details of the procedure are actually added, and the actions performed by the various parties (as described in *v 19*) are an almost exact repetition of the original instructions in v 7:

v 7	*ut'nu bahen esh*	'put fire in them
	v'simu alehen q'toret	and lay incense upon them.'
v 18	*vayitt'nu alehem esh*	'they put fire upon them
	vayasimu alehem q'toret	and laid incense upon them.'

What then is the purpose of this repetition? I think we should take seriously the fact that it is addressed to Korah alone (*v 16*), and not 'Korah and his congregation', as in the previous instance (*v 5*): it is to him personally that Moses speaks, not as leader of a congregation, not as representative of the Levites, but as Korah. Moses has isolated him from the Levites who no longer participate, and only the two hundred and fifty men still support him. This is emphasised by the threefold repetition of '*attah*', 'you', that resounds through

---

[36] This is analogous to Samuel's defence of his record as a judge in the face of public anger at his attempt to induct his corrupt sons as his successor (*1 Samuel 12:3*)

his speech. Twice it occurs in the opening sentence, each time in association with Korah's group:

attah v'chol adat'cha heyu lifne YHWH

attah vahem v'aharon machar

You and all your congregation be before the Eternal

You and they and Aaron tomorrow (*v 16*)

There follows another threefold repetition of the phrase '*ish machtato*', 'each man with his censer', seemingly stressing the individual responsibility of each person for the step he is taking. But in the detailing of the actions when the 250 supporters are mentioned, it is not as people that they are described, but in terms of the 250 censers they will be holding, so that Korah becomes singled out as the only real human protagonist. And whereas at the beginning of Moses' speech he is separated in the sentence from Aaron by his congregation (*attah vahem v'aharon* – you and they and Aaron), at the end he stands isolated beside the priest – '*attah v'aharon ish machtato*' 'you and Aaron, each with his censer'. It is as if Korah who has hidden behind the various groups he leads is now being forced to step out into the public spotlight, and the issue that is really at stake, namely between him and Aaron, is finally exposed. What Korah really wants, says Moses, behind all his talk of the democracy of holiness, is to replace Aaron as the high priest: so, let him stand there as he wishes beside Aaron, and let the Lord choose.

Now that the issues have been clarified and the problem of leadership of the people raised, both protagonists make their preparations. Korah assembles the *edah* to witness the coming events and, presumably, to decide. Moses and Aaron continue a private conversation with God, one which again hinges on the theme of leadership. To God's threat to destroy the whole congregation, Moses and Aaron ask:

O God, the God of the spirits of all flesh, shall one man sin and will You be angry with all the congregation? (*v 22*).

The unusual phrase used here, 'the God of the spirits of all flesh', reappears in *Numbers 27:16*. What both passages have in common is the problem of leadership. In the case of the Korah rebellion, it is Aaron's position that is challenged; in the second a successor for Moses has to be found. In both it is God who sees beneath the surface to the character of the individual who is evoked, once to refute the claims of Korah, once to select Joshua, Moses' successor.

That Moses' tactics of isolating the particular parties has succeeded becomes evident from the people's response to his suggestion (*v 26*) that they move away from the camp of Dathan and Abiram. But why do they warrant such a terrible fate, to be swallowed up by the earth, if their only crime is to challenge Moses' political leadership, even if they insult Moses in the process? Two possibilities suggest themselves. The first is that although mocking Moses' 'manifesto', it is actually God's plan for the people that they are challenging and putting at risk. Effectively this political conflict is a continuation of the problems still dividing the people after the episode of the spies. So, it is a divine intervention in nature that will punish them.

But there may be another more immediate problem. As noted above, Moses has swallowed his pride and gone to Dathan and Abiram, rather than expecting them to come to him. Following Moses are the 'elders' of the people, who appear for the first time in this story. They represent the older leadership of the people, dating back to the Egyptian period, and suggests that this confrontation is important for the future of the people. Dathan and Abiram emerge from their tents and 'take their stance'. The Hebrew word '*nitzavim*' literally means 'to stand', but it includes the idea of 'standing for a purpose.' (From it is derived the noun '*matzevah*', a 'standing stone' or 'monument'.) However, there are two places where the verb refers to people who are armed and standing ready to fight (*Judges 18:16*; *1 Samuel 17:16*). This might suggest they are planning some kind of military coup or the onset of civil war which would be disastrous. What argues against this is the presence with them of their wives and children, which suggests they are actually planning to pursue their own political agenda and return to Egypt, which would also seriously damage the divine project. In any of these eventualities, Moses would not have the resources to combat or stop them, so he has to leave the judgment to God's intervention. In retrospect it appears that God is willing to support Moses, but in the event he could not have known the outcome.

The end comes with the dramatic opening up of the earth to swallow Dathan and Abiram and their households. As noted above, it is an ironic punishment given their refusal 'to go up' at Moses' request, but is also a fulfilment of their sarcastic accusation that Moses had brought them out of Egypt 'to kill us in the desert' (*v 13*)[i].

The death of the two hundred and fifty, in identical fashion to that of Nadav and Abihu, Aaron's sons in the tabernacle, by fire from heaven, forms a brief but dramatic conclusion to the chapter. It is possible to read this as some kind of divine punishment, but there is also another possibility. If we are correct in assuming that these were firstborn who had lost their opportunity to serve in the sanctuary when their role was taken over by the Levites, then their persistence in attempting to continue to do so, is evidence of their spiritual commitment to serving God. Effectively the divine fire that consumed them, made them into sacrificial offerings to God. There is some support for this suggestion in God's response:

> The Eternal spoke to Moses saying: 'Speak to Elazar, the son of Aaron the high priest, that he take up the censers … for they have become holy; the very censers of these men who have sinned at the cost of their lives, and let them be made into beaten plates for a covering of the altar

– because they have become holy because they were offered before the Eternal. (*Numbers 17:1-3*)

There is a certain irony in that those who those who sought earthly power, Dathan and Abiram, go down living into the earth; those who sought spiritual power, go up as a burnt offering to heaven. Whatever the origins of the stories about these groups that came together to rebel against Moses and Aaron, in the narrative art of the writing in this chapter, a rounded symmetry and balance has been created.

The Aftermath

Though some of the leaders of the rebellion have perished, the effects are still felt throughout the community, and the people complain that Moses and Aaron have killed the people of the Eternal (*17:6*). Yet (as noted above) the unleashing of the *qetzeph*, 'the wrath of God', and the *negeph*, 'the plague', which now occur, are precisely the consequences threatened when any but the Aaronide priests approached the sanctuary (*Numbers 1:53; 8:19*). To halt the plague Moses instructs Aaron using his full sacred persona as a high priest to go and repair this damage to their relationship with God by 'atoning for the people' (*Numbers 17:12*). Aaron does as instructed and stands 'between the dead and the living' (*v 13*). Although on one level this means that the plague halted when it reached him, there is clearly a deeper mystery here of the role of the high priest as mediator between the people and God, between life for the community or its death. This narrative serves to illustrate vividly the information conveyed prosaically in the earlier chapters of the Book about the power and significance of the priestly role.

By looking at the story of the rebellion within the context of the Book of Numbers, the issues that are raised can be seen to belong to the Book as a whole and do not suddenly appear in the chapter before us. The questions of political and spiritual leadership are major ideas that the Book explores, and the Korah rebellion serves to dramatize them. Furthermore, it is possible to see within chapter 16 more of a unity of thought than merely the juxtaposition of two or three separate strands, and that some of the apparent 'joins' are less clumsy than at first appears.

To conclude I would like to return to the question with which the chapter begins – what is it that Korah 'took'? There may not be a definitive answer to this question, but there is a strong hint that it lies in the power Korah wished to claim for himself. For if we turn again to the moment when Moses sends Aaron to save the camp from the plague an interesting parallel occurs. In *17:11* Moses instructs Aaron to take his censer, put fire upon it from off the altar, and incense – the very instructions that had been given to Korah and the pretenders to the position of high priest. This action with the censer symbolises the power of the high priest, and is also the means whereby atonement, restoration of the right relationship with God, is achieved. *Verse 12* begins with the phrase *vayyikah aharon ka'asher dibber mosheh*, 'and Aaron *took*, as Moses had said'. Once again, there is no object to the verb 'he took', rather it is understood from the task Aaron is undertaking. 'And Aaron took' exactly matches the Hebrew phrase 'And Korah took'. Perhaps here we have the final confirmation that the real object of Korah's rebellion, despite all the arguments about the democracy of holiness or the abuse of power by Moses and Aaron, was his own desire and ambition to be the high priest, and himself take the censer, the fire and the incense and stand before the Lord.

That, at any rate, seems to be one of the judgments of the rabbinic sages. In the *Pirke Avot*, the 'Sayings of the Fathers', we read

Every controversy that is pursued for the sake of heaven, will be perpetuated; but that which is not for the sake of heaven, will not be perpetuated. What controversy then is for the sake of heaven? The debates between the great religious teachers Hillel and Shammai. But what controversy is not for the sake of heaven? That of Korah and his congregation' (*5:17*).

As if to underscore Korah's personal motives, the formulation is different from that of the example of Hillel and Shammai. For this controversy is not described as being between Korah and Moses – it is purely the affair of Korah and his congregation alone. For in the end it was not a religious issue at stake here, but one of personal power, pride and ambition.

10 Why is Balaam's Talking Donkey in the Hebrew Bible?

Why is Balaam's talking donkey in the Hebrew Bible? Of course this is a question that cannot be answered. Just as we cannot answer a similar question about any other Biblical text. It is a given, a text that is simply there, and from this distance in time and space all we can do is speculate, selecting from the material such clues as suit the nature of our curiosity.

Nevertheless, the question remains important when it comes to a text like the three chapters in the Book of Numbers (*22-24*), where Balaam and his donkey are found, because serious issues arise about how we are to deal with such an unlikely story. Are we to treat it as a fairy tale which is acceptable for children but not serious on an adult level, or do we have to believe that God can work such miracles as a talking donkey if we are committed to the Bible?

I find it helpful to examine some aspects of the narrative itself, but then contextualise it, firstly within the Book of Numbers, and then within the broader narrative of the Torah, the first five books of the Bible. The Book of Numbers recounts the wanderings of the Children of Israel in the wilderness on their forty-year journey to the Promised Land. The Book includes a number of tests of Moses' political leadership and describes conflicts with the local nations they encounter on their way. What is noteworthy at the outset is the complete absence of Moses from the Balaam narrative, moreover even the Children of Israel are only seen from a distance. Instead the two major protagonists are Balak ben Tzippor, the King of Moab and Balaam ben Beor whom he summons from Pator on the Euphrates to curse the Children of Israel.

The first thing to point out is that despite their threatening postures and actions, both Balak and Balaam are comic creations. The story plays off their inability to understand one another, with escalating degrees of exasperation on both sides. They are a little reminiscent of the comedy duo from the silent movies and early 'talkies', Laurel and Hardy. Balak is certainly a prototype for the fat, overbearing, blustering, figure of Oliver Hardy, always frustrated by events and blaming his partner. Though Balaam is a stronger character than the thin, sad partner, played by Stan Laurel, he is similarly rendered inept and victimised by events over which he has no control. If they are comic puppets in this drama, God is the puppeteer.

However, the role of God is decidedly confusing in this story, and this is reflected in part in the use of alternating divine names. Once again we have a text in which the two names '*Elohim*' and 'YHWH' alternate, and if we are to treat the text before us as a whole, we need to understand how these terms are used in the immediate context. Effectively, they are related to a major contradiction at the heart of the story. When Balaam asks permission to curse Israel, God first gives his approval, but then gets angry when Balaam actually undertakes the mission and sends an angel to kill him, at which point the talking donkey intervenes. Nevertheless, despite this obvious contradiction that affects everything that Balaam attempts to do, in the end he concludes:

> God is not a man who lies, or the son of man who changes his mind. Does he say (something) and not do it, speak and not fulfil it? (*Numbers 23:19*)

It might be possible to attribute this puzzling contradiction to two separate original sources of the story each of which had their own name for God. The editor who combined them was either unaware of the contradictions or unable to omit any of the inherited sources. But before we have to resort to that solution we should at least see if there are any literary clues within the story itself as to how to resolve the puzzle.

Balaam and the donkey.

The story begins with King Balak , his fears and those of the surrounding nations, that Israel's advance through their territories poses a major threat to them. These fears seem to be fully justified by Israel's successful battles in the preceding chapter. When military means of stopping Israel seem to have failed them, another powerful force must be brought into play, one that was considered real and effective in the Biblical world, namely the power of a curse. Had Balak read his Israelite history he might have had second thoughts. God's first words to Abraham included the promise that: 'those who bless you I will bless, and those who curse you (*m'kalel'cha*) I will curse (*a'or*)' (*Genesis 12:3*). But in Balak's world the curse was a potent weapon and the man best qualified to deliver it was Balaam.

Balak sent messengers to Balaam to Pator on the Euphrates to summon him saying:

> See, a people has come out from Egypt and they cover the eye of the land, and are settled opposite me. Now, please come and curse (*arah*) this people for me for they are more powerful than me. Perhaps I can strike them and expel them from the land, for I know that whoever you bless is blessed and whom you curse (*ta'or*) is cursed (*Numbers 22:5-6*).

Balak sends an important delegation of elders from Moab and Midian with *k'samim* (the implements for divination or the fee for doing so) in their hand. They come to Balaam and tell him Balak's words. Balaam, being a good professional, does not give an answer immediately, but consults the appropriate 'god' for the task, whom he names as YHWH, indicating his familiarity with Israel's God (*22:8*). However in verse 9 it is *Elohim* who comes to him at night (the first change of name in adjacent verses) and asks, 'who are the men with you?' This question could be understood literally, though God should already know the answer, so it may be a way of considering the significance of such a visit to Balaam himself. Balaam repeats almost verbatim Balak's request, changing only one word, the term for 'curse' from '*arah*' to '*kavah*' (*v 11*). But *Elohim* responds clearly and unequivocally: 'Do not go with them and do not curse (*ta'or*) the people for they are blessed.' (*v 12*)

Balaam now has a problem. His reputation as one who can curse on demand for a fee has been challenged. But rather than say that God does not allow him to fulfil the task of cursing, he reports only the first half of God's words: 'Go to your land, because YHWH refuses to allow me to go with you.' (*v 13*)

One of the useful methods when reading Biblical narratives is to look for differences between the way an event is described by the narrator and the way it is later reported. This is especially important when it comes to comparing conversations. Here is a good example. Balaam has already amended God's words, now the elders of the delegation return to Balak and report their own additionally amended version of Balaam's words. Presumably their version is in a form that they assume Balak will understand and accept, and also not blame them or punish them for their failure! They say:

Balaam refuses to come with us!' (*v 14*)

Missing is God's refusal to allow him to go, and one can read in their words a different emphasis than the one Balaam intended: this is purely Balaam's decision not to come.

In the next verse we encounter a verb that will become significant subsequently: '*vayosef*', from the Hebrew root '*yasaf*', which means 'to add', or in this context, to repeat or do something again. 'Once again Balak sent...' (*22:15*).

The Jewish philosopher Franz Rosenzweig, together with Martin Buber, produced a German translation of the Hebrew Bible, and both of them wrote essays concerning issues raised for them by the text. They identified a system of key words whose repetition within a particular text provided a kind of subliminal message about the meaning of the surface events. Rosenzweig identified the repetition of '*vayosef*' in the Balaam story as playing such a role.[37]

Balak sends a second delegation, this time made up not of elders but of princes, more numerous and more important than those of the previous one. His understanding of the matter is quite transparent. Balak thinks like a 'business man' and from his point of view Balaam has a product to sell. Balaam's refusal

---

[37] Franz Rosenzweig 'Das Formgeheimnis der biblischen Erzählungen' Kleinere Schriften (Schocken Verlag / Jüdischer Buchverlag, Berlin 1937) p 176-178.

is simply a negotiating tactic and he wants Balak to improve his offer. Here is the first comic play, the different perceptions of the two protagonists and the establishment of their character types.

Balak's words contain an urgency and possibly even a veiled threat.

'Thus says Balak ben Tzippor, Let nothing prevent you from going with us. For I will honour you greatly and everything you say to me I will do. Come now and curse (*kavah*) for me this people!' (*v 16-17*).

If Balaam had a problem before, the arrival of this new delegation has made it much worse. The money may indeed be tempting. Moreover, his willingness to consider cursing Israel may suggest either indifference to their fate or even a degree of animus against them.

Balaam's answer suggests that he is trying to get out of the difficulty. He tells the delegation that he cannot go against the mouth of God. But the words with which he begins must have confirmed Balak's suspicion that Balaam was actually bargaining for a better price:

'If Balak was to give me his entire household of silver and gold I could not go against the mouth of YHWH, my God, to do something small or great.' (*v 18*)

Had Balaam stopped at that point, dignity intact, he might have got away with it. But something made him tell the delegation to stay another night while he went and in his own words: 'I will know what more YHWH will tell to me'. The phrase, 'what more', translates the second appearance of the verb '*vayosef*'. And indeed *Elohim* comes to Balaam at night as before, but this time God seems to have softened the earlier decision.

'If the men have come to meet you, arise and go with them but only the word I tell you shall you do.' (v 20)

Again *Elohim*'s opening words can be read as a simple statement of the obvious fact that the men have come to Balaam. But they carry also the possible sense: 'If such important people have come all this way to see you, you really should cooperate with them.'

143

The following morning Balaam leaves with the delegation, but God (*Elohim*) is angry that he goes with them and an angel of YHWH takes up a position in the way so as to obstruct him (*l'satan*) (*v 22*). The word translated as 'angel', *mal'ach*, means 'messenger, sometimes human, sometimes, as here, divine. We are clearly operating in the same territory we have explored in the chapter about Moses and the 'burning bush'. In both cases we, the reader, know that an angel of YHWH is present, but the human protagonists, Balaam and Moses, are unaware of the true nature of the phenomenon. In the case of the 'burning bush', the word '*Elohim*' is used to express some kind of divine phenomenon or manifestation as experienced subjectively by Moses. This would suggest that a similar literary ploy might be being used here by the narrator through the alternating divine names: the name YHWH reflects the objective information that the author shares with the reader. The name '*Elohim*' represents some aspect of Balaam's own subjective experience or inner psychological desire.

In another comic play, Balaam the one who has the power to curse entire nations and talk directly with God, cannot see the angel poised to kill him, but his donkey can! The donkey, the most sympathetic character in the story, tries to save her master from the sword in the angel's hand by changing direction. Not understanding the donkey's actions Balaam strikes her to turn her back to the right path. The angel takes up another position between the vineyards with fences on either side. The donkey tries again to avoid it, knocks into the fence, at the same time knocking Balaam's leg. The next sentence has our key word '*vayosef*', when *again* Balaam hits her (*v 25*). The next verse uses the same verb when '*again*', '*vayosef*', the angel moves to a narrow place where there is no way to turn, either left or right. Unable to move, the donkey sits down, only to be hit a third time by Balaam. Finally YHWH opens the donkey's mouth and she asks:

'What have I done to you that you hit me these three times?' (*v 28*). Balaam seems unconcerned that his donkey can talk and replies:

144

'Because you have mocked me. If I had a sword in my hand I would kill you!' (*v 29*).

In the circumstances the donkey's reply is very reasonable:

Am I not your donkey on which you have ridden all your life long! Have I ever behaved like this to you?

And Balaam simply said: 'No!'

With that word comes Balaam's realisation that something is wrong. YHWH then opens Balaam's eyes and he saw the angel of YHWH with the drawn sword standing in the way, and Balaam bowed and prostrated himself on his face.

The angel scolds him for hitting the donkey three times, spells out precisely what has been going on, and concludes:

'If the donkey had not turned aside from me I would have killed you and let her live! (*v 33*)

Balaam offers to return home, but the angel of YHWH tells him to go on with the journey, but insists again that he may only speak what God tells him to say.

Already in the Middle Ages, Moses Maimonides, the greatest Jewish philosopher of the period and someone celebrated as a rationalist thinker, assumed that the entire episode, including the talking donkey, should be treated as part of a prophetic vision experienced by Balaam. A similar conclusion about the nature of the story is to be found in Rosenzweig's interpretation of the repetition of the verb '*vayosef*'. From the moment Balaam knows that he is forbidden to curse Israel, his refusal to admit this to the first delegation results in a whole series of subsequent events: the additional more impressive delegation, his decision 'again' to ask God, his striking 'again' of the donkey and the angel 'again' moving into his way. Effectively the repeated use of the verb puts a bracket around the entire episode with Balaam moving through a kind of contradictory internal journey.

The same possibility is also expressed through the changing names of God. The '*Elohim*' whom Balaam consults can be understood as reflecting his own internal contradiction: on the one hand the desire to perform the curse, but on the other hand the knowledge that it is not possible because they are protected by God. God's actual intentions are expressed throughout by the use of the name YHWH. The alternating names precisely reflect this with one possible exception, when it is *Elohim* in verse 22 who is angry with Balaam for going despite apparently giving him permission, confirmed by the angel of YHWH who then appears in the same verse. I think that this change can also be explained in terms of Balaam's internal state of mind that has been ambivalent throughout. *Elohim*'s two statements to Balaam at night: 'Who are the men who are with you?' and 'If the men have come to meet you…' are precisely the kind of musings of someone arguing with himself about the wisdom of an action he knows at some level to be wrong. That ambivalence then emerges from Balaam's own mind when he sets out on the journey and experiences within himself the anger he knows that God must have that he has undertaken the mission. He is blind to the consequences of what he has decided to do, and consequently blind to the presence of the angel. It requires the physical damage he does to the donkey and the damage the donkey inflicts upon his leg for the realisation of what he has done to come fully home to him.

What I have suggested here is a variation on the pattern we saw in the narrative of Moses' 'burning bush'. The two names of God, especially in narrative texts like this where they alternate in some way, may represent different perspectives on events, the subjective experience of the main character expressed through the use of the name '*Elohim*' and the objective information given to the reader using the name YHWH.

If we accept that the 'talking donkey' is part of an inner state of mind or vision of Balaam, the problem of having to believe in supernatural events or miracles disappears. The literary clues suggest that this was indeed part of the comic literary intention of the author of the story. It may be objected that this is a very subtle way of reading the text that might have been lost on the original audience. Yet it can also be pointed out that for Western cultures the opening phrase 'Once upon a time', or, for Japanese culture, '*mukashi mukashi*', signals the fanciful nature of the story before us. Such elements as a talking donkey or, in the case of the Book of Jonah, a 'great fish' may well have the same effect within the Biblical cultural worlds and the reader is similarly alerted to spot the literary elements, such as repeated key words or alternating names of God, that underpin it. In the case of Jonah, for example, the commonest word in the story is 'great' – describing the fish, the wind sent by God and the accompanying storm, the size of the city of Nineveh and the fear of the sailors. In the English idiom the repetition makes the story 'larger than life'.

Balaam and Balak

Now that Balaam and Balak have met, a second series of comic miscommunications takes place. These too are built around a threefold repetition: the three times that the donkey stops and is hit are matched by the three altars that Balak builds for Balaam's first three oracles. It has also been noted that in this second part of the story, Balaam plays a role similar to that of the donkey, the object of another's anger. In a similar way, an uncomprehending and increasingly angry Balak shares something of Balaam's earlier experience.

Balaam puts on a spectacular performance to give Balak his money's worth of divining activity. Perhaps he still hopes to influence God. Or perhaps he is trying to prove to Balak that he has done everything possible, while actually he is really preparing his defence for what he knows is going to be his failure to fulfil Balak's orders. He instructs Balak to build seven altars and prepare seven bullocks and seven rams which are then sacrificed, a task that will be repeated two more times. Balaam encounters *Elohim* and, again, seemingly unnecessarily, tells God exactly how many sacrifices he has made (23:4)! Perhaps this is also still part of Balaam's inner dialogue of self-justification, but to no avail: YHWH puts a word into Balaam's mouth that he has to speak to Balak.

This first oracle of Balaam is composed as a typical Biblical poem using the technique known as *parallelismus membrorum*, in which each half verse is followed by a parallel variation, thus reinforcing and advancing the idea. It is notable that in the oracles that follow the word 'El', another common Biblical designation for 'God' is used, presumably to distinguish it from the use of '*Elohim*' in the narrative.

From Aram Balak brings me,

the king of Moab from the mountains of the East:

'Come, curse me Jacob,

And come, execrate Israel.'

How shall I curse, whom God (El) has not cursed?

And how shall I execrate whom YHWH has not execrated?

For from the top of the rocks I see him,

and from the hills I behold him:

Lo, it is a people that shall dwell alone,

and shall not be reckoned among the nations.

Who has counted the dust of Jacob,

or numbered the stock of Israel?

Let me die the death of the righteous,

and let my end be like his! (*23:7-10*)

Balak is understandably angry with the result:

'I took you to curse my enemies and see, you have blessed them!'

Clearly Balak is not used to metaphorical language or Biblical poetry. Ignoring completely Balaam's assertion that he can only say what God puts into his mouth (v 12) he extracts from this disastrous oracle just one sentence 'Who has counted the dust of Jacob?', and interprets it literally. For some reason because of the huge numbers of Israel that Balaam has seen he cannot do the job. So Balak invites him to go to another place and says: 'you may see them, but see only the far edge of them, and not see all of them. Curse me them from there!' (*23:13*)

Seven more altars are constructed and seven more bullocks and rams are sacrificed. But once again YHWH tells Balaam exactly what to say. Again Balaam speaks in poetic language.

Arise Balak, and hear;

give ear to me, you son of Tsippor.

God (El) is not a man that He should lie;

neither the son of man, that he should change His mind.

When He has said will He not do it?

Or when He has spoken, will He not fulfil it?

Behold, I am taken to bless,

and when He has blessed, I cannot call it back.

None has seen iniquity in Jacob,

neither has anyone seen perverseness in Israel;

YHWH his God is with him,

and the shouting for the King is among them.

God (El) who brought them out from Egypt is for them

like the lofty horns of the wild-ox,

for there is no enchantment with Jacob,

neither is there any divination with Israel.

Now it is said of Jacob and of Israel:

'What has God (El) performed!'

Behold a people that rises up like a lioness,

and as a lion lifts himself up;

he shall not lie down until he eats the prey,

and drinks the blood of the slain. (*23:18-24*)

The military threat implied by this last sentence seems to have been too much for Balak, who says to Balaam:

'Neither curse them at all, nor bless them at all!' (*Numbers 23:25*)

149

But still hoping for success Balak has finally recognised that God is somehow behind what is happening. So yet again he latches onto a couple of phrases from Balaam's words which he interprets literally. Perhaps he puts together: 'None has seen iniquity in Jacob' with 'For there is no enchantment with Jacob, neither is there any divination with Israel.' (*23:23*) So this time he directs Balaam to yet another place in the hope that God may indeed see some iniquity, with the words:

'Perhaps it will be right in the eyes of 'the God' (*Elohim* prefaced by the

definite article), so that you may curse them for me from there!' (*23:27*)

So another seven altars are built and animals sacrificed.

But this time Balaam finally recognizes that it is good in the eyes of YHWH to bless Israel, and puts aside the enchantments that he had used before (*24:1*). Instead he saw Israel dwelling tribe by tribe and unlike the previous occasions when YHWH put the words into his mouth, this time the spirit of *Elohim* came upon him and he speaks his own words (*24:2*). To be consistent with the theory of the two names of God, this suggests that the external word of YHWH now coincides with Balaam's own inner understanding. No longer is he merely reciting words that have been put in his mouth, but instead is inspired to speak his own oracle. This time he begins with what may be an ironic reminder of his previous blindness:

The saying of Balaam the son of Beor,

and the saying of the man whose eye is opened;

the saying of him who hears the words of God (El),

who sees the vision of the Almighty (*Shaddai* – another divine name),

fallen down, yet with opened eyes. (*24:3-4*)

He goes on to repeat the theme of the future military success of Israel, and, based on his own experience, ends by acknowledging the truth of the blessing bestowed by God on Abraham:

Blessed be everyone that blesses you,

and cursed be everyone that curses you. (*24:9*)

Balak is now banging his hands together in his rage and warning Balaam to flee back to his place.

'I thought to promote you to great honour, but see, YHWH has kept you back from honour.' (*24:11*).

Balaam can only repeat once again what he had told the second delegation, but now also confirmed by his own experience: that he can only speak what God tells him. But now that Balak has fired him, he gets his revenge by giving a series of his own prophecies about the future success of Israel and the disastrous fate awaiting the surrounding nations. The narrative ends with Balaam returning to his place, and Balak going on his way. (24:25)

An overview

It is time to step back from the details of the story and look for some underlying themes.

A key phrase repeated throughout is that Balaam can only say the words that God puts into his mouth, irrespective of his own personal wishes. Such is the divine power in this regard that God can even put words into the mouth of a donkey when necessary.

Another major contrast is the use of divination and enchantment that are the necessary tools of the trade of Balaam, but which, as he himself points out, are absent in Israel. (The prohibition on using such things can be found in *Leviticus 19:26*). Indeed Balaam himself sets such things aside at the end and instead he is inspired by the spirit of *Elohim* to give the third oracle (*24:2*).

A third theme that recurs throughout is the real power ascribed to blessings and curses. Israel is protected by God's blessing, originally given to Abraham, and not even the most famous and gifted master of the curse can do anything against this power of God. Perhaps this fact also explains the absence of Moses from the story – in this particular case no human intervention is required because God personally guarantees Israel's protection from such curses, and can even make fools and clowns out of those who try to challenge God's blessing.

Can we contextualise this story further within the broader narrative of the Torah? At the beginning of the Exodus story, the enemy that God had to defeat was Pharaoh, who represented the great military power of the time, and against this physical power God unleashed the divine 'military' weapons, the forces of nature: the ten plagues, culminating in the death of the firstborn children of Egypt and the waters of the Sea of Reeds that drowned the Egyptian army. But now at the other end of their journey, as they prepare to enter the Promised Land, another power confronts them, not military, but spiritual. This enemy, represented by Balaam, expresses the power of the word itself, to bless or curse, and together with it all the superstitions, enchantments, magic and divinations to which people turn rather than turning to God.

Perhaps now is the moment to return to the question with which we began: Why is Balaam's talking donkey in the Hebrew Bible? One possible answer lies in the difference between the power of Pharaoh and that of Balaam. Between the encounter with these two enemies there is an event that has transformed the nature of Israel's society, namely the acceptance of the covenant with God at Mount Sinai. This covenant begins with the principle that 'You shall have no other gods before Me'. The people Balaam is sent to curse are now represented by a new generation, one born in the wilderness, not exposed to the religious practices of Egypt. They are to be a people for whom there is only one power in the universe, God, and all other forms of idolatrous worship, including divination and magical arts, are to be forever abandoned. It is the word of God that is to dominate their lives in the future, and against God, a Balaam and all he represents is powerless. Moreover, part of God's promise to Abraham, to protect his descendants from the curses of others, has also been dramatically fulfilled.

There may be a support for this interpretation in the strange episode recorded two chapters earlier in the Book of Numbers that led God to refuse to allow Moses to enter the Promised Land. When the people complained at the absence of water, God instructed Moses to take with him the staff with which he had performed the miracles in Egypt and which he had used on a former occasion to strike a rock and draw out water. However this time he is instructed only to speak to the rock, but instead Moses strikes it just as he did before (*Numbers 20:7-11*). God's punishment for such an apparently small lapse seems severe, but one possible explanation is that the staff represents the magical powers that were needed in the Egyptian environment in competition with the Egyptian magicians. But such powers are no longer needed because the Children of Israel are protected by the word of God. Moses, in his anger at the people, regresses to the older mode of magical activity at that fatal moment. In that respect he still belongs to the Egyptian generation and not the new generation to be established in the new land.

Balaam, the master of the word, the manipulator of blessings and curses, has to experience God's power in this public manner so as to liberate Israel, and those who read his story, from the worlds of magic, of divination and superstition. As Balaam himself is forced to admit:

There is no enchantment with Jacob,

neither is there any divination (*kesem*) with Israel (*Numbers 23:23*).

Epilogue

Perhaps the last word on the subject should be about the donkey. The rabbis were concerned about its fate and imagined that it died shortly after this episode. They offered two reasons why. The first speaks directly to our theme. There would be people who were so impressed with a talking donkey that they would at once start to worship it. Rather than allow yet another form of idolatry into the world, it was better that the donkey died.

But in another interpretation they spared a thought for Balaam. They felt that anyone seeing the donkey would remember Balaam's failure and inability to understand what was happening. For the rabbis, to shame someone in public was tantamount to killing them. So in order to spare Balaam such embarrassment, it was better that the donkey should die. She had served her master well in her lifetime, now she could serve him further by her death.

11 Avimelech: The Rise and Fall of a Biblical Dictator

The Rise of Avimelech

There are kings in the Book of Genesis who bear the name Avimelech. But the biblical character called Avimelech that we are considering is the one to whom an entire chapter is devoted in the Book of Judges. Though the story is told in chapter 9, it actually begins with some essential information that comes in the previous chapter. Avimelech's father is Gideon ben Yoash, who had fought a successful war against the Midianites. Gideon had acquired a second name Yerubaal, 'Ba'al will contend', because he destroyed the family altar dedicated to Ba'al (*Judges 6:32*). He was so successful as a leader that the people had invited him to rule over Israel, and his sons and grandsons after him, in effect to establish a ruling dynasty. But Gideon responded: 'Neither I nor my son shall rule over you, the Lord shall rule over you.' (*Judges 8:23*). So the Gideon story is already foreshadowing the desire of the people to appoint a king over them, something that will be played out in the Book of Samuel.

> Gideon had seventy sons who came out from his loins, because he had many wives. But his concubine in Shechem also bore him a son, and he gave him the name Avimelech. (*Judges 8:30-31*)

The actual phrase used in the text for naming is unusual, literally 'he placed his name'. Moreover given the circumstance that Gideon had refused to become ruler, why did he call him 'Avimelech', the most obvious meaning of which is 'my father (*avi*) is king (*melech*)'? Does it reflect Gideon's personal ambition despite turning down the offer to rule the people, one that he projects onto his son? It is even possible that Avimelech himself is the subject of the verb and that at some time he gave himself the name because of his own desire to become king.

Avimelech's mother, Gideon's concubine, comes from the city of Shechem. Shechem was originally a Canaanite city with a history stretching back long before the beginning of the Biblical period. So it is not clear whether it remained a Canaanite enclave within the territory of the Israelite tribe of Manasseh (*Joshua 17:7*) or was fully Israelite. More probably, because of the way the story unfolds, it contained a mixture of both peoples. But Avimelech's use of his mother's family to aid his political aspirations suggests that they were Canaanite. If so this makes Avimelech doubly an outsider in Gideon's family, as the son of a Canaanite woman who does not even have the status of a wife. Perhaps it is because of his mixed and marginal identity, belonging fully to neither of the two peoples, that the seeds are sown for the dramatic events that are to follow.

The first six verses of chapter 9 tell in a remarkably condensed form the story of Avimelech's ruthless rise to power.

> Avimelech, the son of Yerubaal, went to Shechem to the brothers of his mother and spoke to them and to all the family of his mother's father, saying: 'Please speak in the ears of all the leading citizens of Shechem: which is better for you, that seventy men, all of them sons of Yerubaal, rule over you or that one man rule over you? And remember I am your bone and your flesh.' The brothers of his mother spoke on his behalf to all the leading citizens of Shechem all these words, and turned their hearts towards Avimelech, for they said, 'He is our brother'. And they gave him seventy pieces of silver from the house of Baal Berit and with them Avimelech hired empty and reckless men who went after him. He came to the house of his father in Ophra and killed his brothers, the sons of Yerubaal, seventy men on a single stone, but there remained alive Yotam, the youngest son of Yerubaal, for he was hidden. Then all the leading citizens of Shechem gathered, and all of Beth Milo, and they went and crowned Avimelech as king at the terebinth of the standing stone in Shechem. (*Judges 9:1-6*)

Let us look at these verses in more detail. The opening is pure politics, very familiar whenever an election is approaching. Someone with leadership ambitions finds a favourable constituency upon which to build his political base. In this case Avimelech goes to his mother's family since he is an outsider to Gideon's Israelite community. His first argument represents an interesting debate about the nature of political leadership. We can fill in some of the possible arguments that underpin it. To have seventy people in the leadership position must lead to considerable inefficiency for where does authority lie in decision making? Moreover people may well act out of their own personal self-interest rather than acting together for the sake of the whole. Also there might be enormous opportunities for corruption, with people buying favours from particular factions. Instead look at the advantage of a single person in overall charge of the society, particularly as this is the pattern to be found in other nations in the region. But when such political niceties are set aside, Avimelech makes his real argument. 'Remember I am your bone and your flesh'. I am one of you, part of your family, so naturally I will have your best interests at heart. Perhaps he is also playing here the ethnic card of potential conflict between Canaanite and Israelite people. It is not difficult to find contemporary examples worldwide of how this approach would play out. In the case of Avimelech his family prove to be effective advocates on his behalf. Not unexpectedly it is not the political theory that wins the day but the appeal to their self-interest 'for they said: "He is our brother!"'.

Up till now we are in the realms of normal political activity. The leading citizens of Shechem, literally the *baalei shechem*, the 'masters of Shechem', could be forgiven for their favourable response. Such is their conviction that Avimelech is the man to get things done that they are willing to fund his campaign. The money comes from the temple of Baal Berit, the local Canaanite god. That means, if we translate it into contemporary terms, that the ruling class and the religious leadership together back Avimelech with financial support. We are still within the framework of legitimate political activities. It is only at this point that Avimelech's ambitions and actions take the wrong turn.

With the money he hires men who are described as 'empty' and 'reckless'. I assume that the first term, reikim, literally 'empty', means people who are landless, without a formal stake in the structure of society. The same term will apply two chapters later in the Book of Judges to the men who gather around Jephthah, also in exile from his family. In this sense they are like the families who will gather around David during his flight from King Saul. If this is the case, then the word 'empty' is neutral in terms of behaviour, merely describing their status in the society. It is the second word, ufochazim, 'reckless', which only appears four times in the Hebrew Bible, that hints at the violence that they are willing to undertake. The word is likened to water in Jacob's blessing of his first son Reuben whom he criticizes for his reckless behaviour (*Gen 49:4*). Elsewhere both the prophets Zephaniah (*3:4*) and Jeremiah (*23:32*) use the word to attack contemporary prophets who mislead the people. Effectively Avimelech has recruited a small private army of dangerous people with nothing to lose with which he will now pursue the second stage of his rise to power.

Avimelech, with his army, went to his father's house in Ophrah and he killed his seventy brothers. The verb used for killing is '*harag*', and not '*ratzach*', which means 'to murder', which we might have expected in this situation. There may be no significance in this, were it not for another unusual detail. The killing of his seventy brothers takes place upon a single stone. It is suggested that this may refer to some kind of ritual killing, but there is no evidence for such a practice in the Hebrew Bible. On another level, this reference to a stone will find its echo in the fate of Avimelech himself. He is killed after a millstone has been dropped on his head from the top of the tower in the city of Tevetz that he is besieging. That would then be an example of 'measure for measure', an appropriate punishment for his actions. But I would like to suggest another possible explanation, though I am aware that this may simply be the projection into the past of a contemporary phenomenon. Avimelech's original argument was about the nature of political leadership, and the possible disadvantages of being ruled by a collection of seventy people as opposed to a single person. One of the features of a political coup is the need to make the takeover appear to be justified legally to give the aura of legitimacy to the new regime. That requires the denouncing of the previous regime for corruption or some such cause, and part of the process would include a public 'show trial', suitably rigged to 'prove' their guilt. In such a case those found guilty may be sentenced to death by public execution, and it is possible that this is what is intended by the use of the word 'killing' rather than 'murder' in the case of the seventy brothers. It was not a death by random violence but with full quasi-judicial formal execution upon a 'single stone'.

Incidentally it seems to be too much of a coincidence that the leading citizens of Shechem paid Avimelech seventy pieces of silver and seventy brothers (excepting one who escaped) were killed. It sounds like a piece of silver for each brother was the price put on their heads. If this is the case it would give the leading citizens of Shechem a far greater responsibility for the subsequent events.

Having taken power in this violent way Avimelech now seeks the formal ratification of his new leadership role, and the leading citizens of Shechem, together with the people of Beth Milo, with due ceremony, appoint him as king, as 'melech'. That they do so knowing who he is and what he is capable of doing makes them share in his guilt for the violence he has done, and this will be remembered by God at the end of the chapter. Nevertheless, again looking at the methods of those who seize power, the threat of violence against those who were not prepared to accept Avimelech as king could have played a part. His paymasters may have thought when they supported him at the beginning that they could control him. But as other dictators have proved, once in place they become the ones who control events.

At this point I would like to step back and locate this story, and indeed the Book of Judges, within the Hebrew Bible. In Jewish tradition the Bible has three divisions. The first section consists of the Five Books of Moses, called the Torah, seen traditionally as the direct revelation of God. But the second major division comes under the general title '*nevi'im*', 'prophets' and includes the books of Joshua, Judges, Samuel and Kings, designated as the 'former prophets' (*nevi'im rishonim*), followed immediately by the 'latter prophets' (*nevi'im acharonim*): Isaiah, Jeremiah, Ezekiel and the twelve Minor Prophets. Thus this entire section is traditionally seen as a form of prophecy, of divine revelation mediated through the teachings of the prophets themselves and the authors of these various books.[38]   I mention this because of the contrast in the location of the Book of Judges in Protestant Bibles. It also follows Joshua, but then comes the Book of Ruth, because that book begins with the phrase 'in the days when the judges judged'.   Next come Samuel and Kings but also Chronicles, Ezra, Nehemiah and Esther.   The order is chronological, and I would like to suggest that designating certain of these books as 'history' rather than as 'prophecy' gives them a very different weight and significance.   As 'history' Avimelech's story is an interesting past event, but as 'prophecy' it is a powerful warning about the nature of political ambition and the way in which power can be manipulated for destructive purposes at any time and in any human society.   In fact these few verses are effectively a template for how a dictator can arise. Reading them in this light one can trace, for example, the stages in the rise of Hitler: through appeals to the self-interest of particular groups who financed him, the acquiring of a private army and the use of terror to achieve his first goals, culminating in the legitimising of his actions through using the formal structures of the law to eliminate opponents, and eventually fulfil his genocidal plans. The story of Avimelech is a cautionary tale that needs to be read and constantly remembered.

---

[38] The third division, '*ketuvim*' or 'writings', includes Psalms, Proverbs and Job as well as the five '*megillot*', small scrolls including Song of Songs, Ruth, Lamentations, Ecclesiastes and Esther, and the remaining 'historical' books listed above and Daniel. This division is considered to be 'inspired' writings reflecting more directly human experience.

Yotam's Fable

The surviving son of Gideon is called Yotam, perhaps a play on the Hebrew word '*yatom*' which means 'orphan'. He plays a significant role in this chapter but then disappears from the Biblical record. He leaves behind one of only two fables, both of them about trees, to be found in the Hebrew Bible[39]. Yotam's fable about the trees seeking to elect a king fits the context of Avimelech's rise to power but like all good fables is also universally applicable. Yotam escaped from the killing of his brothers and learnt about the appointing of Avimelech as king by the leading citizens of Shechem. Standing on Mount Gerizim he calls out his fable.

> The trees set out to anoint a king over them and said to the olive tree, reign over us. But the olive tree said to them: 'Must I give up my rich oil through which gods and human beings honour me, and go off to hold sway over the trees?'
>
> Then the trees said to the fig tree, go and reign over us. But the fig tree said to them: 'Must I give up my sweetness and my sweet fruit, and go off to hold sway over the trees?'
>
> Then the trees said to the vine, go and reign over us. But the vine said to them 'Must I give up my wine that cheers gods and human beings and go off to hold sway over the trees?'
>
> Then all the trees said to the thornbush, go and reign over us. Then the thornbush said to the trees: If in truth you are anointing me to reign over you, come and shelter in my shade, but if not, let fire come out from the thornbush and devour the cedars of Lebanon! (*Judges 9:8-15*)

---

[39] The other, in 2 Kings 14:9 is the answer given by Jehoash to the challenge of Amaziah.

A scholarly approach to this fable has been to see it in the framework of the critique of kingship, already hinted at in Gideon's refusal to become king, and a major theme of the Book of Samuel. On this reading it is the least likely and worthy person who will end up as king, to the potential harm of the society. This is appropriate in the context of Avimelech, as Yotam's subsequent explanation will make clear. But as a standalone text it can be read differently, namely that if productive and gifted people are unwilling to take on the responsibility of leadership then it will indeed be unworthy and unscrupulous people who will do so. The absurdity of choosing the thornbush is shown by his derisory offer to let them shelter in his shade. But the actual arguments of the individual trees to justify their refusal are also significant. All produce fruits that are of value for human nourishment or pleasure. But the olive tree fears losing the honour he receives; the fig tree does not wish to lose his sweetness, perhaps the comfort of an easy life; the vine does not wish to lose the popularity that comes from giving pleasure to others, something it will lose because power requires hard choices and decisions that upset others. Their fears about the price they would pay for leadership are justifiable, but their refusal would result in a greater price to be paid by society.

Yotam with great sarcasm draws the conclusions from his fable:

> 'If you have acted in truth and integrity with Yerubaal and his household this day, then rejoice in Avimelech and may he rejoice with you. But if not, let fire come out from Avimelech and devour the leading citizens of Shechem and Beth Milo, and let fire come out from the leading citizens of Shechem and from Beth Milo and devour Avimelech.' Then Yotam fled and went to Be'era and lived there because of Avimelech his brother. (*Judges 9:19-21*)

The Fall of Avimelech

The next sentence informs us that Avimelech ruled over Israel for three years. The verb for 'ruling', '*sarar*', is unique in this context. As a noun, '*sar*' it is often translated as 'prince', but the sense of it is best derived from its use in the powerful criticism aimed at Moses' leadership in the wilderness. As we have noted, the word is found at the very beginning of Moses' career when he tried to intervene between two Hebrews who were fighting. One of them challenges him: 'Who made you a lord, '*sar*', and judge over us. Do you intend to kill me as you killed the Egyptian!' (*Exodus 2:13*). Moses has to leave Egypt and live in exile. A lifetime later, leading the Israelites through the wilderness, Moses has to face a rebellion led by Korah. But several factions are involved including the former political leaders of the tribes, the Reubenites, whose role Moses has effectively replaced. In chapter nine we have seen how they accuse Moses:

> 'Is it too little that you have brought us up out of a land flowing with milk and honey to kill us in the wilderness, that you should lord it over us as well!' (*Numbers 16:13*)

'Lord it over us' translates the Hebrew phrase: '*tistarer alenu gam histarer*', with the emphatic repetition of the verb '*sarar*'. In this context the use of this verb clearly implies that Moses abuses his power, which would suggest that Avimelech's rule is also oppressive and arbitrary. Just as he came to power, so does he wield power. Therefore it comes as no surprise when the next verse in Judges informs us that God sent an evil spirit between Avimelech and the leading citizens of Shechem and that the leading citizens of Shechem betrayed Avimelech. (*Judges 9:23*)

Their betrayal takes the form of setting up ambushes on the mountains so as to rob passers-by, presumably damaging a source of Avimelech's revenue and calling into question his ability to protect his trade routes. It is also a reminder that when power is acquired by violence it is likely to evoke further violence. Moreover, if leadership is gained by usurping the previous regime, a model has been set for future equally violent changes of government. This begins to happen with the arrival on the scene of Ga'al ben Eved together with his brothers. Like Avimelech before him he wins the trust of the leading citizens of Shechem. After a successful harvest they hold a festival in the house of their god and while drunk they curse Avimelech. In this happy state Ga'al asks, why should we serve Avimelech and Zebul his officer? (Zebul is described as the *sar*, presumably Avimelech's appointee to rule the city in the same way that Avimelech ruled.) Instead Ga'al invokes the name of Hamor the father of Shechem, presumably referring to the foundation of the city. Here too, as with Avimelech earlier, we get a hint of the rivalry between those Shechemites who are Canaanites and the Israelites. In fact the mention of both these names, Shechem and Hamor, reminds us of an incident in the life of Jacob, when his daughter Dina went out and was raped by Shechem ben Hamor (*Genesis 34*). But Shechem wished to marry the girl and his father made the arrangements with Jacob and his sons, the latter being ashamed and angry about what had happened to their sister. One of the conditions Jacob's sons impose for the marriage to take place is that Shechem will arrange for his people to become circumcised like the Israelites. All the adult males of 'the city of Shechem' comply, but while recovering from the operation, Jacob's sons attack them, killing every male and taking their flocks, herds and camels. By invoking the name of Hamor, Ga'al appears to be rallying those within the city who value its Canaanite origin and may even be appealing to memories of ancient conflicts.

Whatever else one may say about Avimelech he is an effective military man. He brings his troops under cover of darkness to Shechem, divides them into four companies and attacks in the morning before their presence can be distinguished in the pre-dawn darkness. Ga'al, together with the leading citizens of Shechem, is forced to fight him, only to be heavily defeated. Ga'al's fate is not recorded, only that Zebul drove him out of Shechem. But Avimelech clearly cannot tolerate any kind of rebellion against his authority, another common characteristic of dictators, so the following day he ambushes the people coming out of Shechem to work in the fields. This time not content with a military victory alone he killed all the people in the city, destroyed it physically and sowed it with salt so that it could never be rebuilt in his time. He then turns to a place known as the Tower of Shechem where other leading citizens have taken refuge in their temple, the House of El-berith, from which Avimelech's original funding had come. Its destruction will be another example of the Biblical principle of measure for measure, the punishment exactly fitting the nature of the crime. Perhaps Avimelech's destruction of the temple also illustrates the possibility that when people come to power they resent the fact that they needed help to get there in the first place and set about destroying any traces or memories of this. Again Avimelech's leadership skills are displayed. He himself cuts down branches and encourages his men to do the same and burns down the place of refuge killing a thousand men and women. This is the literal fulfilment of Yotam's fable and curse that fire will come out of the thornbush, out of Avimelech, and destroy those who supported him.

But Avimelech's luck is running out. When he attacks the next town, Tevetz, and is winning the battle, he tries once again to burn down a fortified tower. But a woman on the tower throws a millstone down on his head, fatally wounding him.[40] However, rather than leave as his memorial the shame of being killed by a woman, he has his armour bearer kill him instead. The chapter ends with the moral, that God brought a punishment on Avimelech for the evil act which he did to his father by killing his seventy brothers. And finally the men of Shechem also receive their punishment for their evil in making Avimelech, king even knowing the violence of which he was capable. In a final ironic twist, these same people who have been referred to twelve times in the chapter as the 'ba'alei shechem', the 'leading citizens of Shechem', at their death are simply referred to as 'anshei shechem', 'the men of Shechem', their importance and power meaning nothing at the end.

---

[40]   This event will be recalled in the Book of Samuel in the ugly story of King David's murder of Uriah the Hittite in a deliberately sabotaged military operation (2 Samuel 11:20-21)

The story of Avimelech's rise to power has many similarities to the story two chapters later about the rise to a position of power of a man called Jephthah (*Judges 11*). He is notorious for the apparent sacrifice of his daughter because of a rash vow he had made to God. We will explore this in the next chapter. At the beginning of the Jephthah narrative we learn that he, like Avimelech, is an outsider in his family because he is a child of a prostitute and not his father's wife. His brothers throw him out so that he would be unable to inherit from his father. Yet, faced with a similar difficult personal history as Avimelech, Jephthah managed to restrain his justifiable anger and behave correctly. His story works as an effective counterpoint to that of Avimelech and adds a further critical perspective on Avimelech's behaviour.

Some conclusions

If we look at the overall structure of Judges chapter nine, it only requires six verses and an unknown period of time for Avimelech to rise to power as a dictator. But it requires three years, twenty-seven verses and untold bloodshed to bring his rule to an end. The asymmetry is itself a warning that it is easier to allow evil people to acquire power than it is to stop them once they have it – and the price for doing so is that much the greater.

Moreover the chapter divides into three parts. The beginning and end focus on Avimelech's rise and fall and between them is Yotam's fable which has an independent life that survives long after the details of Avimelech's bloodstained career have been forgotten.[41] But both parts, the narrative and the fable, serve as a warning about the responsibility we need to take for the governance of society and the price that is paid when this is not done.

---

[41] Avimelech is remembered in the name of the Abimelech Society, the self-selected members of which are dedicated to the bizarre task of removing from hotels and other public places copies of the Gideon Bible, a kind of spiritual patricide. Though apparently committed atheists it is ironic that they must have read enough of their stolen or liberated Bibles to have come across the name of Avimelech. Of course had they read the story seriously they might have had second thoughts about identifying themselves with a murderous dictator.

Some might find it uncomfortable that such a violent and unpleasant story is to be found in the Hebrew Bible and question what it is doing there, especially if we turn to the Bible for moral guidance and look for model religious figures. But that is the wrong way round to pose the question. Given the fact that Avimelech's story has a prominent place in the Hebrew Bible we should instead ask questions about the nature and purpose of the Hebrew Bible itself. The fact that such materials and others equally problematic are present is a reminder that all human realities and experiences need to be addressed if we are serious about our religious commitment. Moreover the teachings and warnings to be found in this ancient library seek to address all aspects, private and political, material as well as spiritual, of our lives.

12 Did Jephthah sacrifice his daughter and the King of Moab his own son?[42]

Jephthah and Avimelech

There are two chapters in the Book of Judges, 9 and 11, that basically tell the same story of the rise and fall of a leader. Their proximity suggests that this is a deliberate juxtaposition which highlights their similarities and differences. In common, each of these men is born to a woman considered to not belong to the core family: in the case of Avimelech, a concubine (Jud 8:31) and in the case of Jephthah, a prostitute (Jud 11:1). Both men grow up as outsiders within their family and Jephthah is actually expelled by his brothers and forced into exile. Both men are warriors but by very different paths reach a leadership position: Avimelech through violence directed against his brothers; Jephthah, when he is invited to take command in a time of war. Finally, both suffer a dramatic downfall: Avimelech mortally wounded when a woman drops a millstone on his head during the course of a war[43]; Jephthah sacrificing his own daughter.

The parallels are sufficiently clear to force the reader to compare the two figures. But such is the skill of the narration in both cases, that they come alive as real people, with their ambitions and flaws, and the reader is encouraged to explore what motivates them and what lessons to draw. Nevertheless, as is always the case with narratives, while the reader is engaged, sufficient ambiguity remains within the text itself to leave room for debate about particular details. In the case of Jephthah, most controversial is the vow he made before a

---

[42] An earlier version of this article can be found on line at https://thetorah.com/did-jephthah-actually-kill-his-daughter/

[43] A study of Avimelech can be found in Jonathan Magonet 'Avimelech: The Rise and Fall of a Biblical Dictator' Tr. Hiroshi Hihara *The Seinan Theological Review* Volume 73 Number 1 March 2016 101-116 (Seinan Gakuin University, Fukuoka, Japan)

battle, as a result of which he is notorious for killing his own daughter as a ritual sacrifice. Certainly, that seems to be the consensus view of Bible commentators, ancient and modern. Moreover, it accords with evidence in the Biblical record that child sacrifice was practised in the Hebrew Bible[44] even though condemned[45]. But a closer look at the actual text of the Jephthah story will indicate some of the factors that might have motivated him, and an alternative possible understanding of the actual fate of his daughter. Since this is one of only two Biblical narratives in which a child is actually 'sacrificed', the other one, concerning the son of the King of Moab (*2 Kings 3:27*), will be considered later.

Jephthah's story really begins at the end of the previous chapter of the Book of Judges. In Judges 10:17 we learn that the Ammonites are besieging Gilead. In response the leaders of Gilead decide that 'the man who begins to wage war against the Ammonites will become the head (*rosh*) of all the inhabitants of Gilead' (*Judges 10:18*).

Jephthah is introduced immediately afterwards at the beginning of chapter 9, where he is described as a '*gibbor hayil*', 'a mighty warrior'[46], in Biblical terms a high accolade. Jephthah's misfortune is to be the son of a prostitute. His father, Gilead, had a number of sons from his wife and when they grew up they drove Jephthah out so that he would not inherit from his father. Jephthah was forced to flee and settled in the 'land of Tov'. There gathered around him other similarly displaced men, the Biblical term being, '*rekim*', literally 'empty', presumably meaning they were landless or otherwise without a place in society. Here we can make a comparison with Avimelech from Judges 9. Unlike Jephthah, who seems to have welcomed into his orbit

---

[44] 2 Kings 16:3 = 2 Chronicles 28:1-4; 2 Kings 17:17, 31; 2 Kings 21:6; Psalm 106:38; Jeremiah 19:4-5.

[45] Explicitly condemned in Leviticus 20:2-5, and implicitly in the conclusion of the controversial story of God's command to Abraham to sacrifice his son Isaac (Genesis 22).

[46] The same term is used of Gideon (Judges 6:12), Boaz (Ruth 2:1) and Saul's father (1 Samuel 9:1), suggesting a combination of military ability and wealth.

people who were similarly in need, Avimelech actually hires such people as part of his political plan, using money donated for the purpose from the local temple. But the men he hires have an additional description, for they are *'pochazim'* which means something like 'unruly', constituting his own private army. Avimelech's purpose with them soon becomes clear when he sets out to murder his seventy brothers as part of his bid to become king.

In contrast Jephthah appears to be content to live in the land of Tov until a delegation of elders comes to visit him. The attacks of the Ammonites have become so severe that something more proactive needs to be done. Presumably Jephthah's reputation as a military figure has attracted their attention and they come to him with an offer. Their conversation is well captured in the following text (*Judges 11:6-10*) which reveals Jephthah's anger at his expulsion and the way he has been treated, but also hints at the stirring of some kind of ambition triggered by their visit. As always with such recorded conversations in the Bible, it is necessary to try to read what is actually going on behind the words.

Elders: Come, please, and be our *katzin*, commander, and we will fight the Ammonites.

Jephthah: Did you not hate me and drive me out of my father's house, why come to me now that you are in trouble?

Elders: That is precisely why we have turned to you now, so that you may come with us and fight the Ammonites, and be our *rosh*, head, over all the inhabitants of Gilead.

Jephthah: If you are bringing me back to wage war against the Ammonites, and if the Lord deliver them before me, I will be your *rosh*.

Elders: The Lord will be the witness between us if we do not do as you say.

We have seen from the discussion at the end of chapter ten of Judges that the leaders of the people were prepared to offer the person who led them in battle the position of *rosh*, the head of the inhabitants of Gilead. In their initial offer to Jephthah, however, the offer is reduced to that of *katzin*, some kind of limited role as a military commander. Jephthah's reply, his reminder of the way he had been treated, could simply be a flat refusal on his part to do anything for them at all. But the elders recognize that Jephthah may actually know what they had been prepared to offer and his response is only his opening position in a negotiation, or they are shrewd enough to read behind his anger what it is that might persuade him to agree to return – some kind of reinstatement of the position within their society that he had lost because of the way his family had expelled him. So, their response is to raise the level of the offer and invite him to become the *rosh*, head, over all the inhabitants of Gilead.

This time Jephthah is prepared to agree. Presumably the title would represent his complete rehabilitation as a leading figure of the society, despite his origins. This would explain what was personally at stake for him in this transaction. But it also emerges that he is a religious man and wants God's approval for this sudden change to his destiny. His condition for accepting the role is if God grants him victory over the Ammonites. Herein lies the seeds of his vow to God that will have such tragic consequences.

Jephthah went with the elders of Gilead and the people placed him over them as both *rosh*, the head, and as *katzin*, commander. (*Judges 11:11*) Both the elders and Jephthah have gained what they wanted.

Jephthah's Vow

There follows a prolonged negotiation with the king of the Ammonites about the disputed territory that is at the basis of the conflict. But the king was not prepared to accept Jephthah's argument and war began. The spirit of YHWH comes upon Jephthah and he makes a successful advance into the territory of the Ammonites. At this point he makes his vow.

> 'If you will give the Ammonites into my hand, then 'that which' (or the 'one who') comes out of the doors of my house to greet me when I return in peace from the Ammonites, shall be the Lord's and I will offer it as a burnt offering.' (*Judges 11:30-31*)

The vow is unique in the Biblical record because of its puzzling specificity. To vow to make an animal sacrifice as a thanksgiving offering was a biblical convention with the appropriate cultic apparatus available for fulfilling it. However, in this case, as the rabbis pointed out, who knows who or what might come out to greet him. If an animal, it might be classified as 'unclean', and therefore unacceptable as an offering to God. Moreover, there is some ambiguity in the actual wording of the vow. The opening phrase '*ha-yotzei asher yeitzei*', reads literally 'the [one] coming out which comes out', leaving it completely open as to whether this refers to a person, 'the one who comes out' or an animal 'that which comes out'. But the fate of that subject is then expressed by two separate verbs, linked or separated by a conjunction. The first verb says that this one 'shall be the Lord's', the second phrase says: 'I shall offer it/him as a burnt offering.' They are linked by the conjunction '*vav*' which commonly means 'and', thus making a single statement of the two actions, so that 'belonging to the Lord' meant becoming a burnt offering, as is mentioned immediately afterwards. But that same conjunction '*vav*' could also be read as 'but' or 'or', so that whatever or whoever came out would be 'dedicated' to God, but, would only be sacrificed if it should prove to be appropriate. This ambiguity, which may turn out to be significant, is clearly present in the text.

But what was he thinking of by making a vow of this nature? Did he have a favourite pet in mind that might come out to greet him? What is particularly puzzling is why Jephthah did not realise that it might be his daughter who would come to greet him with timbrels and dance on his return from a military victory.

After all, as a precedent for such joyful musical celebrations of victories, we have Miriam leading the women with timbrels and dance, after the safe crossing of the Sea of Reeds (*Exodus 15:20*). From a slightly later period we have the women coming from all the cities of Israel to celebrate Saul's victory over the Philistines, also with timbrels and dance, chanting the words that angered Saul: 'Saul has slain his thousands and David his tens of thousands' (*1 Samuel 18:6-7*). Who else other than his daughter might want to greet Jephthah on his return from victory?

In the event, on his successful return from the war, it is indeed his daughter who emerges to greet him.

> Jephthah came to Mitzpeh to his house and, behold, his daughter came out to greet him with timbrels and with dances. She was an only child, and beside her he had neither son nor daughter. (*Judges 11:34*)

The terrible moment is dramatized by including the word '*hinneh*', 'behold', which we have encountered before, allowing us, the reader, to see the shocking event through the eyes of the principal character of the story. Yet immediately afterwards, within the same verse, we are told that she was his only offspring. Clearly this is important information that the narrator wishes to impart to the reader. We will have to see how this might play a role in what is to follow.

> When he saw her, he tore his clothes and said: 'Alas my daughter, you have utterly brought me down, and you have become one of those who trouble me. For I have opened my mouth to the Lord and I cannot retract it. (*Judges 11:35*)

Jephthah's horrified reaction confirms just how much he had at stake in the successful outcome of the battle. Translations do not do justice to the harsh guttural sounds of his cry of horror, and the word play on the verb '*kara*', to bow down low, and '*b'okhrai*', 'amongst my troublers': *hakh'rea hikhrat'ni v'at hayyit b'okh'rai*. Perhaps the language of being bowed down is an indirect

173

allusion to his desire to be *'rosh'*, the head, for it is now literally his own head that is bowed down. But he puts the blame, for his own rash oath, on his daughter, describing her as one of his 'troublers'. It is a strong word of accusation, used, for example in the angry exchange between King Ahab and Elijah the prophet (*1 Kings 18:17-18*). But since his victory actually ensures that he will become the *'rosh'*, the head of the people, what else might the appearance of his daughter have 'disturbed', beyond the fatherly love that he might be expected to have felt for her?

Her response is an extraordinary mixture of filial love and religious commitment.

> She said to him: 'My father, you have opened your mouth to the Lord. Do to me that which came out of your mouth, after the Lord has granted you a great victory against your enemies, the Ammonites. (*Judges 11:36*)

There follows in the Hebrew text one of those repetitions of the introductory words to a speech 'and she said' that suggest that before she makes this new comment some time might have passed, or some background interchange has taken place. How significant this new introduction is in any particular case may not be clear. Indeed what she now says in the sentence which follows could quite simply have been the direct continuation of her previous statement. Nevertheless, the repetition of 'and she said' makes a break in the flow of the narrative, as if we, the characters in the story and the readers, need time to absorb the shocking implications of what we have just witnessed.

> She said to her father: 'Do this for me, release me for two months and I will wander through the hill-country and weep for my virginity, I and my women companions. (*Judges 11:37*)

The request of a two-month delay before the sacrifice takes place, time with her women companions before departing from this life, is painful to read.

What is curious is that among all the things for which she might wish to weep about, including family, the society in which she had grown up, why the emphasis on her virginity? We will have to return to this later when the subject is once again raised.

Jephthah agrees, and she and her women companions joined her for that period of time and the same details are repeated. When she returns to her father the text simply says: 'He did to her the vow which he had vowed'. (*Judges 11:39*) What is curious is that immediately following this statement we are told that 'she did not know a man'. If she is dead, then this information is hardly relevant, so presumably it belongs to some broader issue in the narrative.

There follows the statement that this was a 'statute in Israel', and presumably the nature of this statute is to be found in the following sentence, that every year the daughters of Israel would go four days a year '*l'tannot l'vat yiftah*', 'to commemorate the daughter of Jephthah'. Here too there are ambiguities. The word '*l'tannot*' only appears once elsewhere in the Hebrew Bible, also in the Book of Judges (*5:11*). There the context suggests that it means to 'give voice' to praises for God's victories, where 'victories' are the direct object of the verb. However, because there is no direct object to the verb here in Judges 11, all translations are speculative. Most assume some kind of ritual lamentation for her fate. Moreover, the use of the preposition '*lamed*' before 'the daughter of Jephthah' could mean either to speak about her or speak to her were she still alive.

The fate of Jephthah's Daughter

As indicated above, we are left with the question as to the relevance of this repeated information about her remaining a virgin. One clue would seem to lie in the earlier remark when the text first introduced her. She was Jephthah's only child, 'apart from her he had neither a son nor daughter' (*Judges 11:34*).

To lose her would mean the end of any long-term family or dynastic intentions that Jephthah might have.[47]

Before returning to the question of her actual fate I would like to speculate on what might lie behind Jephthah's anger and the blame he expressed against his daughter as his first reaction to her coming to greet him. Here I am relying on the considerable detail that the narrator has given to us, so that we can treat the text as one would an elaborate detective story. Jephthah was born to a woman who was outside the family framework and as a result he had suffered rejection and ultimately exile from his family and society. However, the invitation to become the head of all the inhabitants of Gilead would have meant a total rehabilitation for him. But part of such a rehabilitation meant the possibility of handing on this new status to his next generation. Now the effect of his vow, however it might be carried out, would rob him of this future. Indeed, a psychological study of Jephthah might suggest that this was, if only unconsciously, the purpose of the vow, especially if he knew that the likely person to come to greet him, with timbrels and dance, would be his only daughter. The man who was considered to be unworthy because of his birth, and maybe in his heart of hearts accepted this, made sure, through the vow, that there would be no continuity beyond his own lifetime. Or to put it another way, the stain of his illegitimate birth would end with his death.

If the daughter was actually sacrificed as a burnt offering, the matter of the vow would have been settled. But all the additional material about the journey to the mountains with her companions to weep for her virginity, and some kind of statute that it evoked, suggest instead a different possibility. This takes us back to the two elements in Jephthah's vow, the first being that the one

---

[47] This is worth mentioning because the possibility of dynastic concerns is already a feature of the Book of Judges. The judge Gideon was offered the possibility of becoming the first king of Israel. He refused, but his son Avimelech attempted to become a king, but through violent means.

who comes to greet him will belong to the Lord. We know of Nazirite vows by men in the Hebrew Bible, who dedicate themselves to God for a limited period of time[48]. A variation is cases like Samson and Samuel, who are dedicated to God for their lifetime by their parents. If the same possibility was available to women, it could mean accepting a different fate from that of other women, namely a life of seclusion, and effectively sacrificing what was considered to be the most important priority affecting women in the Biblical world, the necessity of having children. If this is the case then the unusual word '*l'tannot*', need not refer to some annual event, subsequent to her death, when women formally commemorated her. Rather, once a year she would receive a visit in her isolation from her companions who would 'call out' to her. To support this view, the duration of this ritual is expressed as '*miyyamim yamimah*' (*11:40*), literally from day to day. When associated with a 'statute', it can mean 'in perpetuity' (*Exodus 13:10*). But it is also used of the annual visit to the temple at Shiloh by the family of Elkanah and Hannah that marks the opening of the Book of Samuel. This would imply a regular occurrence, time and time again, during the lifetime of a particular family (*1 Samuel 1:3, 2:19*), or, as here, during the lifetime of Jephthah's daughter. The actual time allowed for the visit to Jephthah's daughter was four days. The reference to the 'statute' would then mean that, given the seriousness of the vow, a special concession was made to allow these short annual visits. Together these possibilities might also explain why there is no further trace of this ritual in the Hebrew Bible if it only happened for as long as Jephthah's daughter herself continued to live and no other women followed in her footsteps.

Credit for the above explanation and that Jephthah provided her with a house outside the city and sustenance throughout her life, must go to Abraham

---

[48] The nazirite took a vow of separation and self-imposed restrictions for a limited period of time as an act of dedication to God. (*Numbers 6; Amos 2:11-12*)

Ibn Ezra (1089-1167), later followed by Rabbi David Kimchi (1160-1235) quoting the interpretation of his father.

Some support for the idea that she was not actually killed can be found in the lack of any protest against Jephthah's 'sacrifice', either from the people or from God. Moreover, Jephthah continued to function as a judge for a further six years till his death (*Judges 12:7*). Nevertheless, contemporary scholarly opinion notes that the Book of Judges is full of tales of violence and horror, in anticipation of the need to establish a monarchy, so that this narrative about her shocking death would be just one more such episode.

What conclusions can we draw from the narrative itself in Judges 11? Clearly a summary which only focuses on the vow itself and the fact that Jephthah fulfilled it, would point toward his killing her. But the details we have been examining, about Jephthah's problematic origins and hence the importance to him of restoring his status in society, combined with the tragedy that his daughter would not bear children to continue his family, tell another story. Moreover, the repeated emphasis on the virginity of his daughter, and that she 'did not know a man', would move this aspect far more to centre stage. So, I would argue that the balance of probabilities favours her survival and a life of seclusion dedicated to God. If she was dead such details would have little or no relevance, alive she would be the symbol of what may have been a unique experiment in women's spirituality, 'belonging to the Lord', as expressed in the opening words of Jephthah's vow, even if further traces or examples have disappeared from the Biblical record.

The son of the King of Moab

Because it is assumed that Jephthah's daughter is sacrificed as a burnt offering this chapter in the Book of Judges is often linked with another Biblical narrative presumed to be about child sacrifice, this time from the Book of Kings.

In this case instead of the psychological underpinning of the narrative the background is essentially political, and again it is helpful to study the circumstances of the events that are described. The Moabites were vassals of King Ahab, ruler of the Northern Kingdom of Israel, and paid a heavy annual tribute. But following the death of Ahab, when he was succeeded on the throne by his son Jehoram, Mesha, the king of Moab took the opportunity to rebel and refused to pay[49]. Jehoram decided to take military action against Moab, and he invited Jehoshaphat, the king of the Southern Kingdom, Judah, to join him. Judah also has a vassal state, that of Edom, and their king too joins the coalition that has to pass through his land. But seven days into the journey they ran out of water and it looked as if the expedition could go no further. In such circumstances it was common to consult the word of God through a prophet. Whereas the Southern Kingdom of Judah had remained loyal to the Lord, the Northern Kingdom of Israel had accepted other gods. As on a previous occasion[50], involving King Jehoram's father Ahab, Jehoshaphat asks to consult a prophet loyal to the Lord, a reminder of the tensions between the two kingdoms that can easily erupt into conflict. As a result, the three kings visit the prophet Elisha. Elisha has no respect for the king of the idolatrous Northern Kingdom, but for the sake of Jehoshaphat he summons a musician, and under the influence of the music receives a word from the Lord. The message was to dig a series of trenches, and although no rain fell, the following morning the trenches filled with water coming from Edom. Elisha also predicted that they would succeed in devastating Moab. When the sun rose, the Moabites, seeing the water in the trenches from afar, tinged with red as if with blood, assumed that there had been some kind of falling out and fighting amongst the soldiers of the three kings. They attacked the camp, only to be defeated, and the coalition forces successfully invaded Moab.

---

[49] The general historical background, notably the rebellion of Mesha, king of Moab against the dynasty of Omri, king of Israel, is recorded on the 'Mesha Stele' or 'Moabite Stone'.
[50] 1 Kings 22:7-18.

In the end, the king of Moab is isolated and under siege in his fortified city. At this point the event leading up to the sacrifice is briefly recorded.

> The king of Moab saw that the war was too powerful for him and he took with him seven hundred sword-bearing men to break out to the king of Edom, but he could not. So, he took *his* firstborn son, who would rule in his stead, and offered him up as a burnt offering upon the rampart, and a great anger broke out against Israel and they (Edom) departed from him (Israel) and returned to the land. (*2 Kings 3:26-27*)

There are two ways of reading what happens here, dependent on how one understands the use of a particular Hebrew pronoun. A commonly held view is that in his desperation the Moabite king made a public sacrifice of his own firstborn son to his god, Chemosh, upon the rampart. As a result, either the anger of his god caused the alliance troops to leave, or the invaders were so horrified by this barbaric act they had witnessed that they fled, or even that Israel's God was sufficiently enraged for some reason to bring about their departure. There are problems with all these readings. Why should the act of a pagan king sacrificing to his pagan god have any effect whatsoever on Israel? If it is argued that the king of Moab's god unleashed anger, where else in the Hebrew Bible are such powers attributed to any other god but Israel's? (The argument that this is the preserved remnant of an earlier period in Israel's history when such powers were attributed to pagan gods, does not explain why such an obvious exception would have been overlooked in the editing or, if this was not the case, why the source of the 'anger' was not made more explicit.) And even if that were the case why would this anger be directed at Israel alone and not the other members of the coalition? Why should the coalition forces be so horrified by this act, which effectively handed them the victory that they needed, that they ran away? If the anger, *ketzef*, that breaks out against them is assumed to come from Israel's God, why is there no direct attribution to God in a chapter where

God's miraculous intervention to help the coalition has already been mentioned?

There is a simpler explanation for what happened, which depends on how one understands the pronoun '*his*' in verse 27. In verse 26 the king of Moab has taken a raiding party to try to capture the king of Edom, presumably the most accessible or vulnerable of the three kings in the coalition. Unable to reach him, instead the king of Moab manages to capture '*his*' son, that is, the son of the king of Edom (his firstborn son who would rule in his stead). Since the king of Edom is the last person mentioned in verse 26, the obvious subject of the pronoun '*his*' is that same king of Edom. This, then, is the 'firstborn son' of the king of Edom whom the king of Moab killed and burnt in full public view upon the rampart. This strategy of trying to capture the leader of one part of the coalition also fits in with the previous view of the Moabites that the alliance between the three kings was sufficiently problematic that they might already have turned on one another and fought. In the light of the public murder and burning of the son of the king of Edom, the great anger that broke out against Israel, the kingdom that had initiated the war, came not from Moab's god or even Israel's God, but instead was the very human anger of the Edomites in the face of this tremendous loss to their royal family. As a direct result the coalition broke apart, 'they' (the Edomites) departed from 'him' (Israel), and everyone returned to their land.

While some modern commentators accept this reading of the text[51], credit for the earliest version must probably go once more to the 13th century Rabbi David Kimchi, again quoting the commentary of his father. It seems linguistically, militarily and theologically a far more reasonable explanation of what the text describes, both in the immediate context and in terms of Biblical attitudes.

---

[51] Most recently Steven Anderson 'Edom's heir, Edom's wrath' – https://truthonlybible.com/2017/05/16/edoms-heir-edomswrath/

Some Concluding Thoughts

The view that both the story of the fate of Jephthah's daughter and of the son of the king of Moab or of Edom are examples of human sacrifice in the Bible, persists, despite the questions and doubts raised by the texts themselves. There are clearly ambiguities present, as I have tried to indicate, but the more likely result of a close reading in both cases leads in a very different direction. The more one focuses on the Hebrew text itself, as opposed to relying only on translations, the more nuanced, and richer, the narratives become.

Neither story is comfortable to read. Whether intentional or not, Jephthah's use of his daughter as a kind of bargaining chip in a negotiation with God is clearly being severely criticised. Perhaps one of the key lessons to be derived from the story is the warning not to try to manipulate God, whether through an oath or any other means. Even if Jephthah's daughter survives, what damage must it have done to their relationship? In Biblical narratives the personal dimension always remains, to affect and challenge the reader.

The story of the death of the son, be it of the king of Moab or the king of Edom, is an example of the kind of tragedy that happens when war engulfs a society. Nevertheless, the horror of the event, described in only two short sentences, forces us to focus on the fate of each individual victim of war, and not simply hide behind the abstract numbers of those killed, of the nameless dead when armies meet in battle.

There is an important distinction that needs to be drawn when it comes to the Hebrew vocabulary about sacrifices. In both these stories, the term use is '*olah*', 'a burnt offering', meaning that everything is totally consumed, and no human benefit is derived. But the Hebrew word commonly translated as 'sacrifice' is '*korban*' from the root '*karov*' meaning – to be near. The purpose of a *korban* is to try to draw near to God. The burnt offerings named in these stories do not even attempt this. Instead they are purely self-serving: one of them the consequence of a man's pride; the other the result of the territorial ambitions of nations. If there are lessons to be drawn from these stories it is the Biblical demand that we challenge the myriad burnt offerings that are carried out every day everywhere in our world, acts of violence that provide no benefit to humanity and bring no one closer to God.

13 Elijah the Prophet in the Bible and Rabbinic Thought

Elijah among the prophets

If we have a mental image of what a prophet looks like, it is probably based on the figure of Elijah. In our imagination we see a bearded man dressed in a ragged cloak and loin cloth, his face burned dark by the sun. He appears suddenly in the marketplace, striding out of the wilderness. When he speaks we have to listen, because he is passionate and angry. He is single-minded in his condemnation of the wrongs he sees in society. If we accept his opinion, we may think of such a person as God-intoxicated and rightly impatient with the failings of humanity. If we disagree, we dismiss him as a fanatic, and today we would be anxious about what he might be willing to do in the name of his religious convictions. He is bitter about the false beliefs and worship of his people, angry at the misuse of their power by the priests and the political leadership. But, just as suddenly as he enters society he disappears back into the wilderness. And we are left either to ignore this strange, almost comic, figure, or tremble at his message of doom that will descend upon us soon from his angry, always angry, God.

Much of the above description would indeed fit Elijah. King Ahaziah only had to hear that some man had sent a message condemning him for seeking an oracle from a foreign god; that the man was extremely hairy and wore a leather belt around his waist, to identify him at once as Elijah the prophet. (*2 Kings 1:6-8*) And yet, in terms of the Biblical record, Elijah, and his disciple Elisha, are actually exceptional figures. If we look at the great prophets who have left a record of their teachings, at least in the edited form in which we have received them in the Hebrew Bible, they are on the whole educated, sophisticated thinkers; poets or at least highly skilled in the art of rhetoric. When they speak, they may do so in a formal situation where they have the right to speak, like Jeremiah preaching in the Temple. It is only the content of their address that may be unexpected and disturbing to the audience. They seem to have an official title, *ha-navi*, the prophet, suggesting that they are graduates of a programme of training. Also they use a formulaic speech to introduce their divine oracles. Unlike the priesthood which is hereditary, no such requirements seem to apply to becoming a prophet. With the possible exception of Amos, who claims to be an outsider to the system, they are probably members of something like an official guild of professional prophets. Some, like Jeremiah and Isaiah, are very close to the sources of power in their society, with ready access to the leadership circles of the Temple and the Palace. It is true that at times prophets exhibited somewhat bizarre behaviour, but this was in order to publicise their message in the most dramatic and powerful way in a society lacking the means of instant communication to a wide audience.

So in many ways Elijah seems to be exceptional. Clearly, he has his own disciples, so somewhere in his background he may also be the graduate of a school or the disciple of another individual prophet. He seldom uses a formal introduction to a divine oracle but instead simply argues his case before the people or bluntly accuses the king of wrongdoing. Both he and Elisha, his disciple, use variations of the phrase: 'As the Lord, God of Israel lives, before whom I stand!' as a way of establishing their authority to speak in the name of God (*1 Kings 17:1; 18:15; 2 Kings 3:14; 5:16*)[52] But both Elijah and Elisha have one gift that differentiates them from the other prophets we know about. Both are miracle workers, bringing the dead to life, feeding the multitudes, parting the waters of a river. Before them only Moses had such powers, and after them people with such abilities either disappeared or their activities were

---

[52] Both prophets use the phrase in an oath formula. The second time that Elijah uses it he changes the reference to God to 'the Lord of Hosts' (*1 Kings 18:15*), as does Elisha (*2 Kings 3:14*); Elisha also uses simply 'as the Lord lives' (*2 Kings 5:16*).

ignored or suppressed. Miracle workers might be an embarrassment in the Hebrew Bible that is concerned to limit power and authority to God alone.

The influence that Elijah has on our imagination comes from the legendary stories about him, which are much easier to understand and appreciate than the often difficult oracles of the other prophets. But this also means that we are in the hands of the narrator for the way in which the character and events of Elijah's life are portrayed. So we have to use our critical faculties in studying what the narrator chooses to present to us.

Elijah's zeal

Elijah's first appearance already indicates certain patterns of his behaviour. Suddenly, without warning, he appears before Ahab, King of the Northern kingdom of Israel, and proclaims:

'As the Lord, God of Israel lives before whom I stand, there shall be neither dew nor rain except through My word!' (*1 Kings 17:1*).

The narrator has given us no prior information about Elijah, nor does he indicate when God had given him this message for the king. We are accustomed to trust the words of Biblical prophets, but the Bible itself warns us to be cautious about such an assumption. For example, in another story involving King Ahab, he consults his own four hundred royal prophets about whether or not to go to war. Their unanimous response is that he should. But such unanimity is a bit suspicious. So in addition the king consults the prophet Micaiah, who pretends at first to agree with his colleagues but finally admits that to go to war will be a disaster. He claims that a lying spirit from God has caused the official prophets all to say the same thing. (*1 Kings 22*).

In Jewish tradition the rabbis taught that

'No two prophets prophesy in the same style' (*Sanhedrin 89a*).

Each true prophet, by definition, had to be unique. Jeremiah constantly struggles with 'false prophets', and condemns their behaviour, how they steal oracles from one another! (*Jeremiah 23*) He himself has a public debate with Hananiah, who is also given the title 'the prophet' (*Jeremiah 28*). Both of them claim to be speaking in the name of the Lord. Had we been there whose message would we have believed? So the issue of true or false prophecy is a concern of the Hebrew Bible. Since the narrator has not informed us that God has spoken to Elijah we cannot know if this is really the case. Of course his prophecy is vindicated because a severe drought follows. But in contrast, the narrator is careful to inform us when God instructed Elijah to end the drought (*1 Kings 18:1*).

If I have raised a question about this prophecy by Elijah, it is because I am influenced by a rabbinic comment about it. The rabbis studied the Biblical texts very carefully, and they were sensitive to any gaps in the story that they felt needed an explanation. In this case they wanted to know what led Elijah suddenly to proclaim a drought in God's name, and in their typical way they looked for an answer from elsewhere in the Bible. In their version of what happened, King Ahab had been mocking Elijah, quoting the Book of Deuteronomy. Did not Moses say that if Israel worshipped other gods, then God would shut up the heavens so that there would be no rain and the earth would not yield its crops? (*Deuteronomy 11:16-17*). Well, boasted King Ahab, there is not a single idol that I do not worship, yet we enjoy everything that is good and desirable. Elijah was so incensed that he burst out with his prophecy about the drought. Since God had given this warning to Moses, God had no choice but to do as Elijah asked and bring on the drought (*Sanhedrin 113b*).

This is only one possible interpretation of events that led Elijah to speak. But it also begins to address questions about Elijah's zealousness on behalf of God and how God deals with such a personality. Elijah's sudden appearance without any previous divine word raises the possibility that because of his great passion and zeal for God he may actually have pre-empted God's actions because he believed that he knew what God should do. And once Elijah's prophecy had been spoken in public, God's honour was at stake, and God had to act.

A similar possibility arises with the great contest that Elijah sets up against Queen Jezebel's four hundred and fifty prophets of Baal. God has merely told Elijah: 'Go and appear before King Ahab and I will bring rain upon the face of the ground' (*1 Kings 18:1*). That is all Elijah has to do, visit the king, and God will do the rest. But when they finally meet, King Ahab greets Elijah with the words: 'Are you the troubler of Israel?' (*1 Kings 18:17*) At which point it seems that Elijah lost his temper.

'I am not the troubler of Israel, but you and your father's house are, by forsaking the commandments of the Lord and going after the Baalim, the foreign gods!' (*I Kings 18:18*)

Immediately afterwards Elijah commands the king to summon all Israel and the prophets of Baal to Mount Carmel. He seems to have forgotten the message he was supposed to deliver to the king about the end of the drought, and there is no indication that God has told him to set up the contest.

On Mount Carmel, two altars are built, oxen are slaughtered and placed upon them. The test is: which god, Baal or the Lord, will send down fire from heaven to consume the sacrifice. The prophets of Baal use all their ritual methods, including self-mutilation, but to no avail, and they are mocked by Elijah for their failure. But now it is Elijah's turn. To assume that he can call down fire from heaven exactly when he wants it is a very risky enterprise. It shows great faith, or great self-assurance, that he can get God to do what he wants when he wants it. Of course, knowing what happens, we may take his success for granted, but before Elijah only Moses could assume that he was guaranteed such instant supernatural, divine intervention when he needed it.

For Moses this only occurred once when the earth opened up and swallowed Dathan and Abiram and their households during the Korah Rebellion against Moses in the wilderness period (*Numbers 16*). On the contrary, usually Moses could only complain to God about his difficulties and hope that God would intervene. The prophet Jeremiah lamented bitterly that God was never there at times when he needed God the most (*Jeremiah 15:18*) Moreover, the previous occasion when fire had descended from heaven was at the dedication of the tabernacle in the wilderness, at a time of God's choosing. That was probably also the moment when the same divine fire devoured the two sons of Aaron, Nadav and Avihu because they had performed a wrong kind of ritual in the sanctuary. (*Leviticus 9:23* and *10:1-2*) Elijah is undertaking a high-risk strategy.

But if the fire from heaven itself was not enough, presumably in order to prove God's power, Elijah adds a further dimension by drenching the altar with water from four jugs, each one filled up three times. One can almost imagine God wondering what Elijah will think of next! Perhaps Elijah wanted to convey that he was able to waste water because he alone knew that the drought was about to be over.

Was Elijah worried that God might not respond? It is possible to detect a degree of desperation in his prayer, because just as much as God's authority, he is putting his own reputation on line as a prophet:

'Lord, God of Abraham, Isaac and Israel, let it be known this day that You are God in Israel, and I am Your servant, and at Your word I have done all these things. Answer me, Lord, answer me, and this people will know that You, Lord, are God, and are turning their hearts back again.' (*I Kings 18:36-37*)

And indeed, fire fell from heaven. Again, as the rabbis had suggested in the case of Elijah's proclamation of the drought, with so much at stake God had no choice but to send down the fire, and it is God who obeys Elijah and not the other way round.

I recognize that this is an unusual reading. But as the narrator makes clear, Elijah is a difficult person to deal with. Yet he belongs to a well-known kind of figure from religious folklore, someone who has a special kind of relationship with God. There are children who seem to be able to get away with behaviour that their parents would normally never tolerate in anyone else. Such children evoke a kind of loving indulgence that has to be stretched very far before it breaks. Something of this exceptional tolerance for his behaviour seems to apply to God's relationship with Elijah. Clearly, he serves God's purposes, at least up to a point. Where God draws the line will be seen in their encounter on Mount Horeb.

Elijah's despair

Elijah is in fear for his life because Queen Jezebel has threatened revenge for the killing of her prophets. He is also clearly in deep despair, if not clinically depressed, at the failure of his mission to change the attitudes of his people. Their great affirmation after the death of the prophets of Baal, 'The Lord He is God! The Lord he is God!' does not seem to have convinced or reassured him that something has really changed. Indeed, it is a reminder that a miracle may have a momentary impact but precisely because it is an exceptional event, it may have little long-term influence when hearts and minds need to undergo a radical and deeper change. At his lowest point Elijah even asks God to take his life from him. (*1 Kings 19:4*) While in hiding he is fed by a divine messenger, which gives him the strength to go on a journey of forty days and nights to the mountain called Horeb. It was here that Moses first received his call from God. When God asks Elijah: 'What are you doing here?', his reply is a mixture of self-righteous anger, anguish and despair.

190

I have surely been zealous for the Lord God of hosts, for the Children of Israel have forsaken Your covenant, torn down your altars and killed your prophets with the sword and I, I alone remain, and they seek my life to take it. (*1 Kings 19:10*)

The response he receives is no mere 'burning bush', but a manifestation of God's power far greater than that given to Moses. The typhoon-like wind, the earthquake and the fire that he witnesses may be intended to reassure him of God's ultimate control over the forces of nature. Surely the prophet should take courage from this experience, both in the rightness of his cause and in God's inevitable victory. After all these phenomena comes the 'still small voice'. Perhaps here is also a message to Elijah, if he is able to hear it. The great miracles, conjuring fire from heaven, and the slaughter of vast numbers of foreign prophets, may not be as effective as the silence in which God truly speaks. Perhaps Elijah needs a new, less dramatic, strategy to convince people about the truth of his teaching and so win their hearts. Perhaps God thought that this dramatic and subtle display would convince Elijah, so breaks the silence and asks again: 'What are you doing here Elijah?'

When I teach my students about Biblical narrative techniques, I ask them to pay close attention to repetitions, because in the minor changes between two similar passages something can often be learnt that is relevant to the story as a whole. A good example is the three versions of what happened between the wife of Potiphar and Joseph (*Genesis 39:10-18*). First we get the narrator's account, then the version she gives to her servants and finally the revised version she gives to her husband. From the narrator we have the objective account of events, or at least a base line from which to judge the other two versions. Clearly, she tailors each of her versions to a different audience so as to persuade the hearer of her own innocence and Joseph's guilt in the matter. So when we come to Elijah's new answer to God, I ask the students to check for the differences between what he says before and after the divine revelation. They read the Hebrew once or twice, checking word for word, but finally have to admit that they cannot detect a difference. Of course my task was a bit unfair, because there is no difference, the two passages are identical. But in this case, that is precisely the point. How could Elijah have been subjected to such an extraordinary display of God's power, and yet remain completely unchanged by the experience? Ironically, it would seem that God's miraculous display to Elijah is no more effective at changing the mind of the prophet than was Elijah's miraculous display before the people!

God appears to accept Elijah's response as his official resignation. God then gives him two diplomatic tasks, neither of which Elijah fulfils in person.[53] But since the work that Elijah began has to be completed, God tells him to appoint Elisha as his successor. Finally, God adds a significant corrective to Elijah's very self-centred view of the situation. God points out that actually he is not alone, saying:

> 'And I have left in Israel seven thousand, all the knees that have not bent down to Baal and all lips that have not kissed him.' (*1 Kings 19:18*)

Is this to encourage Elijah or, instead, a criticism of his insistence that apart from himself alone none of the people were still loyal to God? This latter possibility is taken up in a rabbinic commentary on Elijah's attitude. The rabbis were sensitive to such extensive criticisms of the Jewish people, even when they came from the Biblical prophets. They derive a proof of God's displeasure at Elijah's attitude from a detail of the story and by means of a play on words. When Elijah flees from Jezebel he sleeps under a bush and awakes to find a cake ready for him to eat (*1 Kings 19:6*). The cake is described in Hebrew as *ugat retsaphim*, 'a cake (*ugah*) baked on hot coals (*retsaphim*). The rabbis linked the word '*retsaphim*' to another Hebrew word *ritspah*, a burning coal,

---

[53] One is to appoint Hazael as King of Aram which Elisha does in person. The other is to appoint Jehu as the future King of Israel, which Elisha does by sending his agent

and this led them to Isaiah chapter 6 and the story about the prophet's vision of God enthroned on high. In despair and fear at seeing God when this is forbidden, Isaiah said 'Woe is me, I am lost, because I am a man of unclean lips and I live in the midst of a people of unclean lips, yet my eyes have seen the Sovereign, the Lord of hosts.' But a *seraph*, a divine servant, took a burning coal (*ritspah*) from off the altar with tongs and touched it to the prophet's mouth saying: 'Your transgression is gone and your sin is covered over.' (*Isaiah 6:7*)

But why, the rabbis asked, use such a painful method to purify the lips of the prophet? As with the case of Elijah, the rabbis accused Isaiah of using too harsh a judgement on his people in his prophecies. So they interpreted the hot coal that touched Isaiah's lips, and the 'hot-coal cake' given to Elijah, as a kind of punishment for slandering the people. To do this they split the word '*ritzpah*' (burning coal) into two separate words: the verb '*ratsats*', which means 'to smash' and the word '*peh*', which means 'mouth'. For using their mouths to slander the people both prophets were punished in the same way, both received a nasty blow to the mouth! Once again, the rabbis have used their linguistic skills and their imagination to dramatize an idea that they thought was implicit in the Biblical text.

This rabbinic criticism of Elijah's attitude led to an important symbolic item that is present at the Jewish ritual of circumcision, which takes place on the eighth day after a boy is born. Elijah had insisted that 'the Children of Israel have forsaken God's covenant' (*1 Kings 19:10, 14*). As we noted, God actually contradicted Elijah at the time. But the rabbis had a more dramatic response to his remark. The Hebrew word for covenant is '*berit*', and it is the same word used for the rite of circumcision, '*berit millah*'. Part of the ceremony is to set aside a chair, called the chair of Elijah, because he is expected to attend the occasion. Having such a chair present appears to make Elijah an honoured guest. But it can also be seen as a punishment for him. Because he slandered Israel by saying they had forsaken God's covenant, Elijah has to be present as a witness every single time, anywhere in the world, that a circumcision, the sign of the covenant, is taking place!

Returning to the Biblical narrative, God seems to interpret Elijah's words as his official resignation and sends him away with the words '*lech, shoov l'dark'cha*', 'Go! Return on your way…' (*1 Kings 19:15*). No one likes to be fired from a job, not even a prophet, and not even if you have complained that the job is too hard for you and you would rather die than continue. Judging by the way Elijah treats Elisha, his successor, on their first encounter, Elijah is not at all happy at being dismissed.

> 'Elijah went from there and found Elisha ben Shaphat who was ploughing with twelve yoke of oxen before him, and he himself was driving the twelfth pair. Elijah passed by him and threw his cloak to him' (*1 Kings 19:19*).

This action by Elijah is often translated as 'he cast his cloak over him', understood as a formal way of designating Elisha as his successor. But the Hebrew reads literally 'threw his cloak to him', which suggests a far more abrupt and ambivalent act. Yet, despite the absence of any explanation, somehow Elisha got the message that he had been called. 'He left the oxen and ran after Elijah and said: "Let me kiss my father and mother then I will go after you." But Elijah (using the identical words that God had used when dismissing him!) said '*lech shoov*', 'Go! Return… For what have I done to you?' Elisha, however takes this as permission to say farewell to his family, turned back, took and slaughtered the yoke of oxen. He burned the ploughing equipment to cook the meat and gave it to the people, and they ate. Then he arose, went after Elijah and served him.' (*1 Kings 19:21*)

There is a rabbinic observation about the sequence of Biblical texts – *ayn mukdam um'char ba-torah*, literally, 'there is no before and after in Scripture' (*Pesachim 6b*). By this literary comment they meant that the order in which texts appear in the Bible may not be organised chronologically. Instead a different basis may be used sometimes, for example, by following a particular theme or because of word associations between passages. However, if we follow the chronology of the Book of Kings, Elijah is called out of his retirement by God on two occasions. One time it is to confront King Ahab again and predict his destruction and that of his family and his wife Jezebel. (*1 Kings 21:17-29*) Here too Elijah says considerably more than God had told him. The other occasion is to give a message to Ahab's son King Ahaziah that he is going to die from his current illness. When the king sends troops to bring Elijah to him, Elijah, feeling under threat, twice calls down fire from heaven upon them and kills them. Apparently, he has not lost his powers in his old age, though this time his actions cannot be justified on any religious grounds. (*2 Kings 1*)

Elijah's Departure

When the time comes for his final journey, Elisha and his disciples living in different cities are aware of it. Perhaps some of Elijah's ambivalence about Elisha can be seen in this final encounter. Together they leave Gilgal, but Elijah tells Elisha, 'Please stay here, for the Lord has sent me to Bethel.' Instead Elisha makes an oath: 'As the Lord lives and as your soul lives I shall not forsake you!' When it is clear that Elisha will not leave him, Elijah tries again, claiming that the Lord has now sent him to Jericho. But Elisha insists on accompanying him with the same oath and they went on together to Jericho. Elijah tries a third time, this time to go to the Jordan river, but again Elisha stays with him. When Elijah realises that he cannot get rid of Elisha, he parts the waters of the Jordan with his cloak, and they cross together. Elijah asks Elisha: 'What can I do for you before I am taken from you?' (*2 Kings 2:9*) Elisha asks: 'Let a double portion of your spirit be upon me.' Behind this phrase may lie the tradition that the oldest son would receive a double portion of his father's inheritance. So Elisha is asking to be confirmed as Elijah's successor. Perhaps Elijah's reluctance reflects his wish to appoint someone else, or a lingering resentment at the way God had made him choose Elisha. But his reply may simply have been a warning about the dangerous powers that Elisha would acquire if Elijah fulfilled his request[54]:

'You have asked something difficult! If you see me taken away from you, so shall it be! But if not, it will not be so!' (*2 Kings 2:10*)

As they were walking and talking, a fiery chariot and fiery horses separated them, and Elijah goes to heaven in a whirlwind. According to the Biblical text it is the storm that carries him off, not the fiery chariot (compare *1 Kings 2:1* and *11*). If the fiery chariot was meant to distract Elisha at the last moment, what message did it convey? For Elijah, for whom fire was a suitably violent symbol of his miraculous powers, a fiery chariot was a fitting distraction for Elisha. But this kind of fiery behaviour was not to be the way of Elisha, who had a different sort of role to play. If he had been distracted by the fiery chariot and been tempted to follow its message it might have affected his own individual character and task. Instead Elisha was able to see what really happened, retrieved Elijah's cloak that had fallen from him and could now take his place.

Elijah's miraculous and dramatic departure to heaven is appropriate for someone who was always appearing suddenly and disappearing. But it opens up a whole new afterlife for the prophet. Starting with the passage in the prophet Malachi (*3:22-24*) he becomes in both Jewish and Christian tradition the herald for the arrival of the messiah.

We have noted some instances in which the rabbis criticised Elijah's behaviour in the Biblical narratives. But in Jewish tradition he undergoes an

---

[54] Elisha did indeed receive double of Elijah's spirit, repeating some of the same miracles, beginning with parting the waters of the Jordan. But his power is such that a careless remark by him, when teased by some children, will cause bears to appear from nowhere and kill them. From then on Elisha is careful to avoid direct contact with people using his servant or messengers as intermediaries.

extraordinary transformation in this new afterlife. Instead of the unpredictable and dangerous character of the Bible stories, he becomes a benign guide, supporter and friend of the Jewish people. He is there to help the rabbinic sages resolve their debates and disputes about legal matters. Sometimes he even brings down secrets from heaven to share with them. He saves the lives of poor people by miraculously providing for their needs, but will also re-educate the rich if they do not use their wealth for the benefit of others. He appears in many guises to intervene when the Jewish people are in trouble. In fact, any stranger you encounter may actually be Elijah in disguise. In Jewish ritual life, as well as attending the rite of circumcision, a cup is poured for him so that he can attend the Passover meal, and a song celebrates him in the short service that marks the end of the Sabbath, a time when the messiah may actually come.

We have been dealing with some of the Biblical narratives about Elijah, so it is fitting to end with the mysterious obituary given by the one person who must have known him best, his disciple Elisha. At the moment of Elijah's departure, he cries out:

'My father, my father, the chariots and horsemen of Israel!' (*2 Kings 2:12*)[55].

Perhaps he meant that Elijah had indeed been the one true soldier who, in his own idiosyncratic and sometimes problematic way, had fought to win back for God the soul of his people.

---

[55] The same words are said by King Jehoash over the dying Elisha (2 Kings 13:14).

14 Literary conventions and riddles in the Book of Jonah

The outline of the story.

The Biblical 'Book of Jonah' contains one of the most accessible and popular stories in the Hebrew Bible. And yet despite the apparent simplicity of the storytelling it contains a variety of narrative techniques and strategies, word plays and intertextual links with other parts of the Hebrew Bible that suggest additional dimensions of meaning. Many of these elements are overlooked or lost when the Book is only read in translation. Working with the Hebrew text we will explore how some of these literary devices impact on the closing chapter of the Book.

God sends the prophet Jonah to the city of Nineveh to proclaim that their evil deeds have come to God's attention. But Nineveh is no neutral city in the mind of the Biblical reader. It is the capital city of the great Assyrian Empire, notorious for the ruthlessness and cruelty of its military aggression. The earliest readers of this late book in the Biblical canon would have been aware that the Assyrians had conquered the Northern Kingdom of Israel, deported its inhabitants and repopulated the country with other conquered peoples thus destroying any continuation with its previous history. These deported people became the source of legends about the 'ten lost tribes'. It comes as no surprise that Jonah is unwilling to undertake God's mission. His reaction is to go to the port of Jaffa and hire a ship to take him across the Mediterranean to a place called Tarshish, literally at the opposite end of the world from Nineveh. But God sends a storm that threatens to destroy the ship. The sailors discover that Jonah is responsible for the storm. Rather than ask to be returned to dry land and complete the mission, Jonah tells them to throw him overboard. The sailors are reluctant and pray to Jonah's God to help them. When no response comes, they throw him overboard, and immediately the storm stops. The sailors are so overawed by this that they transfer their religious loyalty to Israel's God.

Jonah is miraculously saved by an enormous fish that swallows him – giving the world one of the most memorable and lasting popular Biblical images of 'Jonah in the whale'. Finally, after three days in the fish, Jonah offers a thanksgiving prayer to God, though he says nothing in it about his initial disobedience. In a comic conclusion to the episode the fish vomits him up onto dry land. But Jonah's closing words in his prayer had been that he would bring thanksgiving sacrifices to God, which could only mean his intention of going back home to the Jerusalem Temple. So, God is forced to repeat his command 'a second time', and this time Jonah goes to Nineveh.

In chapter three, Jonah enters Nineveh briefly, he calls out: 'In forty days Nineveh will be overturned', only five words in the Hebrew, and leaves. Somehow this warning is taken up by the people of Nineveh, they call for a fast and dress in sackcloth and ashes, standard public religious responses to threatened danger. But the king, who repeats these actions himself, adds the crucial point in his decree that they must also turn from their evil ways and maybe God will forgive them. Indeed, it is this action that causes God to change his mind about punishing them. Here, in this threefold response (the people fast, the king fasts, the king makes a decree to fast) the author is using another common folkloric convention – something happens twice, unsuccessfully, establishing the 'norm', but the third time a new additional element, the king's call to repent, totally transforms the situation.

Until now, there has been no direct explanation given for why Jonah had refused the mission, beyond the background history indicated above. The narrator may be assuming that Jonah already foresees the destructive role Nineveh will play to the Northern Kingdom of Israel and has been trying to prevent it by refusing to help the city survive God's threat. In the fourth and final chapter, now that the city has repented and destruction seems no longer to happen, Jonah expresses his great anger with God's decision and begs God to take his life. God asks him whether his anger is justified, but Jonah's response is to leave the city and sit down outside it waiting to see what happens, as if he is trying to force God to change His mind. Since he is in for a long wait, he builds himself a little shelter to protect himself from the sun.

Since Jonah has not answered God's question with words but, instead, by the act of walking away, God likewise continues their conversation with actions. God creates a wondrous plant which grows overnight to protect Jonah from the sun, making him very happy; but then God sends a worm which destroys the plant and a fierce wind which blows the dead plant and his shelter away, exposing Jonah to the heat of the sun so that once again he asks to die. There follows a final dialogue between the two protagonists, and the book ends with a long question posed by God to Jonah to which no answer by Jonah is recorded.

'Key words' and repetitions.

As suggested above, there are a number of word associations and plays in the Hebrew text that add special dimensions to the story, and which may easily be overlooked in translation. A simple example is the use of the verb *yashav*, 'to sit', in the form *vayeshev* meaning 'he sat'. It first appears in this grammatical form in chapter three with the description of the king of Nineveh, dressed in sackcloth and sitting in ashes (*3:6*). It then appears twice in chapter four, firstly, when Jonah sits down outside the city (*4:5*) having expressed his anger because God has forgiven Nineveh's evil behaviour; and again, in the same sentence, after he has built his shelter and sat down beneath it. So the author has created an ironic juxtaposition: within the city of Nineveh, the king sits in ashes in great discomfort praying for God to save it; outside the city of Nineveh Jonah sits in the comfort of his shelter praying for God to destroy it.

A characteristic of the book is that the author has chosen to use a relatively limited vocabulary. He has been very precise in his choice of words and has used repetitions of some of them so as to underscore particular elements of the story. These 'key words' provide a kind of subliminal message underpinning the events that are being described. For example, when Jonah flees from the mission, the verb *yarad*, 'to go down' is emphasised (Jonah 1:3 (twice); 5). It describes how Jonah went *down* to the port city of Jaffa, went *down* into the ship, and during the storm went *down* into its innermost part. There is even an additional word play on '*yarad*'. In the middle of the storm Jonah falls into a deep sleep. The verb for this sleep is '*radam*', used here in the form '*vayeiradam*' (1:4). One can hear in this word the essential letters of *yarad* as a kind of reinforcement of the idea of Jonah's descent. When Jonah is thrown into the sea *yarad* appears for the last time to describe his descent into the lowest regions, the base of the mountains that in the ancient Near East support the world (*2:7*). Thus Jonah's 'horizontal' flight from God is actually a series of stages of descent, leading downward, seemingly inevitably to his death.

In another word play, the commonest word in the Book is the Hebrew '*gadol*' meaning 'great'. Here the repetition may serve a different purpose: Nineveh is the *great* city, God hurls a *great* wind upon the sea, resulting in a *great* storm; the sailors fear a *great* fear when they discover Jonah's guilt, and an even *greater* fear of God when the sea calms down. The fish that saves him is a '*great* fish'. Jonah's response to God's sparing Nineveh is a '*great*' evil, and when God produces the plant to protect Jonah, he experiences a '*great*' joy. One effect of this repetition is to emphasis the 'fairy tale' quality of the story, everything is 'larger than life'. This would suggest that it is to be treated as a parable, not a real historic event.

There is another example of repetition in the first chapter. The verb '*tul*', meaning to 'hurl' appears rarely in the Hebrew Bible, yet it is used four times in chapter one: God *hurls* the wind onto the sea (*1:4*); the sailors are forced to *hurl* the cargo overboard to lighten the ship (*1:5*); Jonah asks the sailors to *hurl* him overboard (*1:12*); and reluctantly, after praying for help to God, they do *hurl* him overboard (*1:15*). The effect of the repetition of this key word is to show the underlying causal link between God's first act of '*hurling*' the wind to the response of the sailors and ultimately its direct effect on Jonah. All these acts and events serve as agents of God to remind Jonah of his mission.

The problem of ra'ah, 'evil'.

The reader is sensitised from the opening chapter of the book to pay close attention to repetitions or other word plays at work in the story. I need to introduce one more such word play used by the author which forms a bridge between chapter three and chapter four. When the Ninevites repent the text tells us that

> 'God saw their deeds, that they turned away from their evil ways, and God changed his mind about the 'evil' (or 'punishment') which he had said he would do to them and did not do it' (*3:10*).

The sentence contains an obvious translation problem involving the Hebrew word '*ra'ah*'. It is sometimes contrasted with the word '*tov*' meaning 'good', so in some contexts it is correct to translate *ra'ah* as 'bad' or 'evil'. Back in chapter one we read that God sent Jonah to Nineveh because their '*ra'ah*', their 'evil doing', had come up before God. In chapter three the same Hebrew word recurs when the Ninevites turn away from their '*ra'ah*', their evil ways and God changes his mind about the same word, the '*ra'ah*', that he intends to do to them. It seems that in this second case it is necessary to translate the word as 'punishment', rather than 'evil'. Perhaps this usage suggests that the intended punishment exactly matched the evil that they had been doing, measure for measure. But, however we translate it we cannot escape the direct link which the Hebrew makes between the evil of Nineveh and the divine punishment.

But what are we to make of the reappearance of the same word, *ra'ah*, immediately afterwards in the first verse of chapter four. Here it refers to Jonah's reaction on learning that Nineveh will not be destroyed. A literal translation would read:

'And it was evil to Jonah, a great evil, and it angered him.' (*Jonah 4:1*)

The author has now linked the evil behaviour of the Ninevites, the punishment God was intending to inflict upon them, and the evil feelings of Jonah when he learns that God has decided to rescind the punishment. English translations use various ways of softening the appearance of this word in this sentence, for example: 'Jonah, however, was *greatly displeased* and he became angry.' Perhaps closer to the Hebrew is The New International Version: 'But to Jonah this *seemed very wrong…*' But however one translates the sentence, it is hard not to see, at least in the Hebrew, the continuity of thought between the evil behaviour of the Ninevites, the 'evil' of God's punishment, and the 'evil' of Jonah's angry reaction to the Ninevites being spared. The three uses of the word '*ra'ah*' can be distinguished depending on how one understands the story, but nevertheless in the Hebrew original they are deeply interrelated and remain a challenge. We will see below how God sets about tackling Jonah's feeling that God's response has somehow been '*ra'ah*'.

Miracles and the names of God.

It is now time to address some literary devices in chapter four. When God sends the great fish to swallow Jonah, it is introduced by the verb '*manah*', in the form '*vayeman*', meaning 'God prepared' or 'assigned'. Although rare in the Hebrew Bible, this verb in this form appears four times in the book. God 'prepares' the big fish (*2:1*); God 'prepares' the 'plant' (*4:6*); God prepares the worm (*4:7*) and prepares the 'East wind' (*4:8*). This repetition reinforces the miraculous nature of each of these four events, again underlining the larger than life basis of the story. But this simple repetition takes on an added dimension when it is noted that in the Hebrew, in each of the four instances, a different version of the name or names of God is used as the subject of the verb. The author is clearly playing with the possible meanings of these different divine names.

As we have noted before the two commonest names used for God within the Hebrew Bible are the word '*Elohim*' and the word made up of four Hebrew letters, *yod, hey, vav, hey*, the so-called tetragrammaton, written in English as YHWH. According to Rabbinic tradition, the name in this form is only pronounced once a year by the High Priest in the Jerusalem Temple on the Day for Atonement. Otherwise, Jewish tradition forbids the pronunciation of the sacred name in this form and substitutes for it the word *Adonai*, a form of the word '*adon*' meaning master or lord, when the name is spoken aloud in ritual contexts. In very general terms, *Elohim* seems to be a universal designation for God, either referring to local deities or as the one ultimate God of the universe. The tetragrammaton is the name for that same God of the universe which is uniquely used by Israel. It is, so to speak, the intimate personal name which God shares with Israel alone.

But these are not the only ways in which the two divine names are used within Biblical texts, especially when they occur together within the same narrative context. To give a few examples.

We have already seen in Moses; encounter with God at the burning bush (*Exodus 3:1-15*), that the tetragrammaton is used to designate for the reader the objective information that it is an angel of *Adonai* who has 'appeared' to Moses (*3:2*). Subsequently within the passage, the word '*Elohim*' is used to express Moses' subjective experience of 'seeing' some kind of divine manifestation that is speaking to him (*3:4*). The verb 'to see', is a key word in this account of the burning bush and the reader watches Moses' struggle to understand what is happening until the meaning of the tetragrammaton as God's name is finally revealed at the end of the passage (*Exodus 3:15*). The alternating divine names serve to indicate the switch between the two perspectives, objective and subjective, that of the narrator and reader and that of the character Moses, within the story.

In a very different way, the two names alternate in a series of events recounted in the First Book of Samuel, chapters 4-6. In a time of war against the Philistines the two sons of Eli, the High Priest, decide to take the ark of the covenant (designated with its full title as the 'ark of the covenant of YHWH *Tzevaot*, Lord of Hosts, *1 Samuel 4:4*) into battle with them so that God will fight for them. The ark proves to be ineffective and is actually captured by the Philistines. In this situation the ark is referred to instead as the 'ark of *Elohim*' (v 11), that is to say, this name is used when the ark is being instrumentalised for human purposes and it has no divine power. The ark is deposited in a Philistine temple in Ashdod. The following morning the idol of the God Dagon in the temple is found to have fallen on its face before the ark (*1 Samuel 5:3*), but in that circumstance, where the ark reveals its true divine power, it is designated again as the 'ark of *Adonai*'. The author is using the alternating of the two divine names as part of his narrative technique to critique the misuse of the ark, and the resultant refusal of God to be manipulated.

We have studied a third variation in the story of Balaam (*Numbers 22*). In that story the frequent changes of the two divine names seem to be used by the narrator to designate the psychological struggle going on within Balaam himself between what he personally wishes (*Elohim*) and what God (*Adonai*) intends for him to do.

Finally, there is a fourth example we have also noted in which the respective meaning of the two names may be differentiated. When God asks Abraham to sacrifice his son (*Genesis 22*), it is as *Elohim* that God first addresses him (*22:1*), but it is an angel of *Adonai* that stops him making the sacrifice (*22:11*). One possible interpretation of this change of name is to be found in rabbinic literature. They suggest that in certain contexts *Elohim* represents the divine attribute of strict justice, whereas *Adonai* represents God's attribute of divine mercy, the former aspect testing Abraham, but the latter, in the end, sparing him.

These examples indicate that the names attributed to God by the Biblical writers may represent very different attributes, qualities or meanings as determined by the particular context.

If we now return to the usage of the two names for God in the Book of Jonah, we have already noted that in Chapter one, the sailors initially pray to their individual gods, using the word *Elohim*, whereas Jonah speaks throughout about *Adonai*. However when the sailors learn that Jonah is the source of their problem and that he seems to be fleeing from his God, it is to *Adonai* that they pray for help (*1:14*) and, when they are saved from the storm, it is to *Adonai* they make vows and sacrifices at the end of chapter one (*1:16*). That is to say, the universal and the particular aspect associated with the use of the divine names is operating in this chapter. In an interesting contrast, in chapter 3, the king of Nineveh commands his people to call to *Elohim*, and adds, perhaps 'the *Elohim*' will turn from His divine anger so that we do not perish. Here the word *Elohim* is used with a singular verb, indicating that the King of Nineveh has a concept of the one God of the universe. He even uses the same words of the sailors (compare *1:6,14* and *3:9*) when he expresses the hope 'that we do not perish'. But the king never makes the second step taken by the sailors of addressing his prayer to *Adonai*, to Israel's God. (This would explain a rabbinic view that the sailors actually converted to Israel's God, but the Ninevites did not.) So in chapters one and three of the Book of Jonah the use of the two divine names is associated with the distinction between a universal concept linked to the word *Elohim*, and the particular intimacy of Israel's association with that universal God through the use of the name *Adonai*.

However, if we look more precisely at the use of divine names in association with the four cases when God appoints some miraculous creature or event, a different principle seems to be operating. In *2:1*, it is as '*Adonai*' that God appoints the great fish that saves the life of Jonah. In *4:6*, the combined names, '*Adonai-Elohim*' appear together when God appoints the plant that grows over Jonah; but the use of two names may reflect the dual purpose of the plant which we will discuss below. The worm that destroys the gourd (*4:7*) is introduced by a common variant form of *Elohim*, namely '*Ha-Elohim*', using the definite article, the letter '*heh*', to mean literally 'The *Elohim*'. Finally, the East wind is introduced by the word '*Elohim*' (*4:8*) standing alone, without the definite article. How might we account for these four variations, particularly since we have demonstrated the precision with which different words are used by the author throughout the book? Or otherwise expressed, what narrative technique is he applying, or even what literary game is he playing with the reader?

Before we can answer that, there is another piece of information that we need. This is in the form of a Hebrew word play that is difficult to reproduce in translation, but immediately evident in the original language. It is to be found in chapter four verse six, the verse which utilises the two names for God together.

> The Lord God appointed a plant and it grew up over Jonah to be a shade upon his head and to rescue him from his *ra'ah*, his 'evil'.

We have discussed above the problem of translating the word '*ra'ah*'. So perhaps we will learn something more about it from what God is about to do. The Hebrew word play here is in the juxtaposition of the two phrases 'to be a shade upon his head' and 'to rescue him from his evil'. In Hebrew it reads '*lih'yot tzel al rosho l'hatzeel lo me'ra'ato*', The phrase '*lih'yot tzel*' is the verb 'to be' plus the noun for shade, '*tzel*'. The word play is with the following phrase '*l'hatzeel lo*', from the root '*natzal*', to rescue and the pronoun '*lo*', 'him'. The word play is obvious when the Hebrew words are juxtaposed '*lih'yot tzel*', '*l'hatzeel lo*'. It serves to emphasise the twofold purpose of the plant, to shade him from the heat of the sun, but in some way to rescue him from his bad feelings and anger because Nineveh is not destroyed. It is surely no coincidence that this twofold purpose is introduced by the two names of God in combination – one, *Adonai*, reflecting an act of compassion, the other, *Elohim*, at the very least, with a didactic, or even justice, purpose. I would argue that in this chapter, which deals with a highly personal intimate argument between Jonah and God, the outside world recedes, and it is legitimate to assume that the author is employing a different meaning to the use of the two divine names together for this internal dialogue. The distinction here between the use of the two names is along the lines suggested by the rabbinic tradition. *Adonai*, as shown by its use in God's appointing the fish that saved Jonah's life, hints at the divine attribute of compassion, which also provides him with shade. But the addition of *Elohim*, represents the divine attribute of justice that is attempting to change Jonah's '*ra'ah*', Jonah's anger at God's compassion towards those who for Jonah represent evil within the world.

Internal Biblical Commentary.

There is another Biblical literary technique that reinforces this suggestion of the significance of the use of the two names of God in this chapter. It is related to what is the most provocative passage in the Book of Jonah. Jonah has previously prayed to God in the belly of the fish. That prayer was introduced with the words 'Jonah prayed to *Adonai* his God', suggesting an intimate relationship between them. But that intimacy is greatly diminished in chapter four. Immediately after describing Jonah's anger, the text continues 'He prayed to *Adonai*', omitting the phrase 'his God'. He begins with a conventional introduction to a petitionary prayer, using the identical formula used by the sailors back in *1:14*: '*Annah adonai*, Please *Adonai*, let us not perish....' Jonah begins with the same pious plea, '*Annah adonai*, please *Adonai*' (*4:2*). But then his pent-up anger about what he considers to be the foolishness of his mission to Nineveh bursts through: 'Isn't that what I said when I was back in my country!? That is why I tried to forestall by fleeing to Tarshish!' By now we can imagine him shouting in anger and frustration as he tries to justify his actions. To appreciate what follows we need to recognize yet another common literary technique of the Hebrew Bible, the way in which certain key or significant phrases in earlier Biblical passages are quoted in later texts, either intact or with changes reflecting the need of the new context. One of the most commonly quoted passages is to be found in *Exodus 34:6-7* in which God reveals to Moses the compassion with which God responds to the sins, wrongdoing and outright rebellious deeds of Israel but also the limitations that are set on God's compassion because of the terms of the covenant between God and Israel. It is the passage we have already studied in the chapter on Moses' 'negotiation' with God. It reads:

> *Adonai, Adonai*, a God of mercy and compassion, slow to anger, generous in love and truth, showing love to thousands (of generations), forgiving sin, wrongdoing and failings but who does not entirely declare innocent, visiting the sins of the fathers upon the children and the children's children to the third and fourth generation. (Exodus 34:6-7)

The key terms are two paired phrases, each of which is in the form of a hendiadys, whereby the meaning of the combination is greater than that of the two individual parts alone. Thus, the Hebrew '*rahum v'chanun*', 'a God of mercy and compassion', combines '*rahum*' a word meaning 'love and compassion' with '*chanun*' which means to be 'gracious', to act with a generosity that expects nothing in return. Together they speak of God's boundless, limitless love. But the second pairing, '*hesed ve'emet*', 'generous in love and truth', combines '*hesed*', which is the love and loyalty that exists in a covenant between two partners, a faithfulness that goes beyond their mere contractual obligations to one another, with the second word, '*emet*', 'truth' which comes from a root '*amen*' which means that something is 'firm', 'reliable'. This combination speaks of a love that has boundaries, that requires and expects loyalty and faithfulness from the partners, with consequences if that trust is betrayed. The effect is to address the theological question of how an almighty, immeasurable God can create a formal relationship with mere mortals. The answer is in the creation of a covenant, a love-based contract that is eternally binding between the partners and imposes conditions. This accounts for the darker conclusion of the Exodus passage. The boundless compassion allows God to forgive the various sins that human beings commit, but on condition that they are prepared to acknowledge the wrongs that they do and repent. If not, there are penalties, hence the punishment to the third and fourth generation. However, as we have already noted in the chapter on Moses' negotiation with God, this does not mean a punishment continuing through yet unborn generations. Rather, the person being addressed here, as in the Ten Commandments, is the adult Israelite male, the patriarch, in this patriarchal society, to whom belong family, slaves, land and animals. Such a patriarch can live to see in his lifetime four generations of his offspring, so the warning is that what he does has consequences for all of them, whether for good or for ill. 'With great power comes great responsibility!'

Such is the power and importance of this passage from Exodus that it can be called upon, modified and relied upon to appeal to God in different circumstances. Moses uses it to challenge God when God threatens to abandon the people after the episode with the spies (*Numbers 14:18*). Time and again, each time with a variation, it is cited in Psalms and prophetic texts (*Psalm*

86:15; 103:8; 145:8; Joel 2:13-14). It is this text, in the variation to be found in *Joel 2:13-14* that Jonah uses here, overwhelmed by his anger and frustration!

For I know that 'You are a gracious and merciful God, slow to anger, generous to love, who relents from punishment.' (*4:2*)

It is the closing phrase, 'who relents from punishment' that is the special addition to the original text in Exodus that is found in Jonah and Joel. Jonah is furious that God is willing to extend the kind of compassion that he seems to think should only be available to Israel to their arch enemy Nineveh. Jonah literally throws this expression of God's loving care in God's face. It is an act by Jonah that amounts to blasphemy but also reflects the dark humour and extraordinary courage of the author of the book to allow his hero, or perhaps anti-hero, Jonah to attack God in this way. Perhaps what finally makes Jonah explode with anger is yet another quotation from an earlier Biblical chapter. After the disastrous episode of the Golden Calf, when God was on the point of abandoning the Israelites Moses manages to persuade God not to do so. That passage ends with the sentence:

> And *Adonai* repented of the '*ra'ah*' (evil/punishment) which he had said he would do to his people. (*Exodus 32:14*)

It must have been for Jonah the final straw when the identical sentence, but this time in the name of *Elohim*, and referring to Nineveh, concludes chapter three:

> And *Elohim* repented of the '*ra'ah*' (evil/punishment) which he said he would do to them - and did not do it. (*Jonah 3:10*)

Some concluding observations.

From the literary and rhetorical point of view, we have seen how the repetition of key words can create a subliminal message beneath the surface of a text – the descent of Jonah towards death, the way God's initial response to

Jonah's flight carries a message indirectly, via nature and other people, to Jonah; how word plays can create connections between seemingly independent events; how changes in divine names can be used to reflect different ideas or values; how the Hebrew Bible comments upon itself, recycling earlier materials both to suggest the original meaning and correct or critique it.

Given the literary strategies at play in the closing chapter, how does the story resolve?

God asks Jonah whether he was right to be so angry (4:4), but Jonah does not answer. Instead he leaves the city and takes up his position outside to watch what happens, as if trying to force God to change his mind and destroy the city. Since Jonah has defined the terms of their conversation with his actions, God continues the dialogue also by means of actions – with the plant, the worm and the wind. How does God use these small miracles? To answer this, we need to address a problem noticed by Biblical scholars. If Jonah already has a shelter to protect him from the sun, what is the need for a plant to provide the same shade? One historical-critical approach suggests that this chapter is a compilation from previous sources, one of which had Jonah build a shelter, the other had the miraculous plant, the two versions being subsequently amalgamated.

But there is another more coherent way of explaining the need for both sources of shade, again in line with the literary skill of the author. It brings us back to the comparison between the king of Nineveh sitting on ashes within the city praying for its survival, and Jonah sitting outside praying for its destruction. But in the case of Jonah, the word 'he sat' is repeated within the same verse, because Jonah recognizes how dangerous it would be to remain sitting exposed to the sun. So, he gets up, builds his shelter and again sits down. Whatever Jonah's rationale may be for his anger with God, his first concern is actually, and understandably, his own physical safety. So, he builds his shelter. God's response is action for action, as if to say: 'Your real concern is actually your personal comfort. Very well, let's talk about comfort! I will provide for you a

212

miraculous source of comfort and shade', hence the plant. But then God takes it away, and Jonah is exposed to the East wind and the burning sun. He is thus forced to experience the kind of suffering that he was quite happily wishing on the people of Nineveh. On this reading, the plant is not redundant but is an integral part of the dialogue, conducted not with words alone but with actions. The plant will later have further significance as God challenges Jonah's sense of compassion – 'you felt compassion for the plant over which you did not labour…. should I not feel compassion for Nineveh? (*4:10-11*)'

The ending of the book leaves us not only with God's question to Jonah, but also the reader's question about what Jonah's response might have been. Did he come to appreciate that the Ninevites were also God's creatures and were owed the same compassion that God had offered to Israel? Or did he remain stubborn, self-righteous and unconvinced till the end? It is part of the author's rhetorical skills that he tosses God's final question to Jonah, but equally to the reader who has accompanied Jonah on his journey. For that is part of the narrator's tactics and skill. He has chosen as his hero someone who in normal circumstances would be admired and respected as a prophet, a servant of God, with whom the reader automatically wants to identify. Yet at every turn, the alien people that Jonah encounters, the foreign sailors, the hated and feared Ninevites, are shown to be quite admirable in their behaviour, while Jonah is at the very least unsympathetic. Without even noticing it we have become forced to acquire a different perspective on our own instinctive loyalties and assumptions. God's final question is very firmly addressed to us, the readers.

God may have the last word in the text, but the author leaves us with one final literary trick to enjoy, one that is sadly completely lost in translation. Chapter four began with Jonah's long speech to God (*4:2-3*) and ends with God's long reply and question (*4:10-11*). If you count the Hebrew words in Jonah's speech to God they come to thirty-nine words (since some words in the Hebrew are hyphenated it is possible to treat them as a single word in which case the number of words comes to thirty.) If we now turn to God's closing speech, with its enigmatic ending about 'much cattle' and perform the same double count the numbers come to … thirty-nine and thirty. The author has given equal 'air-time' to the two protagonists, God and Jonah. Greater even than God's patience with Nineveh, is God's patience with Jonah. And perhaps greater still, in the view of the author, is God's respect for the stubbornness, irreverence and courage of his difficult but all-too-human partner.

15 Rabbinic Readings of Ruth

At first glance the Book of Ruth seems to be an unlikely source of much rabbinic interpretation. The story is often seen as a simple tale about country folk, complete with a happy end. That Ruth is a Moabitess who will end up as the ancestress of King David is obviously significant. But what special implications might the rabbis have found in it? Indeed there is one Midrashic comment that pretty much asks this question.

> Rabbi Ze'ira said: This scroll contains nothing about uncleanness or cleanness, about what is prohibited or permitted, so why was it written?!

He seems to be parodying the obsession of some of his rabbinic colleagues with finding in every letter of the Torah some legal significance. But he then offers a different reason for valuing the book:

> It is to teach you how good is the reward for those who perform deeds of loyalty and love. (*Ruth Rabbah 2:15*).

The Hebrew for such people is '*gomlei chasadim*', and it picks up the theme of '*chesed*', loyalty and love, that recurs in the Book. Naomi hopes that God will show *chesed* to her two daughters-in-law, just as they have shown *chesed* to their dead husbands (*Ruth 1:8*); Naomi, despite here initial bitterness, recognizes God's *chesed* in bringing Ruth and Boaz together (*2:20*); and Boaz recognizes Ruth's *chesed* in staying with her mother-in-law instead of pursuing her own interests and finding a young man (*3:10*). Indeed, as Rabbi Ze'ira remarks, it is a significant motif throughout the Book. Nevertheless, despite Rabbi Ze'ira's inability to detect anything in the Book about *Halakhah*, Jewish law, it was precisely in that area that the Book was mined for a particular purpose.

The rabbis, in the aftermath of the Roman destruction of Jerusalem, were engaged in re-establishing Jewish life in the context of exile. Without land, king, temple or priest, scattered throughout the known world, a number of strategies were needed to hold these different communities together and ensure their continuity while wating for God to return them to their homeland. They reconstituted a territorially based nation as an extra-territorial faith community, held together by Jewish law, under the authority of the rabbis.

But who belonged to this community and how did newcomers gain entry? In the Biblical world one became part of a people by settling in the territory and accepting the local god. Thus the Bible speaks of the '*ger*', the resident alien who had certain rights and responsibilities under the covenant with God, detailed in the Torah, the constitution of the nation. Full membership of the people in the Biblical period, symbolised by the right to eat the Passover offering, required, for men, the final step of circumcision (*Exodus 12:48*). But in this new situation, without land or nation, how did someone become part of the Jewish people?

One way was simply through birth, though under rabbinic law it became birth from a Jewish mother, whereas in the biblical period it appeared to depend on the father. The reason for this change is not clear, nor even the exact point at which it became normative. However, how did an adult enter the covenant? Since Ruth represents the most obvious example in the Bible of a woman who joined herself to the Jewish people, the Book was scoured for evidence as to how this might happen, even in this radically new situation.

This kind of question may well lie behind the historical background of the Book. Boaz himself draws the analogy between Ruth and Abraham. She also 'left her father and mother and the place of her birth' (compare *Genesis 12:1* and *Ruth 2:11*) as did Abraham when called by God, thus reinforcing the spiritual dimension of her journey. Indeed Boaz characterises Ruth as 'taking refuge under the wings of the Lord' (*2:12*). For rabbinic Judaism, in this new context, it is the affirmation of faith in Israel's God, and not, for example, the wish to marry into a Jewish family, that becomes the primary requirement for accepting a convert.

Did the rabbis really derive laws from the Book of Ruth, or, having devised their laws, simply look within the Book for some kind of sanction for what they had decided? The answer is probably the latter, as some examples will indicate.

Before someone can be considered for conversion, they must obviously approach a rabbinic authority. So how should such a rabbi respond? Though, according to the New Testament, the Jews had been keen on converting, this desire was radically curtailed after the success of Christianity in conquering the Roman Empire, following which conversion proved dangerous for the convert and the one who had helped in the process. The Midrash collection, *Ruth Rabbah*, records a tradition that already expresses a reluctance to accept a potential convert. In the context of the story, Naomi tries to send her daughters-in-law away, and three times uses the same Hebrew term '*shovnah*', turn back.

Rabbi Shmuel bar Nachmani in the name of Rabbi Yudan son of rabbi Hanina [said]: In three places it is written here, '*shovnah, shovnah, shovnah*', 'turn back, turn back, turn back' corresponding to the three times they push the potential convert away. But if he persists more than this they accept him (*Ruth Rabbah 2:16*).

This testing of sincerity is spelled out further in the Talmud:

Our masters taught: If, at the present time, a man comes seeking to be a proselyte, he should be asked: What makes you wish to be received as a proselyte? Are you not aware that at this time Israel is broken down, pushed about, swept from place to place, driven here and there, and overcome by afflictions? If he says, 'I am fully aware. But I am scarcely worthy of [the privilege of becoming a Jew],' he is to be received at once and instructed in a few minor and a few major precepts. Another comment adds:

One should take care not to impose on him too many commandments nor go into fine details about them (*Yebamot 47a-b*).

However Ruth's persistence, despite Naomi's rejection, is rewarded. Her statement 'do not entreat me to leave you, and return from following you' is read as follows:

'Do not entreat me' – She said to her: do not sin against me, do not turn your misfortunes (from the verb *paga*, translated here as 'entreat') away from me. … I am fully resolved to convert, but better at your hands than at those of another. When Naomi heard this she began to set in order before her the laws of conversion.' (*Ruth Rabbah 2:22*)

In the immediately following verses Ruth expresses her determination to follow Naomi, and her loyalty and commitment to her mother-in-law. For the Biblical author it is enough that Ruth says 'Your people shall be my people, your God my God' to represent her joining herself to the fate of Israel. Indeed the sequence, putting 'people' first, and only then followed by 'God', exactly represents the process we mentioned above, First comes the joining with the national community, naturalisation, and only then, as an automatic consequence, the religious commitment.

At its face value, Ruth's words are simply an expression of personal loyalty to and love for her mother-in-law, and her willingness to follow her to her own land. Yet there are at least three different early rabbinic interpretation of this passage that follow the same pattern: in the Targum, the Aramaic translation of the Book; in Ruth Rabbah, the major Midrashic commentary on it; and in the Talmud itself, *Yebamot 47b*. All are similarly constructed, as if Ruth's words were one half of a conversation with Naomi, with the rabbis supplying Naomi's missing words. Having established that this was part of the process of conversion, with Ruth eager to be taught certain basic principles, they took their cue from Ruth's 'answers' and derived from them the laws that Naomi taught her.

The first commandment that Naomi provides tells Ruth that it is forbidden to walk more than two thousand cubits on the Shabbat (*Targum, Yebamot*). Which obviously feeds into Ruth's 'reply': 'where you walk I will walk' Presumably Naomi must have taught her some fundamental rules about the Shabbat. Ruth Rabbah has an interesting variant, for Naomi tells Ruth instead that it is not the custom of daughters of Israel to go to the circuses and theatres of the gentiles. This is more in keeping with the view of Ruth as a Moabite girl with a rich social life behind her.

Ruth's next reply is also to two different suggestions as to which laws Naomi taught her. One is again a more domestic one: it is not the custom of Israel to live in a house where there is no mezuzah on the door (*Ruth Rabbah*). Hence Ruth's answer: where you dwell, literally 'stay overnight', there I will dwell. However the other version hints at a sexual issue that is also very present within the Book: it is not the custom for a female to be alone with a man who is not her husband! (Rashi's version of *Yebamot*). There is a certain irony here in the choice of law because Boaz will use the same verb '*loon*', 'to stay overnight', when he asks Ruth to remain with him on the threshing floor till the morning.

The next teaching by Naomi is common to all these rabbinic texts: 'The Jewish people are distinguished by keeping 613 mitzvoth, commandments.' Hence Ruth's reply accepting the 'yoke of the mitzvoth', 'Your people shall be my people'.

Again there is a variation in the response to her next answer, 'Your God, my God'. The *Ruth Rabbah* version has not specified the 613 mitzvoth so now has Naomi teaching her 'the rest of the mitzvoth'. But the other two versions, perhaps more appropriately for the context, have Naomi teach her that, as an Israelite, it is forbidden to worship other gods.

Ruth's final words are a very powerful evocation of a lifetime commitment to Naomi and her people: 'Where you die I shall die, and there I shall be buried'. But this statement is taken almost literally by all three sources which describe the different kinds of death penalties that can be imposed by a Beth Din: stoning, burning, decapitation and strangling, depending on the nature of the capital crime committed. Since Ruth talks about burial, they conclude by defining the two different kinds of graves that are available depending on the nature of the death described above!

According to these versions Naomi is enough of an expert in Jewish law to be able to impart this information to Ruth. But in addition to the above laws, she must have given Ruth further instruction on the walk from Moab to Bethlehem about how to glean properly. This emerges in a rabbinic observation about Boaz. The Biblical text has him enquire about Ruth when he first sees her: 'To whom does this young lady belong?' Clearly, for the rabbis, a man of Boaz's piety could not have simply been attracted by a pretty face! Though a rabbinic text also notes that on the day Ruth arrived in Bethlehem Boaz's wife died. Besides which Boaz already knew something about her story as he will later reveal to her. The mediaeval commentator Abraham Ibn Ezra thought she might have been wearing Moabite national dress, or possibly had some kind of facial appearance that would have marked her out as different. However he also notes that there is a well-known Midrash, and indeed Rashi quotes a version of this Midrash but introduces it with the question, was it Boaz's way to ask about women, surely not! Instead Boaz observed the modesty and wisdom of her actions. *Ruth Rabbah* elaborates on the former:

> The other women bent over when they gleaned, but she sat and gleaned…..The other women flirted with the harvesters, but she kept to herself. The other women gleaned amongst the sheaves, but she only gleaned amongst the parts that had been declared ownerless (*Ruth Rabbah 4:9*).

Rashi then adds that she picked up two stalks when they were together but not three, as this number would not constitute gleanings but a sheaf and would not be permitted.

But Boaz's own legal knowledge becomes apparent in another matter that is central to the problem of Ruth. She is repeatedly described as a Moabitess. Indeed the rabbis assumed that she came from royal lineage and was no less than the granddaughter of Eglon king of Moab. Not only that, but he in turn was the grandson of Balak, the earlier king, who had incited Balaam the prophet to curse Israel, only to find that God forced him to bless Israel. This is also a favourite idea of the rabbis that former enemies ended up, generations later, becoming part of the Jewish people. But how could the sons of Elimelech possibly marry Moabite women when such a marriage was explicitly forbidden in Deuteronomy.

> An Ammonite and Moabite shall not enter into the congregation of the
> Lord even unto the tenth generation. (*Deuteronomy 23:4*)

Presumably behind this law are a number of associations with these two peoples, beginning with the scandalous story of the birth of their two ancestors as the incestuous offspring of Lot and his daughters. The behaviour of these two peoples in the wilderness stories, seducing the Israelites and leading them into idolatry or fighting them, would have added to, or confirmed, the need for such a prohibition. Yet Ruth was somehow acceptable, and moreover the ancestress of King David himself, so this required an explanation and justification.

The rabbis saw this problem acted out in chapter four of the Book in the story of the anonymous redeemer who had a prior commitment to buy back the field of Naomi. While he was willing at first he turned the opportunity down at the last minute. The reason for that is not made explicit in the Biblical text, but the rabbis assumed he thought that he would be breaking the law of Deuteronomy, as he understood it, by marrying Ruth the Moabitess. However Boaz was a serious student of *halakhah* and kept up to date with new decisions, so he knew that the law had recently been re-interpreted to make such a marriage possible. The text in Deuteronomy uses masculine terminology, which in Biblical terms includes the feminine, when speaking of an Ammonite and a Moabite. But law is developed or challenged through examining the precise formulation of legal enactments in new circumstances. The terminology of the commandment was explicitly masculine so it need not apply to a Moabite woman, and hence his marriage to Ruth was now permitted. While this is told at the expense of the anonymous redeemer, and to Boaz's credit, it also helps the rabbis solve an embarrassing contradiction between the Book of Ruth and Deuteronomy.

Just to return one final time to the issue of conversion, if Ruth's words to Naomi constituted her entry into the Jewish community, what was the status of her and Orpah's previous marriage to Machlon and Chilion? If neither of them had converted beforehand these marriages would have been a breech of the covenant law. Indeed this could have been a possible cause of their early deaths! But again it is Abraham Ibn Ezra who goes against the generally accepted rabbinic interpretation of events. In his view the two daughters-in-law had indeed converted prior to their marriages. What is his proof for this? When Ruth persists in staying with her mother-in-law Naomi tries to send her away, she says explicitly, 'your sister-in-law has returned to her people and to her god' (*Ruth 1:15*). This can only mean, he argues, that they had already converted and adopted the country and God of their husbands. So how does he explain Ruth's confession to Naomi, 'Your people shall be my people, your God, my God'? He explains her twofold saying as meaning: I shall never depart from the Torah of Israel or from the declaration of the unity of God.

All these concerns with the legal ramifications should not ignore that the rabbis in their commentaries also recognized other elements in the story. In particular they responded to the sexual undercurrent. When Naomi says that even if she were to be with a man that night and became pregnant and bore a child, would her daughters-in-law wait till they had grown up and marry them? Though they were aware that this was only an exaggerated question raised by Naomi, they also discussed whether the law of levirate marriage might have to be invoked. When a man died without offspring, his widow had to marry his brother in order to raise up children in the name of the deceased and ensure that his relationship to the family property was maintained. But this only applied, they pointed out, to brothers alive at the time of the first death. However they focused in particular on Naomi's reference to doing something that night and assumed that she was yet again imparting things of significance to Ruth.

Said Rabbi Yochanan: Torah teaches you appropriate behaviour. Namely that intercourse should not take place by day but rather by night. That is the meaning of what is written in the Book of Esther (*Esther 2:14*), [referring to the beauty queens brought to King Ahasuerus to be tested out by him] 'In the evening they would come and in the morning they would return.' Hence the phrase, 'if I was with a man tonight' (*Ruth Rabbah 2:16*).

One rabbi's view of the beauty of Ruth is also brought out in a somewhat shocking statement which shows that the rabbis were not averse to the occasional lapse into locker-room humour. The verse says '*vayiker mikreha*', 'she happened to chance upon the field of Boaz (*2:3*) From the verbal root '*kara*', 'to happen', comes the word '*keri*' which means 'mishap', but it is used euphemistically for a particular mishap common to adolescent males.

Rabbi Yochanan said: [She was so beautiful that] everyone who saw her had a seminal emission!' (*Ruth Rabbah 4:4*)

But what happened when Ruth came secretly at night to Boaz on the threshing floor? The rabbis are at pains to point out that nothing happened and that both behaved appropriately, but that did not stop them recognizing the temptation faced by Boaz. They had already taught that on the day that Ruth arrived, Boaz's wife died. On the threshing floor Boaz makes an oath that they felt needed further explanation. 'If the first redeemer does not redeem you then I will redeem you myself. As the Lord lives, lie here tonight!' (3:13) The apparent lack of relationship between the oath in the name of God and the command to stay the night led them to the following view.

His evil inclination kept inciting him all night long, saying: You are free and are looking for a wife, and she is free and is looking for a husband. Come to her and she can become your wife. He swore to his inclination: 'As the Lord lives, I shall not touch her!' and to the woman he said: 'lie here tonight till morning.' (*Ruth Rabbah 6:1*)

223

There is one further theme that was of concern to the rabbis, which once again reverts back to Ruth's status as a Moabitess. How could the ancestress of King David, and indeed of the longed-for Messiah, have come from such a background? The problem is compounded, as explicitly noted in the Book of Ruth itself, by the equally scandalous background of Boaz as a descendant of the illicit relationship between Judah and Tamar. Indeed the story of both women, Ruth and Tamar, outsiders who take action to ensure the continuity of the family line, invites comparison. A number of Midrashim reflect on David's struggle to be accepted as king because of this background, especially Ruth's Moabite status. Finally, however, because God elevated him to kingship, this past was now overcome.

In my own reading of the Book of Ruth, the author is similarly concerned with correcting both of these previous incestuous events: Lot and his daughters and Judah and Tamar. The past cannot be removed, but it can be repaired when the descendants of those events re-enact them but behave this time in an exemplary fashion. Hence the encounter on the threshing floor where nothing untoward actually happens; only after marriage is it explicitly stated that intercourse took place leading to an immediate pregnancy. Thus the family tree at the end of the Book leading to David, expresses a longing for a future messianic redemption.

This reading of the Book finds its echo in certain rabbinic teachings that became even more developed in the mystical tradition. Commenting on a phrase in Job, 'Who can withdraw purity from impurity, not one? (*Job 14:3*): a Midrash explains:

> Abraham came from Terah, Hezekiah from Ahaz, Josiah from Amon, Mordechai from Shimei, Israel from idolaters, the world to come from this world. Who could do this? Who could command this? Who could decree this? No one [but God] the unique One of the world! (*Bamidbar Rabbah 19:1*).

This view of purity emerging from impurity is later developed in Lurianic Kabbalah. Within the corruption of the world are holy sparks of an original divine light, and our task is to redeem and restore them, a process called 'Tikun', 'repair'.. Thus David and the messiah emerge from this earlier corruption that has been healed by Ruth. This doctrine became itself distorted when messianic claimants felt the need to immerse themselves in corruption in order to do such a repair, alas unsuccessfully.

But if we remain within normative rabbinic tradition, the rabbis are aware that behind the simply human stories within Scripture, there is a deeper drama being enacted. Whatever the surface events may be, behind them are the hidden actions of God. The protagonists of the Book of Ruth do their best to fulfil their responsibilities to one another and to their tradition. Though the rabbis will give each of them prophetic insight into the future, the author does not. Their humanity suffices. But for the Midrash even the most mundane of domestic events may play a part in the ultimate redemption of the whole world:

The tribal ancestors were engaged in selling Joseph.

Joseph was occupied with his sackcloth and ashes.

Reuben was occupied with his sackcloth and ashes.

Jacob was occupied with his sackcloth and ashes.

Judah was occupied in taking a wife.

The Holy One, blessed be He, was engaged in creating the light of the Messiah. (*Genesis Rabbah 85:1*)

16 The Politics of the Book of Esther

This chapter adopts a different approach to a larger unit of Biblical narrative. It will look at the 'political' dimensions of the Book of Esther from three perspectives: the political logic of the narrative plot itself; the internal Biblical referencing; and the significance of the Book in the light of one contemporary reading of the Book.

The Political Logic of the Plot

The Book of Esther is conventionally read as a series of events that fortuitously, or through the hidden hand of God, come together to save the Jewish people from a potential act of genocide. In fact the only action that is an obvious and deliberate intervention is Mordecai's decision not to bow to Haman, that leads to the threat to his entire people. Nevertheless, at the risk of creating a classical conspiracy theory, the narrative as a whole can be read as a consequence of a series of political decisions and subsequent moves and countermoves.

To what extent the political structure of King Ahasuerus's Court is an accurate reflection of Persian society or of a later culture, depends on views about the historical context of the author. However, what is significant in terms of the narrative itself is the clues that the political structure of the regime provides to the unfolding of the story. In this regard with the appointment of Haman there is a significant change in terms of the king's advisers and counsellors. In chapter 1 much is made of the seven named eunuchs (v 10) sent to summon Queen Vashti and the seven named 'closest advisers' (v 14), one of whom suggests that she should be replaced. In chapter 2 yet another group of 'servants and advisers' suggests the search for a successor to Vashti. One may read this overabundance of advisers as a parody of the way matters of state were dealt with and the ease with which the king could be manipulated. However, in terms of the narrative thrust, it is also establishing a pattern that is about to be radically changed by the elevation of Haman in chapter 3.

The significance of his rise is emphasised by the opening words of chapter 3, 'After these things'. This may be translated to indicate an unidentified lapse of time (JPS 'some time afterward'), however the literal meaning points instead to some preceding 'things', 'events' that have led to this new situation. Thus the similar usage in 2:1 is directly linked to the removal of Vashti and the king's subsequent change of heart and the need to find her successor.[56] What is significant for the narrative is that the king, for some reason, elevated Haman and placed his throne higher than any of the 'officials who were with him', his contemporary office holders. That is to say Haman steps out of the ranks to a unique new position in this otherwise well-established court structure. What preceding event might have caused this radical political change? The obvious answer is the immediately preceding story at the end of chapter two of the plot against the life of the king by two eunuchs Bigthan and Teresh who 'guarded the threshold'. This episode is usually read as a kind of convenient plot device to introduce the place in the royal palace of Mordecai, who overheard the plot and reported it, via Esther, to the king, but also as foreshadowing the convenient discovery about Mordecai's actions on the night when the king could not sleep (6:1). But why overlook the immediate significance of the event itself, of an attempted assassination of the king by people close to him, and the impact it might have had on policy changes, including the need for enhanced security measures?

Two elements essential for the plot of the narrative follow from this observation. We learn that Haman feels insulted by Mordecai's refusal to bow to him and wants to destroy him, and with him his entire people. That aspect belongs to the broader context of the Book within the Hebrew Bible and the

---

[56] The same phrase is common in Genesis narratives (15:1; 22:1; 39:7; 40:1) and Kings (1 Kings 13:33; 17:17, 21:1).

struggle between Israel and Amalek whose background we will study below. But in what circumstances might Haman have a legitimate opportunity to bring to the king such an outlandish accusation against an entire population within the empire? The obvious answer is in his role in charge of what today we would term 'homeland security'. (Incidentally, this is a role for which Mordecai might have felt himself to be suitably qualified having saved the life of the king.) Haman's infamous description of the Jews echoes Pharaoh's similar accusation of the Children of Israel (*Exodus 1:9-10*):

> 'See the people, the Children of Israel, are more and stronger than us. Come let us deal wisely with them lest they multiply, and if war occurs they will also join our enemies, and fight us and go up from the land.'

Haman builds his argument carefully, beginning with a true statement about the distribution of the Jewish people throughout the empire, then pointing to their significant difference from other peoples, only then asserting that they represent a threat to the king's authority:

> There is a certain people, scattered and dispersed among the other people in all the provinces of your realm, whose laws are different from those of any other people and who do not obey the king's laws and it is not in the king's interest to tolerate them' *(Esther 3:8)*.

Like Pharaoh's ploy, this is the language of demagogues against vulnerable minorities, throughout history up to the present day, based on innuendo, selective or manufactured evidence. It is also not unknown for outsiders, as is Haman himself as an 'Agagite' in the Persian court, to project onto other outsiders their own insecurities and promote their own acceptability within the host society.

The second element is the introduction of Haman as an Agagite. Within the Biblical listing of the history of various peoples, we learn that Amalek is a grandson of Esau, through Esau's son Eliphaz and a concubine called Timna

(*Genesis 36:12*) The significance of this is something already touched on in the story of Jacob's stealing of the blessing of Esau. When the children of Israel were departing from Egypt, the most vulnerable were attacked by a people known as Amalekites who were condemned by God for this act to an eternal war that would wipe out their memory (*Exodus 17:8-16; Deuteronomy 25:17-19*) The war against the Amalekites becomes significant in the story of King Saul. When he battles successfully against them (*1 Samuel 15*), he spares the Amalekite king Agag, to the great anger of the prophet Samuel. When we learn in the book of Esther that Haman is an Agagite, we are bound to make the link with this association: Esau – Amalek – Agag – Haman. The connection is actually spelled out for the reader when Mordechai gives a 'great and bitter cry' (*Esther 4:1*) on learning Haman's plan to exterminate his people, echoing Esau's 'great and bitter cry' when he learns that Jacob has stolen his blessing (*Genesis 27:4*). The author of this late Biblical book clearly had this thread of historical connection in mind in creating his villain.

But within the inner political logic of the narrative, in appointing an Agagite to this important post, the king may have had a particular consideration in mind that will similarly apply to the later appointment of Mordecai in his place. The fact that he was an outsider also made him vulnerable and disposable should he fail to fulfil his task or in any way displease or pose a threat to the king. Here we also have an echo of the story of Joseph's sudden rise in Pharaoh's court and, in Jewish history, the roles of Court Jews, *Hof-Juden*, equally important to the ruler but equally vulnerable. That Mordecai will succeed Haman is no guarantee that his ultimate fate will be any different after the final chapter of the Book has been written.

If these political realities are recognized as essential plot elements, they may help explain the central riddle of the book, and the one which set in train the violent threat to the Jewish people. What made Mordecai refuse to bow before Haman as Court protocol seemed to demand and as expressly commanded by the king (*3:2-3*)? Indeed that disobedience of the king's command gave legitimation to Haman's accusation that the Jewish people 'do not follow the king's laws!' Whatever Mordechai's reason it clearly had political consequences as his fellow courtiers pointed out to him and indeed they not only noted it but reported it to Haman and watched to see how long Mordecai would hold out. Moreover, only here is there some indication of the reason he gave for not bowing, namely that he was a Jew (*3:4*). What lies behind this reason is never made entirely clear. Elsewhere in the Bible Jews bow before other human beings out of respect or convention. The rabbis were forced to invent as explanation an idolatrous device on Haman's clothing before which Mordecai refused to bow on religious grounds. The most obvious reason relates yet again to the historical enmity between the Israelites and Amalekites here acted out in the setting of the royal court.

However, if we are talking politics, there remains another possibility that represents a high-risk strategy on the part of Mordecai and belongs to the familiar theme of court rivalries and struggles for influence and power. By the end of the book Mordecai will have successfully replaced Haman as the leading political figure second only to the king. Was that another of the fortuitous events in the book or the consequence of a calculated strategy on the part of Mordecai to establish himself in the public mind as an independent figure and potential rival to Haman? That reading would see Mordecai driven by the historical Israelite/Amalekite conflict, but also his own personal ambition. If so, it must have come as a horrible shock to him when Haman's response was the plot to destroy all the Jews. That Mordecai came to know the precise financial details of Haman's plot, like his knowledge of the attempt on the life of the king, suggest that he had found ways of gaining access to the innermost circles of the palace (*4:7*). The shock of recognizing his own responsibility, whatever his original intention, could certainly reinforce his reaction, tearing his clothes, wearing sackcloth and ashes and going through the streets 'crying out loudly and bitterly'.

On this reading, the unique appointment of Haman to a rank just below the king created a degree of potential political instability, whereby whoever had that role might ultimately pose a threat to the king himself. This possible ambition on the part of Haman is actually revealed in his description in chapter six of what should be done to a man whom the king wished to honour. Thinking of himself in that role he has the person robed in royal apparel and riding the king's horse (itself a symbol of royalty). The constant threat of a possible palace coup is already suggested, however absurdly, in the response to Vashti's refusal to attend the king's feast and the dire warnings about potential revolutions in the households of the empire. It is likely therefore that Esther played on precisely such fears of a possible coup in her own plot against Haman.

Again this depends on how one reads the details of the story and to some extent understands its genre – is the Book simply a popular folk tale or instead a well-constructed spy thriller? If the latter, Esther's strategy hinges on her repeated invitations to the king and Haman to attend a banquet. After the first successful one, the king asks her what it is that she desires, 'up to half of his kingdom'. (5:6). Her response is to invite the king and Haman to a second banquet. On one level she is acting simply in a coquettish manner, keeping the king intrigued. But it is also possible that a small change of language in the two invitations has real significance. In the first she says: 'let his majesty and Haman come to the feast that I have prepared for *him*' (5:4). But in the second she says: 'Let his majesty and Haman come to the feast that I have prepared for *them.*' The change from 'him' to 'them' can be dismissed as simply a grammatical variant. However, in general, as we have noted such changes are significant elements in Biblical narrative style. Moreover, in the highly sensitive context of court intrigue, such an apparently minor change in protocol or nuance could not have been overlooked. Extending the invitation from one for the king himself, merely accompanied by Haman, to a banquet for 'them', both now regarded as of equal status, must raise the question of a possibly significant change in the balance of power. Such a possibility is reinforced by the anxiety about the potential power of the queen, indicated already by the opening exaggerated fears about the consequences of Vashti's behaviour. The king's seemingly absurd offer to Esther of 'up to half the kingdom' would also fit a kind of competition as to who might make the best offer for her loyalty.

If further proof be needed of the king's suspicions it can be found when, following the first banquet, the king has a sleepless night, another 'fortuitous' event that now makes sense if the fears about a possible conspiracy is recognized and the king is concerned about what Haman and the Queen might be plotting. What is the king's solution to his sleeplessness - research in the Chronicles to find someone at court to act as a potential counter to Haman! The search brings up the name of Mordecai, someone with proven loyalty, whom the king now decides to honour publicly. Moreover, to confirm that the king is deliberately snubbing Haman, the king refers to Mordecai as 'Mordecai the Jew' (*6:10*) when instructing Haman to honour him, although in the Chronicle he is only referred to as 'Mordecai' (*6:2, 3*).

The downfall is described in chapter six, which is a comic masterpiece. At its core is the five-fold repetition of the phrase 'the one whom the king wishes to honour.', each time with a different implication and intonation. Verse 6, the king's seemingly innocent question. Verse 7, Haman's apparently reflective repetition of the question, then v 8-9, preening as he imagines to himself how he would appear in such a situation riding on the king's horse through the streets of the city, climaxing with his acting out the final ecstatic imagining of the voices proclaiming before him the exact same words. And then the shattering of his fantasy, as the king instructs him to fulfil every one of those suggestions, except that Mordechai the Jew (surely the word 'Jew' was intentionally introduced by a king who is fully aware of what is going on between them) will be the one riding the horse, and Haman the one making the proclamation. And Haman's spectacular fall from grace is magnificently displayed when the same phrase comes yet again in verse 11 but this time, we imagine, through Haman's clenched teeth.

No wonder Haman's 'advisers' (*6:10*), presumably all that are left of those formerly described as his 'friends' (*5:10*), sensitive to such shifts in court intrigue, foretell his downfall (*6:13*).

The Biblical context

As we have already noted the story of the struggle between Mordecai and Haman reflects a theme that has run through the Hebrew Bible. The immediate association is the failure of King Saul to kill Agag the Amalekite king, despite Samuel's divine command (*1 Samuel 15*), Haman being an 'Agagite' so presumably a descendant of the king. This failure contributes to Saul's downfall as king. Among the literary echoes used by the author of Esther is that Queen Vashti is to be replaced by 'her neighbour who is better than her' (*Esther 1:19*) (compare *1 Samuel 15:28* where Saul, as king, will similarly be replaced). Mordecai is introduced as the descendant of the Benjaminite 'Kish', the name of Saul's father and tribe. A further echo can be seen in the insistence throughout the latter part of the Book of Esther that when defeating their enemies the Jews did not take their 'spoil' (*9:10,16*) unlike Saul's troops who sinned by taking the Amalekite 'spoil' (*1 Samuel 15:9*).

It is as if the Book of Esther, while working on a popular and entertaining level, and providing the reason for the Festival of Purim, is also consciously addressing an ancient Biblical conflict. The attempt is to 'replay' it and thus 'repair' earlier failures or mistakes. What has been done cannot be undone, but when the same circumstances arise the substitute protagonists can behave in a more appropriate way.

233

What might lie behind this dimension in the Book of Esther? It echoes a similar 'hidden' dimension within the Book of Ruth. Behind the two protagonists, Ruth and Boaz, lie two inappropriate sexual acts. The intercourse between Lot and his daughters leads to the birth of Moab, the eponymous ancestor of Ruth. In the ancestry of David is the intercourse between Judah and Tamar, an association that is explicitly mentioned in the text of Ruth (*4:12*). Thus when Ruth and Boaz meet on the threshing floor the earlier circumstances are reproduced and, though the text is ambiguous, it opens the possibility that nothing untoward happens before they formally marry, thus 'repairing' these wrongdoings in David's ancestry. This possibility is alluded to in a rabbinic comment on *Psalm 116:16* 'I am your servant, the son of your handmaid, you have loosened my bands.'

> David said: You have loosened the bands that constrict me on account
> of Tamar; of whom it is written 'You shall not uncover the nakedness of
> your daughter-in-law (*Lev 18:15*). You have also loosed the bands that
> constrict me on account of Ruth the Moabitess. (*Tehillim Rabbah 116:9*)

 As the rabbinic tradition, suggests this paves the way for David's future descendant to take on the role known in rabbinic tradition as the 'messiah son of David'. Presumably at the time of the composition of the Book of Ruth messianic speculation was heightened and among its other dimensions the Book played into this hope.

When we turn again to the Book of Esther, we are confronted with the other potential 'messianic' line, that of Saul, who was similarly anointed by Samuel, though his reign was cut short by his rejection by God and ultimate death in battle. But rabbinic thought preserves a tradition of two messianic lines: alongside the Messiah son of David is the 'Messiah, son of Joseph'. One source of this is a rabbinic discussion on the verse in *Zechariah 12:10*

'And they shall look unto Me because they have thrust him through; and they shall mourn for him; and they shall mourn for him as one mourns for an only son.'

In one rabbinic source the mourning is on account of the death of the Messiah son of Joseph who is killed in the battle against evil, to be succeeded by the Messiah son of David. (*Babylonian Talmud Succah 52a*). It is easy to see in this tradition the reminiscence of the short-lived 'messianic' career of Saul and the possibility that the roots of such a tradition can already be found at the time of the authorship of the Book of Esther. Mordecai's success against Haman, including destroying his sons, 'repairs' Saul's failure and would help bring on the messianic period. Again a political dimension would underlie the composition and reception of the Book.

A contemporary view

Any reading of the Book of Esther today from a theological perspective needs to take into account the discussion of the Book by the Jewish philosopher Emil Fackenheim. In his *The Jewish Bible after the Holocaust – A Rereading* ((Manchester University Press, 1990) he argues that in the light of the Holocaust certain Biblical texts that might have been considered peripheral in the past need to take centre stage, while others require a different emphasis as we 're-read' them. He notes the 'strangeness' of Esther, because of the absence of God, but also because of the nature of the main characters.

Mordecai is no prophet or martyr but a leader of his people who shows no special religious qualities. Esther is a beautiful Jewish girl who marries out of the faith, and becomes a heroine only because – after hesitating! - she decides to risk her life for her people. These facts, added to the absence of God, make the book alive for secular Jews. What makes it explosively alive for this whole Jewish 'generation', - the 'religious' as well as the 'nonreligious' part of it – is the figure of Haman. Jews seek a Biblical prototype of their worst enemy of all time... The enemy of our time (Hitler) has only one Biblical type that comes close to being his prototype, but this one comes uncannily close: the Haman of Esther, who wants to kill all Jews because of the trifling slight of a single Jew. (pp 60-61)

In the Book, Mordecai tells a hesitant Esther that, in case she turns a deaf ear to his plea, deliverance will come to her people 'from another place'. (*Esther 4:14*) Traditionally this is an allusion to the unmentioned God. But what if the Biblical Mordecai hoped for no more than some lucky coincidence? ... What if Mordecai of the 'naked text' means no more than this, that just as luck has always saved the Jewish people, so it will not fail in the present emergency? Esther is a literary masterpiece: what makes it so is the weaving together with supreme economy, of a series of small coincidences into one large fortunate coincidence.... During the Holocaust there were thousands of nameless Esthers, less hesitant than the Biblical one to risk their lives for their people: not one had the chance. The much-maligned *Judenraete* included countless would-be Mordecais: to none came the help from another place that would have made him an actual Mordecai... (pp 61-62)

This Jewish 'generation' is thus required to face up to a radical question regarding its Ta'nach as a whole... After what has happened... Esther is strange no more. What if this once-strange book in the Jewish Bible had to be moved from the periphery to the centre, so as to provide the new principle uniting the whole? (p 62)

On this reading, the Book of Esther is the one book in the Hebrew Bible that addresses the experience of life within the Jewish Diaspora. Unlike the other texts relating to the Babylonian exile, whose thrust is the longed-for return to the land of Israel, this one speaks to the reality of Diaspora life, one in which

God is not obviously present, in which political pragmatism and a measure of good fortune may determine whether or not one survives. Prayer to God is present in the Book, but if God's actions are also present they are concealed, at least in the Hebrew version. For Fackenheim these features reflect a stance that he feels must be taken in the wake of the Holocaust:

> We are, first, commanded to survive as Jews, lest the Jewish people perish. We are commanded, secondly, to remember in our very guts and bones the martyrs of the Holocaust, lest their memory perish. We are forbidden, thirdly, to deny or despair of God, however much we may have to contend with him or with belief in him, lest Judaism perish. We are forbidden, finally, to despair of the world as the place which is to become the kingdom of God, lest we help make it a meaningless place in which God is dead or irrelevant and everything is permitted. To abandon any of these imperatives, in response to Hitler's victory at Auschwitz, would be to hand him yet other, posthumous victories.[57]

Fackenheim derives a paradoxical conclusion from his theology. The absence of God from the Book of Esther, and the successful resolution of the story despite that absence, becomes the challenge to maintain our belief in God 'lest Judaism perish' and we help make the world into a meaningless place. Fackenheim, who at age 23 escaped from Sachsenheim Concentration camp, accepted the logic of his reading of Esther as reflecting the dangerous realities of Diaspora experience. He chose to settle in Israel after the Six Day War, the place where he might expect that 'help from another place' would at least in part be available: through self-reliance and a degree of national independence, through military power to combat external threats and by means of a legendary espionage system to rival that of Mordecai.

---

1 *To Mend the World: Foundations of Future Jewish Thought* (1982) p 213

On Purim, the Book of Esther is read in synagogue, but the reading is constantly interrupted by noise-makers whenever Haman's name is mentioned. We are literally 'blotting out the memory of Amalek' as *Deuteronomy 25:19* commands, but also drowning out any significance the Book might have in the carnival atmosphere. Moreover, commentaries that emphasise only the comic elements and parody in the narrative somehow miss the point of its ultimate political seriousness. Perhaps the rabbis had it right when they asked the question: was Ahasuerus wise or a fool? And the political similarity between Haman and Mordecai is also hinted at in the rabbinic injunction that on Purim we should drink so much alcohol that we can no longer differentiate between 'cursed be Haman and blessed be Mordecai'.

Afterword

Jonathan Magonet has a great track-record in expounding the Bible in the traditions of rabbinic practice, yet also showing its relevance to modern life and modern questions. This book continues in the style of some of his earlier books: *Bible Lives* (1992), *A Rabbi Reads the Psalms* (1994), and *The Subversive Bible* (1997). Like them, it makes a type of reading that is unfamiliar to most non-Jews accessible and attractive to any reader. As a Christian I have learned immensely from his approach.

How Did Moses Know that He Was a Hebrew? offers a close reading of a number of passages from the Bible, in every case turning most of our prior expectations and assumptions on their head. As one example out of many, take his reading of one of the most difficult passages, the *akedah* or 'binding of Isaac' in Genesis 22. Assuming that Abraham passes the test, commentators have strained to find some way of justifying what seems like the fanaticism of a man prepared to sacrifice his only son, and the cruelty of the God who commands it. Christians have either interpreted it as a prefiguring of the sacrifice of Jesus (the passage is read on Good Friday in my own Anglican tradition), or else, with Kierkegaard, have seen Abraham as a 'knight of faith', prepared to override ethical norms for the sake of obedience to a divine commission. Underlying these interpretations, however, is the assumption that God meant Abraham to obey the command, only intervening just in time to prevent him from carrying it out once he had shown his perfect obedience. Not so, says Jonathan Magonet. The test was to see whether Abraham would have the courage to *disobey* an unjust command—a test which Abraham failed, even though God gave him till the very last moment to refuse to kill Isaac. From this God himself learned the limits of the human beings he had made, and their fatal ability to ascribe violent impulses to divine inspiration.

Thus Abraham *fails* the test, and God knows more than he did before. Here are two ideas strange to traditional Christianity, and I think also to traditional Judaism. The Bible, read like this, is indeed 'subversive'. Unlike later philosophical speculation about God and humanity, the biblical record shows them in lively debate, each with something to learn from the other. God and his human creatures alike develop and change through experience. Magonet here opens our eyes to new ways of reading these old and familiar stories.

He does so, however, not by applying some fresh method or hermeneutic, but by drawing on the resources of Jewish interpretation down the ages, especially in midrash. The new insights emerge from highly traditional attention to the exact detail of the Hebrew text, seeing it as full of puns and verbal echoes. Traditional midrash joins hands with modern, even postmodern close reading, as has often been observed. Repeated words form a hidden code to meanings beneath the surface of the text, as when the two decisive moments in Abraham's life—his departure for Canaan in Genesis 12 and the binding of Isaac in Genesis 22—are marked out by the only two occurrences in the Torah of the Hebrew expression *lekh l'kha*, 'take yourself off'. The rabbis had noted this, as did Martin Buber and Franz Rosenzweig in their translation of the Hebrew text into German in the mid-twentieth century. Such echoes structure the story.

A biblical critic, such as I suppose I am, is not always comfortable with midrash. We fear that it can represent over-interpretation, the ascription of meaning to sub-semantic features of the text. But time and again striking insights emerge that at least challenge us to justify our own approaches. The variation in the name of God, *elohim* or YHWH, has long been a criterion for detecting different underlying sources in the Bible. Magonet does not deny that this may sometimes be justified, but he shows how in the finished text there is often a theological significance in the variation. Hence source theories are generally unnecessary, or at least not very important. Throughout, he concentrates on the text as it now presents itself to the reader, and, like his rabbinic predecessors, he mines the detail of its words for depths of meaning. Anyone who wishes to learn how traditional Jewish reading of Scripture works will find him a most accessible guide. Every page brings a fresh insight to texts we thought we already knew the meaning of. These pieces originated as lectures, and will have engaged the hearers as they now do their readers. This is a thoroughly enlightening book, full of ideas that Christians as well as Jews can benefit from reflecting on.

John Barton

Emeritus Oriel and Laing Professor of the Interpretation of Holy Scriptures, University of Oxford

About the author

Jonathan Magonet was born in London, attended Westminster School, studied medicine at Middlesex Hospital Medical School and qualified as a doctor, MB.BS. He completed the necessary year of 'House Jobs' to become registered. This was an expected outcome because of his background in a 'medical family'. But during the same years he came under a different influence. As a teenager he became involved with the 'Junior Membership' of the West London Synagogue, the oldest 'Reform' synagogue in the UK, and 'progressed' from 'editor' of the newsletter to chairman, to a 'vice-president' in the larger Jewish youth movement, the Youth Association of Synagogues of Great Britain. Having shown some leadership skills he was approached by two rabbis, first generation of graduates of the newly created Leo Baeck College.

The great European rabbinic seminaries had been destroyed by the Nazis, and the College was established with the aim of creating a new generation of rabbinic leadership. The spiritual figurehead of the refugee Rabbinic community was Rabbi Dr Leo Baeck, the leader of pre-war German Jewry, a survivor of Theresienstadt concentration camp. The College opened in 1956 and when Baeck died that same year, the College was given his name. It inherited a kind of German intellectual and cultural Jewish tradition, that had become transplanted to a very different kind of Jewish life in the UK. The two aforementioned graduates, Rabbis Lionel Blue and Dow Marmur, shared concerns for the need to rebuild the largely destroyed pre-war Jewish communities. One of the instruments was the development of the College to provide rabbinic leadership, the other was a youth movement that would attract young people to help fulfil that task. Jonathan Magonet became the Chairman of the Youth Section of the World Union for Progressive Judaism and, working with Rabbi Blue, set about creating a series of conferences on continental Europe, including the first post-war international Jewish youth conference in

Berlin, a remarkable 'taboo-breaking' venture at that time in the sixties, so soon after the war. It was in that arena that Jonathan recognized a personal call to enter the rabbinate and joined the College in the autumn of 1967. (By chance his last medical activity was earlier that year. He had gone to Israel to begin Hebrew studies prior to entering the rabbinic programme, when the 6-Day War broke out. He volunteered as a doctor and worked in Hadassah Hospital for that short period, relieving doctors who had been called up.)

At the College he discovered another dimension to his vocation, his fascination with the Hebrew Bible, in particular Biblical narrative and poetry. This was partly a consequence of his own skill as a writer, poet and composer of songs that had blossomed during his youth group work. It became evident that his rabbinic career would be best fulfilled in the area of Jewish studies, and having gained his PhD at the University of Heidelberg, with a study of narrative art in the Book of Jonah, he was invited to teach Bible at Leo Baeck College.There he spent his career as Lecturer in Bible, and subsequently, for twenty years as Principal of the College (1985-2005). He is currently Emeritus Professor of Bible.

During that period he brought to the College other aspects of the values of his youth group experience. The readiness to create relationships with a new generation of Germans found its expression in innovative interfaith activities, one significant example was the establishment of the annual International Jewish-Christian Bible Week, in a small Catholic conference centre in Bendorf, near Koblenz, supported by the visionary work on post-war reconciliation by the Director of the Hedwig Dransfeld Haus, Anneliese Debray. Rabbi Lionel Blue was one of the first to recognize the growing presence of Muslim populations in Europe and under his influence the Standing Conference of Jews, Christians and Muslims was created, with its annual student conference based as well in HDH. Both programmes were supported by the College.

These various activities are reflected in Jonathan Magonet's literary output: Several volumes of popular Biblical studies, published by the SCM Press (*A Rabbi Reads the Bible* (1991, 2004); *A Rabbi Reads the Psalms* (1994, 2004); *Bible Lives* (1992); *The Subversive Bible* (1997); *From Autumn to Summer* (2000); *A Rabbi Reads the Torah* (2013); (some of these based on radio broadcasts on the BBC World Service and German Nord Deutschland Rundfunk, often with German editions). His commitment to interfaith dialogue is reflected in *Talking to the Other: Jewish Interfaith Dialogue with Christians and Muslims*, with a Foreword by Prince Hassan Bin Tallal and an Afterword by Karen Armstrong (I.B.Tauris 2003). With Rabbi Lionel Blue they produced a number of books of popular spirituality, including *A Guide to the Here and Hereafter* (1998), *How to get up when life gets you down* (1992), *Sun, Sand and Soul* (1999) and *Kindred Spirits: A Year of Readings* (1998) (all published by HarperCollins).

The other strand of collaboration by Magonet and Blue is in the editing of a series of prayer books under the overall title 'Forms of Prayer for Jewish Worship' including volumes on *Daily and Sabbath Services* (1977, 2008), *Days of Awe: Prayers for the High Holydays* (1985), *Prayers for the Pilgrim Festivals* (1995) for the Reform Synagogues of Great Britain, later Movement for Reform Judaism. Both of the latter two volumes contain extensive Biblical commentaries.

Jonathan Magonet is also editor of the journal *European Judaism* (Berghahn Books*)*, the Journal of Leo Baeck College.

He has published his collected poems in *Ghostwalk and other poems* (Kulmus Publishing 2018). His interest in Japanese 'netsuke', pursued during several years of lecturing visits to Seinan Gakuin University, in Fukuoka, Japan, led to his collection of short stories, *Netsuke Nation: Tales From Another Japan* (Troubador 2013). He performs occasional concerts of his songs and harmonica playing.

He is married to Dorothea, has a son Gavriel and daughter Avigail, and grandchildren to Gavriel and his wife Deborah, called Ephra and Arava.

Printed by
Schaltungsdienst Lange o.H.G., Berlin